D1596222

Bureau of Indian Affairs

Recent Titles in
Landmarks of the American Mosaic

Abolition Movement
T. Adams Upchurch

Chinese Exclusion Act of 1882
John Soennichsen

Tuskegee Airmen
Barry M. Stentiford

Wounded Knee Massacre
Martin Gitlin

Bureau of Indian Affairs

Donald L. Fixico

Landmarks of the American Mosaic

GREENWOOD

AN IMPRINT OF ABC-CLIO, LLC
Santa Barbara, California • Denver, Colorado • Oxford, England

Library of Congress Cataloging-in-Publication Data

Fixico, Donald Lee, 1951–
    Bureau of Indian Affairs / Donald L. Fixico.
        p. cm. — (Landmarks of the American mosaic)
    Includes bibliographical references and index.
    ISBN 978-0-313-39179-8 (hardcopy : alk. paper) —
ISBN 978-0-313-39180-4 (ebook)   1. United States. Bureau of Indian Affairs—History.   2. Indians of North America—Government relations—1869–1934.   3. Indians of North America—Government relations—1934–   4. United States—Race relations.   I. Title.
    E93.F513   2012
    323.1197—dc23   2011036170

ISBN: 978-0-313-39179-8
EISBN: 978-0-313-39180-4

16 15 14 13 12   1 2 3 4 5

This book is also available on the World Wide Web as an eBook.
Visit www.abc-clio.com for details.

Greenwood
An Imprint of ABC-CLIO, LLC

ABC-CLIO, LLC
130 Cremona Drive, P.O. Box 1911
Santa Barbara, California 93116-1911

This book is printed on acid-free paper ∞

Manufactured in the United States of America

To all my relatives of my four tribes, the Shawnee, Sac and Fox, Muscogee Creek, and Seminole.

Contents

Series Foreword

THE LANDMARKS OF THE AMERICAN MOSAIC series comprises individual volumes devoted to exploring an event or development central to this country's multicultural heritage. The topics illuminate the struggles and triumphs of American Indians, African Americans, Latinos, and Asian Americans, from European contact through the turbulent last half of the 20th century. The series covers landmark court cases, laws, government programs, civil rights infringements, riots, battles, movements, and more. Written by historians especially for high school students on up and general readers, these content-rich references satisfy more thorough research needs and provide a deeper understanding of material that students might only otherwise be exposed to in a short section in a textbook or superficial explanation online.

Each book on a particular topic is a one-stop reference source. The series format includes

- Introduction
- Chronology
- Narrative chapters that trace the evolution of the event or topic chronologically
- Biographical profiles of key figures
- Selection of crucial primary documents
- Glossary
- Annotated Bibliography
- Index

This landmark series promotes respect for cultural diversity and supports the social studies curriculum by helping students understand multicultural American history.

Introduction

The Bureau of Indian Affairs (BIA) has a very long history of varying relationships with American Indians and Alaska Natives in the United States. In the early years, the BIA was called the Indian Office, and in later years it has been referred to as the Indian Bureau. Originally, the Department of War housed Indian affairs, but this responsibility shifted to the Department of the Interior when Congress created the department in 1849. The commissioner of Indian affairs presided over the BIA until 1978 when a higher level position of assistant secretary of the Interior took its place. Forty-seven men have served as the commissioner of Indian affairs, and 16 have served as assistant secretary, with the exception of Ada Deer being the only woman. The commissioner and later the assistant secretary were named by the secretary of the Interior and appointed by the president of the United States.

This book presents an overview of the history of the Bureau of Indian Affairs that spans more than 200 years of relations between the United States government and more than 500 American Indian tribes and Alaska Native groups. Key individuals, both Indian and non-Indian, forged an official relationship between the tribal nations and the United States that resulted in an official liaison called the Bureau of Indian Affairs. This volume covers the early U.S.-Indian relationship in the late 1700s of treaty and trade negotiations to Indian removals and wars that involved Eastern and Western Indian groups, leading to various policies. Such policies included boarding schools, Indian health, a reform movement, land allotment, termination, relocation, self-determination, and government-to-government recognition of tribal sovereignty. As relations with more Indian nations increased, the Indian Bureau expanded with agents throughout Indian Country. These relations resulted in 374 U.S.-Indian ratified treaties.

The organization of the Bureau of Indian Affairs is addressed here as well, and the long history of the Indian Office is briefly introduced in meaningful periods to readers to demonstrate the many changes and transitions that the BIA made to administer over 500 tribal nations.

Basically, the bureau's history can be divided into several periods of creation, early treaty negotiations, the removal years, treaties with western tribes, the reform years, the boarding school era, federal management of natural resources and lands, termination and relocation programs, education, self-determination, and tribal self-governance. It is important to view the BIA within a context of historical events and noted individuals who defined and shaped the course of federal-Indian relations. As Indian history unfolded, the BIA served as a liaison representing the federal government but not necessarily defining history. This is not to say that the BIA did not have its own history, but rather it had a proper place within the larger picture of Indian-white relations, because the operations of the BIA affected not only Indians and tribes but also non-Indians, land companies, railroads, mining companies, ranchers, and other agencies of the federal government.

Before reading the following pages, two important questions should be asked: what is tribal sovereignty, and why are treaties important?

Sovereignty, treaties, and the trust relationship make American Indians uniquely different than anyone else in the United States because their nations have signed nearly 400 treaties and agreements with the federal government. Due to the international doctrine of law, sovereigns respect sovereigns in treaty agreements. This relationship is based on a reciprocal trust status that is maintained by both sovereigns. Thus, the U.S. government has a responsibility to live up to the treaties and carry out their provisions, obligations, and promises.

The Indian Bureau cannot officially make Indian policy, but it can recommend policies and programs. Congress and the president of the United States make federal-Indian policy for the BIA to supervise. How it is carried out is up to the BIA. This situation creates a difficult challenge of being criticized much more than praised for its work. Naturally the commissioners or assistant secretaries since 1978 have played a vital role in leading the BIA. And he or she has to depend on other officials, including area office directors, to carry out the details of supervision and work with native leaders and their tribal communities.

As of 2010, 12 regional offices operated throughout Indian Country—Alaska, Eastern, Eastern Oklahoma, Great Plains, Midwest, Navajo, Northwest, Pacific, Rocky Mountains, Southern Plains, Southwest, and Western. The regional offices contain 83 agencies that report to the BIA deputy director of Field Operations. Each regional director is responsible for all BIA activities except education, law enforcement, and administrative procedure. Generally, regional offices also have a deputy regional director for Trust Services and deputy regional director for Indian Services. The former has a staff of specialists who are responsible for natural resources (water resources, forestry and fire, and irrigation and dam safety), agriculture (farm, pasture, and range), fish, wildlife and parks, and real estate services (land acquisition and disposal land title records office, probate, rights-of-way, and lease or permit). The latter has a staff of specialists who are responsible for transportation (planning design, construction, and maintenance) and Indian services (tribal governments, human services, and housing improvement).

With a central office as a part of the Department of the Interior, located at 1849 C Street, NW; Washington, DC 20240, the Indian Bureau operates with a series of 85 area offices strategically located throughout what has been called "Indian Country." Indian Country consists of 326 reservations, 55.7 million acres (about 2.3% of the United States), or 87,000 square miles in 33 states. At the end of the first decade of the 21st century, an estimated 12,000 employees work for the BIA.

Federal-Indian-reserved lands exist in all but 18 states: Georgia, South Carolina, Tennessee, Kentucky, West Virginia, Virginia, Maryland, Delaware, New Jersey, Massachusetts, Vermont, New Hampshire, Ohio, Indiana, Illinois, Missouri, Arkansas, and Hawaii. Treaties, congressional laws, and presidential executive orders have created federal-Indian reservations, and there are 9 state reservations in 16 states: Alabama, California, Connecticut, Delaware, Georgia, Louisiana, Massachusetts, Michigan, Missouri, New Jersey, New York, North Carolina, Ohio, South Carolina, Vermont, and Virginia. As of 2010, there were 564 federally recognized tribes with at least 24 Indian communities wanting federal recognition and 70 state-recognized tribes. As of the 2000 U.S. Census, there were almost 2.5 million American Indians and Alaska Natives. In 2006 the estimated Indian and Alaska Native population was 4.5 million. At this time, Larry Echo Hawk is the assistant secretary who strives to carry out the mission of the BIA to "enhance the quality of life, to promote economic opportunity, and to carry out the responsibility to protect and improve the trust assets of American Indians, Indian tribes and Alaska Natives." The BIA works in conjunction with the Bureau of Indian Education (BIE), created in 2006, whose mission is to "provide quality education opportunities from early childhood through life in accordance with the tribes' needs to cultural and economic well-being, in keeping with the wide diversity of Indian tribes and Alaska Native villages as distinct cultural and governmental entities. Further, the BIE is to manifest consideration of the whole person by taking into account the spiritual, mental, physical, and cultural aspects of the individual within his or her family and tribal or village context" (www.bie.edu).

The lengthy history of the BIA in this volume provides a chronology, glossary of helpful terms, an annotated bibliography of books about

federal-Indian relations and a list of BIA commissioners and assistant secretaries of the Interior. The longevity of the BIA will outlive this book, but
the essence is that this federal agency directed the lives of Indian people
and their communities. There is a strong human dimension that should not
be ignored as well as the people who directed the BIA and its people who
kept—and now keep—it going on a daily basis.

A word is necessary about the usage of American Indian, Native American, and Indian in the following pages. While some people today refer to
Indians as Native Americans, I have refrained from using this term because
the Indian Office in the Department of the Interior is the Bureau of Indian
Affairs, not the Bureau of Native American Affairs. Thus, I have almost
always used the terms Indian, American Indian, and Native people to represent the indigenous people of the United States.

Supportive people have also been involved in the completion of this
book. First my appreciation goes to my research assistants, Brianna Theo-
bald and Clara Keyt, who have both worked with me over the last four
years; and Clara is now Dr. Keyt. In the final stages, Brianna edited much
of this work for errors. At Greenwood Press and ABC-CLIO, I am grateful
for the editorial support and patience of Kim Kennedy-White, Vicki Moran,
Mariah Gumpert, Danielle Fox, Rajalakshmi Madhavan and the team at
Apex. I am also grateful for former assistant secretaries of the Interior,
Eddie Brown and Kevin Gover, who are friends and colleagues at ASU. At
Arizona State University, I am grateful for the support of my Distinguished
Foundation Professorship and the support from President Michael Crow,
Provost and Executive Vice President Betty Capaldi, Vice President and
Dean Robert Page, Dean Neal Lester, School Director Mark von Hagen, and
History Faculty Head Phil VanderMeer. On the fourth floor of Coor Hall, I
am also thankful to the staff for the daily things they do to make my job
easier. I also want to mention my appreciation of the graduate students
that I have worked with in my seminars on federal-Indian policy: Azusa
Ono, Tam Swafford, Matt Garrett, Cody Marshall, Patricia Biggs, Chelsea
Mead, Meaghan Heisinger, Katie Sweet, Karl Snyder, Billy Kiser, Louise
Alflen, Monika Bilka, and John Goodwin. At home I have always had the
support of my wife, Professor April Summitt, who listened to my thoughts,
which I expressed aloud, in writing this book; and to my son, Keytha, who
respects what I do as a scholar. Lastly, this book is dedicated to my family
and relatives of my tribes, the Shawnee, Sac and Fox, Muscogee Creek, and
Seminole of Oklahoma.

Donald L. Fixico
Arizona State University

Chronology

1638 The Puritans create the first Indian reservation for the Quinnipiac Nation of 1,200 acres near present-day New Haven, Connecticut, placing the Indians under British rule.

1755 The British Crown establishes an Indian Department.

1774 A committee is established for Indian Affairs.

1775 The First Continental Congress creates Indian commissioner positions for the Indian Affairs Committee's three geographic departments.

1775–1783 The Revolutionary War is waged, and the Shawnee, Delaware, Miami, and Ottawa join with the British to try to stop U.S. expansion. The war ends with the Treaty of Paris, in which the United States and England agree that Indians will be under the supervision of the United States.

1777–1787 Native Americans are sovereign nations according to the Articles of Confederation. A 1779 law stated that only the U.S. government could distribute Indian lands.

September 17, 1778 The Delaware sign the first ratified treaty, also called Treaty of Fort Pitt, with the U.S. government called the Continental Congress.

October 22, 1784 Treaty is made with the Six Nations of Iroquois at Fort Stanwix, and this agreement establishes the eastern boundary of the Iroquois.

January 21, 1785 Treaty is made at Fort McIntosh with the Wyandotte, Delaware, Ottawa, and Chippewa.

1786 The secretary of war assumes supervision of Indian Affairs. Treaties are signed with the Shawnee, Choctaw, Chickasaw, and Cherokee.

1787 The Constitutional Convention in Philadelphia adopts the U.S. Constitution. The document's Commerce Clause gives Congress the authority to make laws concerning Native American relations and trade and prohibits the colonies from making treaties with Indian groups.

July 13   Congress passes the first Northwest Ordinance, which divides up the land north of the Ohio River in order to create territories that can later become states.

1789   The United States creates the War Department; because many Native American nations are still allied with the British and Spanish, Indian Affairs is moved to the newly developed War Department.

January 9   A treaty at Fort Harmar is made with Wyandot, Delaware, Ottawa, Chippewa, Potawatomi, Sauk, and Six Nations.

July 22, 1790   Congress passes the first trade and intercourse act.

1794   As a result of Jay's treaty signed between the United States and Britain, the British withdraw their military aid to allied Indian groups as they recede into Canada.

1795   The United States signs the Treaty of Greenville with Shawnee, Miami, and other tribes who cede almost all of Ohio to the United States.

March 30, 1802   Congress passes a permanent trade and intercourse act.

1803   The United States negotiates the Louisiana Purchase for $15 million, a large tract of land comprising seven present-day states and portions of an additional eight present-day states, from the French.

November 7, 1811   William Henry Harrison's troops defeat the Shawnee Prophet and burn down Prophetstown while Tecumseh is away.

1813–1814   Andrew Jackson and his men defeat Creek Indians living in present-day Alabama in the Red Stick War, and the Creeks cede 22 million acres of land to the United States.

1815   The Treaty of Ghent ends the War of 1812. The British acknowledge that all lands below the Great Lakes belong to the United States and agree to stop giving aid to their Indian allies.

1819   Congress passes the Indian Civilization Fund Act that provides $10,000 per year for schools in Indian Country. The act signals a partnership between missionaries and the government to change Indians' cultural practices.

1823 In *Johnson v. M'Intosh*, Supreme Court Justice John Marshall rules that Indians have rights to their land because of preexisting use. However, he also rules that Indians can only sell their land to the U.S. government, which ends up limiting Indian control over their own land.

March 11, 1824 The Office of Indian Affairs is formed by War Secretary John C. Calhoun in the Department of War.

1830 The Indian Removal Act is passed, and throughout the 1830s and 1840s, many Indians are forced to leave their lands in the East and moved to lands in the West.

1831 In *Cherokee Nation v. Georgia*, Supreme Court Justice John Marshall declares that the Cherokee Nation is a domestic dependent nation rather than a foreign nation because they depend on the United States for legal status.

1832 In *Worcester v. Georgia*, Chief Justice John Marshall rules in favor of the Cherokee. His ruling declares the Cherokee a sovereign nation with which only the federal government, not the states, can form agreements.

July 9 Congress passes an act to provide for the presidential appointment of a commissioner of Indian Affairs, although a head of the Indian Office had been supervising Indian affairs since 1824.

In the Black Hawk War, Black Hawk and remnant bands of the Sac and Fox tribes try to regain their lands in Wisconsin and Illinois but are unsuccessful.

June 30, 1834 Congress passes an act to organize operation of the Bureau of Indian Affairs and to authorize the establishment of superintendents and 12 agents to work throughout Indian Country.

1835–1842 After seven years of fighting in Florida, the United States is unable to claim a decisive victory in the conflict known as the Second Seminole War.

1840–1860 The U.S. government tries to implement a plan to move all Native Americans to what was known as Indian Territory (present-day Oklahoma and Kansas). The territory was to be later made a state with a Native American government.

1846–1848 The United States is involved in the Mexican-American War. With the Treaty of Guadalupe Hidalgo, Mexico cedes land that encompassed modern-day California and the Southwest with Indians in the area coming under BIA supervision.

1848   California Indians working for a miller named James Marshall discover gold in the American River. The discovery creates the gold rush of 1849.

1849   The Office of Indian Affairs is moved from the Department of War to the Department of the Interior.

1850–1860   Many treaties are made between the U.S. government and the various California Indian groups. However, non-Indian residents of California stop these treaties from being ratified by Congress.

1853–1856   The United States makes over 52 treaties with various Indian nations and it gains 174 million acres of land.

1854   The Gadsden Purchase extends the southern portions of Arizona and New Mexico for nearly 30,000 square miles, increasing BIA responsibilities.

The Kansas-Nebraska Act is passed. Indians in the area are removed to present-day Oklahoma.

1855–1907   The Chickasaw are given independence in a treaty. A year later they create a constitutional government that parallels the U.S. Constitution. This Chickasaw government lasts until 1907, when the Curtis Act eliminates it.

1860–1907   The Choctaw embrace a constitutional government consisting of a principal chief, three district chiefs, a legislature, and a court. This Choctaw government lasts until 1907, when the Curtis Act eliminates it.

1861–1865   After defeating Confederate forces in New Mexico, General James Carleton stays to run the New Mexico Department. He commands Christopher Carson to defeat the Mescalero Apache and Navajo and remove them to reservations.

1862   Suffering from near starvation due to their agent's corruption, Little Crow leads the Minnesota Sioux in a series of attacks on nearby settlements.

December 26   Thirty-eight Sioux are hanged for their participation in the revolt, and this is America's largest mass execution in history.

1863   Non-Indians invade the Nez Perce Reservation in Idaho after the discovery of gold. The government negotiates a treaty (known as the Thief Treaty) that reduces their land to one-tenth its former size.

1864   Colonel John M. Chivington, a former Methodist minister, leads a force of Colorado volunteers in a surprise attack on peaceful Cheyennes and Arapahoes. The attack becomes known as the Sand Creek Massacre.

1866   The Peace Commission is established to implement a new government policy that emphasizes the establishment of treaties with Indian groups.

1867–1907   The Creek create a constitutional government, though many tribal members want a more traditional government. Over the next four decades, the constitutional government remains in power only through U.S. intervention. In 1907 the Creek government is eliminated because of the disapproval of those Creeks desirous of a return to the old system.

1868   At Medicine Lodge Creek in Kansas, the Peace Commission holds the largest treaty council in the West, with nearly 10,000 Indians (Kiowa, Comanche, Plains Apache, Southern Cheyenne, and Southern Arapaho) present.

1869   Brigadier General Ely S. Parker, a Seneca, is appointed commissioner of Indian Affairs under President Ulysses S. Grant.

March 3, 1871   Congress creates an act that disallows further treaty negotiations with tribes. Past treaties are still to be honored, but agreements are now to be made by executive orders or congressional acts.

June 17, 1876   General George Crook's troops, in pursuit of the Sioux and Cheyenne, are surprised by 1,500 Sioux and Cheyenne warriors led by Crazy House, forcing Crook to withdraw.

June 25   Colonel George Custer and the Seventh Cavalry encounter the Sioux and Cheyenne along the Little Bighorn River. Custer and his men suffer a crushing defeat.

1877   Nez Perce warriors reject relocation to their appointed reservation in defiance of the actions of their older chiefs, instigating the Nez Perce War. Allied with the Palouse, the Nez Perce fight several battles with the army and are ultimately captured 40 miles south of the Canadian border and eventually placed at the Ponca Agency in Indian Territory.

1879 Captain Richard Pratt starts Carlisle Indian School in Pennsylvania, and other boarding schools follow the Carlisle model, for the specific purpose of teaching Indian children the mainstream culture.

In *Standing Bear v. Crook*, Judge Elmer S. Dundy rules in favor of Standing Bear, the leader of the Ponca tribe that was removed against its will to Indian Territory. The ruling recognizes Indians as persons within the United States and thus subject to U.S. laws.

The Women's National Indian Association (WNIA) is established by a group of concerned white women focused on the Christianization and assimilation of Indians.

1881 Helen Hunt Jackson publishes *A Century of Dishonor*, which exposes and criticizes the poor treatment of Indians. The late 1880s to the early decades of the 20th century are known as the Indian Reform era.

1882 The Sioux Commission is created to negotiate an agreement with the Oglala Sioux following the final defeat of the Sioux and Cheyenne. This gives the United States prime territory along the western border of Dakota Territory, including the Black Hills.

The Indian Rights Association is formed in Philadelphia. A second office is opened in Washington, DC, to lobby Congress and to serve as a liaison to the BIA and the Board of Indian Commissioners.

1883 In *Ex Parte Crow Dog*, the U.S. Supreme Court rules that U.S. courts lack jurisdiction over crimes committed involving Indians on their land. As a response, Congress passes the Major Crimes Act of 1885, which is amended to 10 laws and then to 14 that allow federal courts to have such jurisdiction, thus undermining tribal sovereignty.

1883–1916 Albert and Alfred Smiley organize the Lake Mohonk conferences of like-minded humanitarians to discuss the best way to solve the Indian problem and offer recommendations to the BIA.

1886 The legendary Apache leader Geronimo surrenders for the fourth and final time.

1887 The General Allotment Act is passed. Also known as the Dawes Act, this act divides reservation lands into individual allotments; surplus land is to be purchased by the government and sold to settlers.

1889 Congress passes the Nelson Act, which allots lands in Minnesota on the White Earth Reservation.

December 29, 1890   Major Samuel Whiteside's Seventh Cavalry slaughters roughly 150 Minneconjou Sioux Ghost Dancers led by Big Foot and wounds another 50 men, women, and children in the Wounded Knee Massacre.

1898   The Curtis Act abolishes the tribal governments, schools, and courts of the Five Civilized Tribes and other tribes in Indian Territory.

1900   The U.S. Census reports the total Indian population to be 237,196, the lowest it has ever been, strengthening the concept of the "Vanishing Indian."

1902   In *Lone v. Hitchcock*, the court rules in favor of the Department of the Interior, certifying that Congress is the major authority in determining Indian affairs and abolishing or changing treaties.

1906   The passing of the Burke Act makes trust patents to fee simple title of land ownership enabling large losses of Indian land allotments.

November 16, 1907   Oklahoma is formed into a state out of what was known as Indian Territory and Oklahoma Territory.

1908   In what becomes known as the *Winter's* Doctrine, a court rules that Indians on Fort Belknap Reservation in Montana have the right to water for agricultural needs, and allows Indians to appropriate as much water as is required for both agricultural and economic needs.

1911   The Society of American Indians (SAI) is founded in Columbus, Ohio, by national American Indian leaders. The organization's leaders criticize the BIA and call for its termination.

1914–1918   Despite the fact that many are not U.S. citizens, an estimated 10,000 American Indian men serve in World War I. The following year Congress passes a bill to thank them for their patriotism, granting honorably discharged World War I veterans full citizenship.

1921   The Snyder Act is passed, which obligates the Department of the Interior to provide social, health, and educational services to Indians.

1923   The BIA introduces the Committee of One Hundred to assist in reviewing past federal policies and make recommendations about better supervision of Indian affairs.

June 2, 1924   All remaining Indians without citizenship are given citizenship under the Indian Citizenship Act.

1927   Laurence F. Schmeckebier publishes *The Office of Indian Affairs*, a general overview with laws involving Indian policy and BIA operation.

1928   Lewis Meriam and his committee publish "The Problem of Indian Administration." The Meriam Report reveals the alarming death rates, inadequate education, and horrible living conditions within Indian boarding schools. It advises Congress to allocate money to counteract these problems and to reform the Office of Indian Affairs and concludes the land allotment policy failed.

1934   The Indian Reorganization Act is passed. Otherwise known as the Wheeler-Howard Act, it attempts to boost the well-being of Indians by respecting their different cultures, economies, religions, and languages. Indian tribal governments are given the authority to create their own constitutions, membership, and laws.

The Johnson-O'Malley Act is passed. This act authorizes the federal government to provide health, education, and social welfare services to Indians through state and territorial contracts.

The Civilian Conservation Corps–Indian Division is created to enable Indians to work during the Depression.

1935   Congress passes the Indian Arts and Crafts Board Act. The law creates a board to authenticate Indian arts and crafts and makes it a crime for non-Indians to produce similar goods for sale.

1936   The Indian Reorganization Act is amended to include tribes in Oklahoma and Alaska Natives.

1941–1945   An estimated 25,000 Indian men and several hundred Indian women serve in World War II.

1944   Tribal leaders gather in Denver, Colorado, to create the National Congress of American Indians, an organization devoted to protecting Indian lands, rights, culture, and reservations.

1946–1949   The BIA is reorganized; authority is decentralized and transferred to 12 newly created area offices.

1946   Congress creates the Indian Claims Commission, which lasts until 1978, allowing tribes to sue the federal government for wrongs committed.

1949   The Hoover Commission is formed, and it advocates immediate Indian assimilation, which the commission suggests should be encouraged by the cessation of funding for Indian programs following the end of their trust status and the relocation of families off the reservation.

1952 The BIA supervises the Relocation Program, which removes Indians from rural areas and reservations and places them in major cities in the West until 1973.

1953 House Concurrent Resolution 108 and Public Law 280 are passed. HCR 108 is used to end the unique government-to-government relationship that existed between Indian governments and the federal government. This begins the termination era that ends in 1973. PL 280 allows six states to have criminal jurisdiction on reservations.

1961 Individuals representing 90 tribes meet at the Chicago Indian Conference. They write their own Indian policy and present it to President John Kennedy in 1962.

An activist group called The National Indian Youth Council is created in Gallup, New Mexico, which questions the ways former advocate groups have dealt with Indian problems.

1962 The federal government forces New Mexico to allow its Indian populations to vote in elections: both state and local.

1964–1966 Tribal governments are given funds directly from the Office of Economic Opportunity to help reduce poverty among Indians.

1964 Treaty rights allow Indians in Washington to fish in traditional areas ceded to the United States, although new state laws and court rulings prohibit the use of traps and certain types of nets.

February 1966 Nisqually tribe members are arrested, along with other fish-in protesters, for illegal net-fishing. The Nisqually contend that they have the right to fish this way according to their 1856 treaty.

April Robert LaFollette Bennett, an Oneida, is appointed as the BIA commissioner and becomes the second Indian to hold this position.

The Navajo establish the Rough Rock Demonstration School by contracting with the BIA. This is the first school in modern times to be completely controlled by a tribe.

October The members of the Alaska Federation of Natives meet in Anchorage, Alaska, to discuss plans for conserving their land.

January 16, 1967   The BIA creates the National Indian Education Advisory Committee to improve educational services to Indian students.

June 10   The U.S. Claims Court upholds a previous decision made by the Indian Claims Commission that stated that the Seminole of Florida, according to an 1823 treaty, has claim to 32 million acres.

August 6   Eight Sioux tribes get $12.2 million in compensation from the Indian Claims Commission for lands totaling 29 million acres taken from them by deceitful treaties in the 19th century.

March 6, 1968   President Lyndon Johnson asks Congress for a 10 percent increase in funding for Native American programs. He signs the National Council on Indian Opportunity into existence, which is responsible for presenting Indian problems to the highest levels of the federal government.

April 11   The American Indian Civil Rights Act is passed, giving Indians living on reservations, under tribal governments, many of the same civil rights that all persons under state and federal governments have according to the U.S. Constitution. It also abolishes Public Law 280.

July   Dennis Banks, Clyde Bellecourt, and George Mitchell, all Minnesota Ojibwa, found the American Indian Movement in Minneapolis.

October 24   A $5-million settlement for the illegal taking of 9 million acres of land by the federal government in 1874 is awarded to the Yavapai tribe of Arizona.

March 23, 1969   The trial of seven Mohawk protesters begins. They demonstrated against the Canadian custom duties on Mohawk goods, stating that the Jay Treaty of 1794 allowed border tribes to freely pass the borders and exempted them from paying import and export taxes on their goods.

May 18   The Indian Claims Commission awards the Klamath tribe of Oregon $4.1 million because of bad surveys that were conducted on their reservation by the government in 1871 and 1888.

August 7   Louis R. Bruce, a Mohawk-Oglala Sioux and cofounder of the National Congress of American Indians, is appointed as commissioner of Indian Affairs by President Richard Nixon.

November 20   Indians of All Nations is organized, and Richard Oakes leads a takeover of Alcatraz that lasts for nearly 18 months.

1970 The Native American Rights Fund officially opens in Denver, Colorado.

Americans for Indian Opportunity is founded by LaDonna Harris in Washington, DC.

April 18–23 Indians hold sit-ins in several BIA offices throughout the nation.

November 8 Seventy-five Indians take over abandoned Army communications buildings in Davis, California, and demand it be turned into an Indian cultural center.

December 15 President Nixon signs a bill returning Taos Blue Lake to Taos Pueblo Indians.

1971 The BIA establishes regulations for direct election of the chiefs of the Five Civilized Tribes and 32 other tribes in Oklahoma.

February 19–20 Tribal leaders from 50 reservations meet in Billings, Montana, and start the National Tribal Chairmen's Association.

May 21 The Office of Economic Opportunity makes $880,000 in grants to establish a Model Urban Indian Center program.

December 18 President Nixon signs the Alaska Native Claims Settlement Act, which gives Alaska Natives 44 million acres and $962 million for relinquishment of the remainder of their claims in Alaska.

May 20, 1972 Congress passes the American Indian Education Act, creating the Office of Indian Education.

November 2–8 Indians participating in the Trail of Broken Treaties march to Washington, DC and take over the BIA building for several days.

February 27 to May 8, 1973 The American Indian Movement (AIM) takes over Wounded Knee in South Dakota for 73 days.

August 13 An Office of Indian Rights is created in the Civil Rights Division of the Justice Department.

December 22 President Nixon signs a bill to restore the Menominee to federal recognition as a tribe.

December 28 Congress passes a law starting the Comprehensive Employment and Training Act, producing the Manpower program to assist unemployed and economically deprived Indians.

February 12, 1974   A U.S. Supreme Court ruling known as the *Boldt* Decision confirms Indian treaty rights and declares that Indians in Washington have the rights to at least half of the fish in many of its state rivers.

April 12   Congress passes the Indian Financing Act, which allocates $250 million in grants of up to $50,000 to help finance economic development in Indian communities.

January 4, 1975   Congress passes the American Indian Self-Determination and Education Act, starting a new federal Indian policy called Indian Self-Determination.

The Council of Energy Resource Tribes (CERT) is founded in Denver, Colorado.

August 6   President Gerald Ford signs the Voting Rights Act that specifically includes rights of American Indians.

September 16, 1976   Congress passes the Indian Health Care Improvement Act.

May 18, 1977   Congress releases the American Indian Policy Review Commission Report of several volumes with one recommendation: to abolish the BIA and replace it with a new agency to be a liaison between tribes and all federal agencies.

October 13   Forrest J. Gerard (Blackfeet) is appointed by President Jimmy Carter as the first assistant secretary of the Interior, which replaces the position of commissioner of Indian Affairs. The recommendation was first proposed by President Nixon in 1970 to advance the BIA to the level of other agencies in the Department of the Interior.

March 6, 1978   In *Oliphant v. Suquamish Indian Tribe*, the U.S. Supreme Court rules that tribal courts do not have jurisdiction over non-Indians on reservations.

May 15   In *Santa Clara v. Martinez*, the court upholds Santa Clara Pueblo authority to deny tribal membership based on tribal law.

August 13   President Jimmy Carter signs the American Indian Religious Freedom Act.

September 28   The BIA sets regulations for the newly organized Federal Acknowledgement Program affecting more than 250 unrecognized tribes in 38 states.

October 18   Congress passes the Tribally Controlled Community Colleges Act.

November 28   Congress passes the American Indian Child Welfare Act.

1979   The Seminole tribe in Florida starts the first bingo operation, leading to big bingos for tribes.

June 30, 1980   The Supreme Court rules in *U.S. v. Sioux Nation* for a $122 million judgment against the United States by the Court of Claims for illegally taking the Black Hills from the Sioux.

May 8, 1981   One hundred fifty tribal leaders attend the National Tribal Government conference in Washington, DC and send a letter to President Ronald Reagan asking for the resignation of Secretary of the Interior James G. Watt for his unwillingness to consult with tribes.

1982   Congress passes the Indian Land Consolidation Act.

In *Merrion v. Jicarilla Apache Tribe*, the Supreme Court rules that Indian tribes are entitled to impose taxes on non-Indians that are conducting business on their reservation.

January 12, 1983   The Federal Oil and Gas Royalty Management Act is passed, allowing cooperative agreements between the secretary of the Interior, tribes, and states pertaining to oil and gas royalty management information.

January 14   The Indian Tribal Tax Status Act is passed, stating that tribes have many of the federal tax advantages that states have.

June 8, 1984   The U.S. Senate agrees to make the Senate Select Committee on Indian Affairs, introduced on a temporary basis in 1977, permanent.

September 2   The Mashantucket Pequot Indians in eastern Connecticut obtain title to 650 acres of their original reservation after an eight-year struggle.

April 16, 1985   In *Kerr-McGee Corp v. Navajo Tribe*, the Supreme Court rules that the Navajo have the right to tax business on their reservation without federal approval, allowing tribes to tax mineral leases on the reservation.

February 14, 1986   The Smithsonian Museum of Natural History agrees to return skeletal remains to tribes for reburial on tribal lands, and an estimated more than 1 million Indian remains are stored at museums and universities.

July 4   The Pequot tribe in Connecticut opens Foxwoods Indian Casino and Resort, which becomes the world's largest gaming operation.

October 27   Congress amends the Indian Civil Rights Act to permit tribal courts to impose fines of $5,000 and one year in jail for violating tribal laws.

1988   The court ruling in *California v. Cabazon Band of Mission Indians* allows Indians to operate gaming operations.

October 17   The Indian Gaming Regulatory Act is passed, establishing the Indian Gaming Commission and its supervision of state-tribal compacts.

November 28, 1989   The National Museum of the American Indian Act is passed, providing for museum construction on the Smithsonian Mall in Washington, DC.

May 29, 1990   In *Duro v. Reina*, the Supreme Court rules that tribes do not have criminal jurisdiction over nonmember Indians on the reservation.

August 3   Congress declares November as American Indian Heritage Month.

September 25   The Tribally Controlled Vocational Institutional Support Act is passed, allowing grants to operate tribally controlled postsecondary vocational institutions.

September 28   The Indian Tribal Leaders Conference in Albuquerque, New Mexico, proposes to reorganize the BIA.

October 30   The Native American Languages Act is passed to promote the preservation of Indian languages, with fewer than 250 left at this time.

November 16   The Native American Graves Protection and Repatriation Act is passed to protect Indian grave sites and return Indian remains and cultural artifacts to tribes.

November 28   The National Indian Forest Resources Management Act is passed to improve management of Indian forest lands between tribes and the Department of the Interior.

December   Department of the Interior Secretary Manuel Lujan states that an advisory task force of 43 members, including 36 tribal leaders and 7 Interior officials, calls for reorganization of the BIA to give it less control, and the tribes more, in decisions regarding the operation and management of federal programs involving $415 million in annual appropriations.

January 1992   President Bill Clinton's administration holds the White House Conference on Indian Education to develop recommendations to improve Indian education services.

1993   Ada Deer, Menominee, becomes the first Native woman to serve as assistant secretary of the Interior over Indian Affairs.

August 6, 1998   President Clinton signs Executive Order 13096, which commits the federal government to improving the academic performance of Indian students and reducing the dropout rate of American Indian students attending public schools and BIA schools.

September 8, 2000   Assistant secretary of the Interior Kevin Gover (Pawnee) makes a national apology on behalf of the BIA for the past mistreatment of American Indians as the BIA celebrates its 175th anniversary.

2002   By a new law, the Sand Creek Massacre site is returned to Cheyenne and Arapaho tribes.

2004   The Smithsonian's National Museum of the American Indian celebrates its grand opening.

August 8, 2005   President George W. Bush signs the Indian Energy Act to improve relations between tribes and the federal government. The act gives tribes more control over the development of their lands.

May 6, 2004   Kansas Senator Sam Brownback introduces Senate Joint Resolution 37 as a national apology by Congress to American Indians.

2010   Ninety-five percent of the BIA's 12,000 employees are American Indian or Alaska Native.

ONE

The Office of Indian Affairs, 1824–1849

The foreign supervision of Indian affairs initially began during the mid-16th century when European nations ventured to North America to extend their empires. The Europeans viewed Native people as potential colonists, trade partners, and possible allies against other foreign nations. Desire for new lands inspired an era of imperialism as Europe led the way in claiming various parts throughout the world. Naval powers—Spain, England, France, and the Netherlands—ruled the seas as explorers staked claims to the Americas for their monarchies.

European officials realized that a policy and an official body made relations with the indigenous people operate more efficiently. Negotiations and trade business involved many Native communities, yet the Europeans had no idea how many different Indian nations existed in the so-called New World. Well over 500 different Indian nations and their communities lived in North America.

The Spanish ruled over the North American Southwest, and by the turn of the 19th century, the imperial wars in Europe and the Americas ended with the British as the victor over France. After the French and Indian War of 1754–1763, the dissolution of Spanish Florida in 1783, and the fall of Napoleon Bonaparte in 1815, the British were alone in their dealings with eastern Indians. The Spanish hold on the Southwest continued for the next two decades. The British monopolized trade relations with Indians at profitable levels. Like the French, the British found it economically beneficial to trade European items to Indians for pelts of fur, particularly those of beavers. Trapped by Indian hunters, numerous shiploads of pelts left North America for the foreign market during this golden age of trade in the late 18th century.

British Indian Policy

Colonial activities convinced the Crown to establish an Indian Department in 1755, which was divided into northern and southern divisions. George II found himself attending more to his colonies across the Atlantic and realized something had to be done to regularize British-Indian relations. And one particular person arose as the possible solution.

Sir William Johnson, an Irish-born Englishman, operated a successful trade business with Mohawk hunters, and he had learned to speak their language. Johnson's influence convinced Governor George Clinton of the New York colony to appoint Sir William as superintendent of Indian Affairs for the Six Nations in 1744. The military power and political influence of the Six Nations required a careful cultivation of fine diplomacy. As Johnson's personal land estate grew because of his presence representing the British, he received the appointment of superintendent of Indian Affairs for all northern Indians in January 1756, and he served until 1774. Johnson's responsibilities involved maintaining the Covenant Chain of peace, friendship, and respect—an alliance between the Iroquois and the colonies, which lasted from 1692 to 1753.

Similarly, Sir Edmond Atkin became the superintendent of the Indians of the South in 1756. Atkin negotiated land grants with traders wanting to enter the region to exchange goods for Indian pelts. Most important, the Crown wanted Atkin to maintain peace with the five southern nations: the Cherokee, Creek, Choctaw, Chickasaw, and Seminole. John Stuart would later succeed Atkin in this position. Powerfully large in population, these tribal nations ruled the broad region south of the Ohio River.

British means of negotiating with Indian leaders set a precedent for the formation of American Indian policy. The practices of a superintendent included monitoring Indian activities as well as making formal relationships, when necessary, to stop independent traders from making their own agreements with the Indians.

First Continental Congress

When the First Continental Congress met on September 5, 1774, the delegates found themselves consumed with threats from the British to rule the 13 colonies. Organizational issues for a new government convinced American officials to focus on maintaining peace with Indians. The Continental Congress's Indian policy was intended to avoid hostilities, which required successful diplomacy. The majority of Indians had sided with the British in the Revolutionary War that lasted from 1775 to 1783. An estimated 13,000 fought as loyalists for the British, consisting mainly of Mohawk, Seneca, Cayuga, and Onondaga. Only the Mohican joined the Americans (Merrell 1991, 393).

While the United States emerged as a new nation, war broke out in the South with the Cherokees. The militia of North Carolina, Virginia, and South Carolina united to defeat the Cherokee. This conflict became known as the Second Cherokee War and threatened the success of the American Revolution. The Cherokee, a formidable military power, had waged an earlier war from 1758 to 1761 that earned the title of the First Cherokee War.

As more settlers moved into the southern region, Indian affairs escalated with the increasing presence of missionaries. Baptists, Methodists, Presbyterians, and other groups appeared on the southern frontier to convert Indians to Christianity. Quakers and Catholics had already been among Indians in the North well before 1776. Eager to work among the Indians, missionaries complicated Indian affairs, forcing officials new at their jobs to formalize some approach toward indigenous people. Early government officials wanted to control relations with the Native groups so that the missionaries did not become too influential among the indigenous.

Officially, 1776 marked the beginning of the United States of America. The late 1770s and early 1780s proved to be a turning point for Native peoples as well. The United States created the War Department in 1778, and Henry Knox of Boston, a former colonel under Washington, became the first secretary on September 12, 1789. Also known as the War Office, the department maintained the U.S. Army, including naval affairs. (The War Department lasted from 1789 until September 18, 1947, when it was renamed the Department of the Army.) Secretary Knox had a large say in developing Indian affairs, especially treaty negotiations and the formation of early Indian policies. Indian affairs remained under the war secretary until Congress created the commissioner of Indian Affairs in 1832.

Simultaneously, the War Department strove to work directly with the Indian nations. Early federal-Indian policy began with congressional action attempting to unify its approach in dealing with the various Indian nations. At the same time, Knox, President Washington, and other officials realized that the military strength of many of the Indian nations like the Iroquois exceeded that of the United States, including the Delaware, who held a respected status among regional Indian nations.

Secretary of War Henry Knox was the principal federal official in charge of Indian affairs before the Indian Office was established in 1824. (National Archives)

First U.S.-Indian Policy

As the first U.S. president, George Washington already had considerable experience with Indians. He owned land along the Ohio River and knew that negotiations with Indians cost a lot less than a war with them. President Washington explicitly stated, "For I repeat it, . . . that policy and economy point very strongly to the expediency of being upon good terms with the Indians, and the propriety of purchasing their Lands in preference to attempting to drive them by force of arms out of their Country; . . . and this can be had by purchase at less expence [*sic*], and without that bloodshed" (Fitzpatrick 1938, 136 and 140).

Washington's instruction to Congress became the first official American Indian policy, stressing diplomacy and peace for the first 25 years of U.S.-Indian relations. In the early years, the new United States encountered new problems such as what role did its new states have in relations with Indians? Delaware, Pennsylvania, and New Jersey became states in 1787, followed by Georgia, Connecticut, Massachusetts, Maryland, South Carolina, New Hampshire, Virginia, and New York the following year. North Carolina came in 1789 with Vermont in 1791, Kentucky in 1792, and Tennessee in 1796. Sixteen colonial areas became states before the end of the century.

Secretary Knox and other government officials had no way of knowing that more than 250 Indian languages existed with various dialects in North America. A new Indian policy of peaceful negotiations entailed working out a protocol that acknowledged the importance of the Native leaders, as federal officials wanted recognition, trade, and land from the Indians. This

Indian Peace Medal, 1833. As early as 1792, Indian peace medals, usually inscribed with the most common phrase in Indian treaties, "peace and friendship," were given to Native leaders by U.S. officials as an act of diplomacy. These medals, often plated of pure silver, were produced—including fake ones—until about 1869. (Courtesy of the U.S. Mint)

initial diplomacy fell to early Indian agents who became strategically important, and many of these individuals were unofficial. They became agents only because they could speak one or more Native languages. The role of the Indian agent or interpreter held considerable responsibility for making both sides understood.

At the same time, early Indian agents, interpreters, and federal officials quickly learned about Native protocol in calling meetings or councils. Gift giving played a critical role on the part of the United States, as federal officials wanted to keep Native leaders in a positive frame of mind (Jacobs 1966, 11–28). Providing gifts to begin talks or councils remained a part of the cultural ways of Native people to create a positive opportunity for negotiations.

Vast cultural differences between the United States and Native nations enlightened American officials who began to understand a kinship system of references when addressing Native peoples. Interpreters and early agents integrated "father" into their speeches in reference to President George Washington. They soon discovered the dependency of Native people on the gifts and trade goods from the British and French crowns with Indian leaders referring to the British "father" and French "father." The symbolic paternal reference allowed American officials to redirect the Indian dependency to the president of the United States.

First U.S.-Indian Treaty

When the American Revolution broke out in 1775, the Second Continental Congress created three Indian agencies that held the authority to negotiate treaties with Indians. These unstable years reflected the new United

States struggling for its own recognition. In 1778 President Washington and Secretary Knox agreed on the necessity of gaining recognition from and maintaining the neutrality of the Delaware, one of the most powerful Indian nations in the northern region. The United States needed the Delaware as a military ally with the British so close at hand. In fact, Lord Dunmore (John Murray) entered into early treaty negotiations with the influential Delaware leader, White Eyes. Washington and Knox ordered eight military officials and three other men led by Brigadier-General Lach'n McIntosh to impress the Delaware and invite their leaders to Fort Pitt to talk peace. On September 17, McIntosh and his officials persuaded White Eyes, The Pipe, John Kill Buck, and other attending Delaware to make an alliance agreement. In the second article of the treaty, the agreement stated:

> That a perpetual peace and friendship shall from henceforth take place, and subsist between the contracting parties aforesaid, through all succeeding generations: and if either of the parties are engaged in a just and necessary war with any other nation or nations, that then each shall assist the other in due proportion to their abilities, till their enemies are brought to reasonable terms of accommodation. (Kappler 1904, 3)

This agreement resulted in the first federal-Indian treaty that Congress ratified, and other treaties soon followed. Ratification depended upon the U.S. Senate voting to approve treaties. "Peace and friendship," the understanding of the British-Indian Covenant Chain, became a common phrase for most treaties between the United States and Indian nations. In all, the 1778 agreement set a precedent for a total of 374 Indian treaties that federal and military officials successfully negotiated and ratified until 1871 when a federal law then stopped the process of Indian treaty making. The first Indian treaty was also known as the Treaty of Fort Pitt. With safe passage through the land of the powerful Delaware, Americans attacked the British at Detroit. The treaty also called for the Delaware to fight for the United States, who provided "articles of clothing, utensils and implements of war" to the Indians. Furthermore, the United States offered an Indian state consisting of Ohio Country tribes to be headed by the Delaware that would have representation in Congress. Supposedly the Delaware leader White Eyes thought the Delaware could become the 14th state in the United States of America. In early November, frontiersmen killed the Delaware leader, provoking many Indians to fight for the British against the Americans in the revolution.

Interestingly, the area of about 2,500 square miles that became known as Delaware became the first official state of the United States on December 7, 1787, and the first one to ratify the new U.S. Constitution. By the end of the 18th century, 15 more new states joined the union stretching southward from Vermont and New Hampshire to Kentucky.

President Washington continually urged diplomacy in approaching the Indian nations. He feared British intrigue to incite Indian attacks against American settlements. In a letter to New York State Senator James Duane, Washington outlined the first Indian policy by stating, "But as we prefer Peace to a state of Warfare, as we consider them as a deluded People; as we perswade [sic] ourselves that they are convinced, from experience, of their error in taking up the Hatchet against us, and that their true Interest and safety must now depend upon *our* friendship" (Fitzpatrick 1938, 133–140).

At the time, Congressman Duane served as the chairman of the congressional committee on Indian affairs. The Continental Congress's informal Indian policy favored a friends and allies approach of cultivating harmonious relationships with the Indian nations, particularly the noted Delaware and the influential Six Nations of the Iroquois (Onondaga, Oneida, Cayuga, Mohawk, Seneca, and Tuscarora).

Following Washington's lead, the Continental Congress issued a proclamation on Indian affairs on September 22, 1783, citing the ninth article of the Articles of Confederation. The proclamation, as recorded in the 25th volume of *Journals of the Continental Congress*, stated:

> the United States in Congress assembled have the role and exclusive right and owner of regulating the trade, and managing all affairs with the Indians, not members of any of the states, provided that the legislative right of any State, within its own limits, be not infringed or violated. (602)

Duane and Washington kept an eye on British influence and British supervision of Canada, its colony. Furthermore, the two American officials recalled that a majority of Indians caught in the Revolutionary War fought against the United States. The American Revolution closed with the Treaty of Paris in 1783 between the United States and Great Britain as Indians officially came under U.S. supervision.

Treaty with Six Nations

In early October, American officials arranged for a meeting with Iroquois leaders. The Iroquois nations held the greatest military strength in the New York region. Treaty commissioners Richard Butler, Oliver Wolcott, and Arthur Lee called the council meeting of sachems and warriors of the Six Nations. The United States recognized peace with the Six Nations and succeeded in negotiating the Treaty with the Six Nations on October 22, 1784. This major treaty designated the boundary lines of the Six Nations with them yielding to the United States outside of the borders.

On November 28, 1785, American officials Benjamin Hawkins, Andrew Pickens, Joseph Martin, and Lachlan M'Intosh met with the Cherokee leaders and their warriors. The two sides reached an agreement made at Hopewell, South Carolina Colony. A second Cherokee treaty followed in 1786. Both treaties called for the withdrawal of U.S. protection of settlers on Cherokee land and established boundary lines, separating the Indians from the settlers (Kappler 1904, 8–11).

Northwest Ordinance of 1787

As new settlers arrived at eastern ports and headed west across the Appalachian Mountains, Washington's government became involved with Indians of the Ohio River region. Washington and Knox continued precariously in dealing with different Indian leaders. Their approach alerted all federal officials to the current Indian policy of careful diplomacy and systematically dealing with settlers moving westward into the region. This resulted in Congress passing the Northwest Ordinance on July 13, 1787.

This important measure established the Northwest Territory and systematically produced an orderly settlement to the Ohio country. The ordinance, recorded in the 32nd volume of *Journals of the Continental Congress*, states, "The utmost good faith shall always be observed towards the Indians, their lands and property shall never be taken from them without their consent; and in their property, rights and liberty, they never shall be invaded or disturbed, unless in just and lawful wars authorised by Congress" (340–341). The continual westward movement of settlers tested the diplomacy of U.S. officials, not only in keeping Native nations as allies but in stopping new territories and states from monopolizing affairs with Indians.

Formalizing Indian Departments

Three years later, Congress passed an ordinance for the regulation of Indian affairs in August 1786, which identified geographic regions as departments. The ordinance identified the two areas as the Northern and Southern districts. Individuals working in these districts began to also refer to these areas or departments as "superintendencies, agencies, and subagencies" (Prucha 1962, 52). This ordinance also created Indian superintendents. The idea of Indian agents and departments among the Indians became the norm under the attention of the War Department and the president. The Indian agent exercised six basic duties: "The report of claims made for injuries inflicted by Indians upon whites and by whites upon Indians; the compilation of lists of Indians to whom rations should be issued; the payment of government annuities chiefs; the arrangement for visits of chiefs to Washington; the settlement of intertribal disputes; and the supervision of local education development" (Gallaher 1916, 37).

In 1789 John Adams of Massachusetts, the first vice president, became the second U.S. president. He served two terms, ending in 1797. Although he was not so much personally concerned with Indian affairs, his administration involved itself with issues pertaining to the Native nations. As described earlier, Congress passed an act on August 7, 1789, that created the secretary of war. Specifically, section one outlined the responsibilities of the position. Quoted in *United States Statutes at Large*, section one states that "the Secretary of the Department of War shall . . . perform and execute . . . duties . . . relative to Indian affairs" (49). This law made Indian affairs a matter of the War Department until the creation of the Department of the Interior in 1849.

Congress passed another important measure on September 11, 1789, that paid $2,000 as an annual salary to the governor of the Northwest Territory, also known as the Ohio Country. This law involved the governor taking charge of the duties of superintendent of Indian affairs in the Northern department. The following year, the law identified the territory south of the Ohio River and stated that the responsibilities of the Indian superintendent would be joined with those responsibilities of the governor (Prucha 1962, 52). On June 1, 1792, Kentucky became the 15th state, and Tennessee followed in 1796. Two years later, Mississippi Territory developed as more settlers homesteaded in the area. In 1800, Congress passed a new law that divided the Northwest Territory and created Indiana Territory. This measure helped Ohio become a state in 1803 with most of the eastern part of the region already settled.

First Trade and Intercourse Act

Congress passed the first of the Indian Trade and Intercourse Acts on July 22, 1790, the last one being made in 1834. These laws set guidelines for U.S. interaction with the Native nations. The initial act authorized superintendents to distribute licenses to those desiring to trade with Indians, and they had the power to revoke licenses from traders or stop illegal trading.

The government was specifically concerned with the trade of liquor to Indians as independent traders made rum available to them. The government attempted to control the whiskey trade when the president appointed four special agents. Three agents were designated for the Southern department and one for the Five Nations of the Iroquois League. The agents focused on diplomacy to keep peace and communications with the Iroquois in the North and the Muscogee Creeks, Cherokees, and Chickasaws in the South.

The second Trade and Intercourse Act, passed on March 1, 1793, authorized the president to name "temporary agents" to live among Indians and instruct them in the ways of civilization by teaching them agriculture. Over time, officials used the word "temporary" less, and the new popular title became "Indian agent" (Prucha 1962, 55). The agents monitored Indian activities, maintained peace, and stressed the importance of Indian relationships with the government in Washington.

The Indian agents reported to the War Department through the territorial governors. Agents' responsibilities increased to include the maintenance of records of the history of the area where the Indians lived and reports on the progress of Indians becoming civilized. Assistants to the agents, called subagents, received appointments and provisions. There was little designation between agents and subagents as the Indian Office directed the latter to move to new areas to live with Native communities. By 1818 a total of 15 agents and 10 subagents lived among the Indian nations (Prucha 1962, 54–55).

Factory System

President Washington had stressed the importance of trade relations to assure a successful commerce with the Indian nations. He articulated the need for government trading houses to assure an American presence throughout what had become known as Indian Country (Richardson 1897, 133). Washington believed that a stable economy and peaceful relations with Indians guaranteed the future of the United States. The government called for a plan or system of trade houses or posts called the factory system.

Passed every two or more years, Congress enacted a permanent act regulating trade on March 30, 1802. The acts, now recorded in *United States Statutes at Large*, had two defining characteristics. First, they established a series of "factories" known as trading posts that had government licenses to trade goods to Indians for their pelts. Previously it had been remnant French and British traders that engaged in the Indian trade. Second, the act established "Indian Territory" for the first time as "all that part of the United States west of the Mississippi and not within the states of Missouri and Louisiana and the territory of Arkansas" (139–146). Four years later, Washington established the superintendent of Indian Trade with funding to carry out its operation (Taylor 1984, 33). The superintendent of Indian trade became the forerunner to the position of commissioner of Indian Affairs.

In that same year, instructions were issued to Indian agents. The instructions required agents "to reside with the Indian Nations . . . are the cultivation of peace and harmony between the U. States, and the Indian Nations generally; the detection of any improper conduct in the Indians, or the Citizens of the U. States, or others relating to the Indians, or their lands, and the introduction of the Arts of husbandry, and domestic manufactures, as means of producing, and diffusing the blessings attached to a well regulated civil Society" (Prucha 1962, 51). Government officials sought to introduce civilization to the Indians because they believed Native people could be more easily dealt with if they were civilized.

The superintendent of Indian Trade represented the most influential position in federal-Indian affairs. When this position became vacant, President James Madison appointed Thomas McKenney on April 12, 1816. From a prosperous family in eastern Maryland, the Quaker-influenced superintendent had served in local militias in the War of 1812. McKenney became responsible for 28 trading posts, although only about a dozen or less were in operation at one time (Kvasnicka and Viola 1979, 2). McKenney envisioned the trade houses offering the finest merchandise to Indians for their furs, which was not easy as the British provided goods of a better quality. The War of 1812 had disrupted the factory system when the British destroyed several trade houses. In trying to keep the system functioning, McKenney began monitoring all of Indian affairs, a difficult task from his office in Washington. He advised Secretary of War John C. Calhoun on Indian affairs, and Calhoun encouraged this relationship.

McKenney's greatest achievement was influencing Calhoun and Congress to pass the Indian Civilization Fund Act on March 3, 1819. This measure provided $10,000 per year for the operation of schools throughout Indian Country. Church leaders and humanitarians pressured congressmen to accept a plan to Christianize and civilize Indians. This effort resulted in a partnership of missionaries and the government to educate and change the cultural ways of Indians. The act enabled the president to "employ capable persons of good moral characters, to instruct [Indians] in . . . agriculture . . . teaching their children in reading, writing, and arithmetic." (Statutes at Large, 3:516–17).

During the following five years, federal officials became increasingly aware that a central point, such as an office, was necessary. One of the most powerful orators in Congress represented South Carolina. In an attempt to provide balanced representation in the new federal government, the president appointed John C. Calhoun as the new secretary of war. Congressional refusal to recognize the need for an office of Indian affairs compelled Secretary Calhoun to take matters in his own hands and form the first Bureau of Indian Affairs in his Department of War. Although Calhoun used the phrase Bureau of Indian Affairs (BIA) for the first time, the BIA remained known commonly as the Indian Office. Fourteen years later, in 1824, the United States placed the Office of Indian Affairs in the War Department.

Jeffersonian Indian Policy

As president, Thomas Jefferson inherited increasing Indian trade and treaty making. Considered to be a political philosopher, idealist, and intellectual, Jefferson envisioned the yeoman farmer to advance republican values as he viewed them: farmers would build homes, communities, and states while practicing democratic freedom. He believed that the federal government should not restrict the states and sought to provide guidelines in the form of laws for peaceful growth. At the same time, Jefferson believed that Indians could have a place in American society if they learned the ways of the yeoman farmer. Jefferson received criticism from skeptics who claimed that Indians were incapable of becoming civilized. A group of American officials began to speak out, and they became known as removalists. Removalists wanted all Indians to be moved westward, leaving their lands available to expanding settlers.

The Jefferson administration negotiated more treaties than the previous presidential administrations of George Washington and John Adams, which combined had negotiated 19 in 11 years. Jefferson's administration negotiated 40 treaties. This busy activity indicated that the United States needed peaceful relations with the Indian nations.

As trade continued between the early Americans and various Indian groups, other factors created problems. As early as 1809, British naval conflict against France involved the British stopping American ships. In

Following George Washington's initial Indian policy, President Thomas Jefferson advocated the assimilation of Native people into farmers as his response to the Indian question of whether Native people could become civilized or not. His administration negotiated 40 treaties for trade and peace with Indians. (National Archives)

response to the British impressments of roughly 6,000 American sailors, the United States and England entered the War of 1812 as Congress voted its slimmest margin ever, in American history, for going to war.

The War of 1812 cost the United States more men, and it endured more damages, than the British. In fact, Americans had to rebuild the White House after the British invaded Washington and burned the capitol before its construction was even finished. James Madison served as president during these turbulent years from 1809 to 1817, and he continued Jefferson's Indian policy of treaty negotiations.

Madison had worked with Washington to design the new federal government, and he was known to be a brilliant mind. He served as secretary of state under Jefferson, and he orchestrated the purchase of Louisiana from France for $15 million, thereby doubling the size of the United States. At the same time, the purchase doubled the responsibility of the BIA to supervise new western Indian nations within the Louisiana area.

First Commissioner of Indian Affairs

Under President Madison, Thomas McKenney became the first unofficial head of Indian affairs, and Elbert Herring would be the first official commissioner. Previously McKenney served as the superintendent of Indian Trade from 1816 to 1822. In 1822, Congress dissolved the U.S. Indian Trade program as Indian removal became the unofficial policy as more treaties aimed to displace Indians. Private interests like the American Fur Company

U.S. Senator John C. Calhoun from South Carolina served as secretary of state, vice president of the United States, and secretary of war. In 1824, as war secretary, he created the Indian Office in his department that eventually became the Bureau of Indian Affairs. (Library of Congress)

lobbied Congress to put an end to the factory trade system, and it ended government-regulated Indian trade in May. McKenney's influence grew in Washington as he seemed to know the most about Native people. While the president did not seem to take notice, John Calhoun did.

On March 11, 1824, Secretary of War John C. Calhoun appointed Thomas McKenney to take charge of the newly created Bureau of Indian Affairs. In his instructions to McKenney, Calhoun outlined his duties for directing Indian Affairs: "You will take charge of the appropriations for annuities, and of current expenses, and all warrants on the same will be issued on your requisitions on the Secretary of War. You are also charged with the examination of claims arising out of the laws regulating the intercourse with Indian Tribes" (Meriwether 1968, 575–576). In his new position McKenney supervised two clerks and a messenger and received an annual salary of $1,600. This salary proved to be actually $400 less than when he served as superintendent of Indian Trade (Kvasnicka and Viola 1979, 4).

McKenney took charge of Indian affairs for six years from 1824 to 1830. During this time, he advocated a "civilization" program for Indians with the idea of removing them west of the Mississippi River for this grand experiment to take place. McKenney's plan grew from Jefferson's belief that Native people could all become agrarians and help to build the United States. But no one bothered to ask the Indians what they thought. Generally the Indian nations fell into two groups: those peaceful to the United States and those who were hostile. The discussion of civilization and assimilation carried over into the following presidential administrations.

Thomas Loraine McKenney was superintendent of Indian trade from 1816 to 1822 and served as the first commissioner of Indian Affairs from 1824 to 1830. (Library of Congress)

After his election to the presidency in 1828, Andrew Jackson engineered a program for wholesale Indian removal to the West. He disagreed with McKenney's view on Indians and dismissed him as the Indian commissioner in 1830. At the time of his dismissal, McKenney's Indian civilization program operated 52 schools with an enrollment of 1,512 Indian students (Kvasnicka and Viola 1979, 5).

Later McKenney co-authored with James Hall, his former business partner, a book of three volumes: *McKenney and Hall's History of the Indian Tribes of North America, with biographical sketches and anecdotes of the principal chiefs* (McKenney and Hall, [1836–1844] 2002). McKenney's work broadened the scope of Indian affairs that fell to the U.S. government. The close proximity of white settlements to the Indian nations prompted Commissioner McKenney and other officials like Lewis Cass and William Clark to report on the activities of Indians from other parts of Indian Country. Both Cass and Clark had extensive experiences in dealing with Indians. Cass served as secretary of war and also territorial governor of Michigan, and Clark had achieved historical recognition in his travel up the Missouri River with Meriwether Lewis during 1804–1806.

Jacksonian Policy of Indian Removal

In the South the Muscogee Creeks waged conflict against settlers to protect their lands. This action developed into the Creek War of 1813–1814, which was actually a part of the War of 1812 that began in 1811 and extended into 1815. The Creeks operated independently of the British and Tecumseh's Indian army. The War Department ordered Andrew Jackson against the Creeks in 1813 where he became known as an Indian fighter and "Old Hickory." Slim like an oak stick, Andrew Jackson's leanness and unwillingness to break under the pressures of war earned him his nickname.

Jacksonian Indian removal policy marred the 1830s as the majority of eastern Indian nations were forcibly removed from their homelands in the Eastern Woodlands to west of the Mississippi River. Jackson kept the War Department busy during his eight years as president from 1829 to 1837. One of Jackson's crowning achievements was the Indian Removal Act passed on May 28, 1830. Congress authorized $500,000 for the purpose of exchanging Indian lands in the East for new lands in the West and for the cost of the removals. Known best as the Trail of Tears, the Cherokee story represented the displacement and suffering of many tribes such as the Potawatomi, who called their removal the "Trail of Courage." Ironically the Delaware found themselves being removed a total of nine times following their signing of the first treaty in 1778. Indian agents like Benjamin Hawkins, who worked among the Creeks in the South, negotiated the removal treaties.

In the end, some missionaries moved with the Indian nations. Some Indians took their slaves with them during removal to the West. Both the Indian Office and the War Department became weighted down in paperwork while sending guidelines to military officials to remove the Indian nations via parties or groups. The Indian Office negotiated contracts with independent companies to provide supplies to the removal parties. This upheaval of removing Indians provoked some tribes to resist. In western Illinois the Sac and Fox went to war in 1832 under the leadership of Black Hawk. The Seminoles in Florida waged a second war from 1835 to 1842 to resist removal as they fought to stay in their Native homeland.

Indian affairs became more complicated when the Cherokees resisted via use of law in the courtroom. In two noted cases, the Cherokees set a legal precedent that would be a landmark in federal-Indian law for years to come. In 1831 in *Cherokee v. United States*, the Cherokee lost when Chief Justice John Marshall ruled against them, calling the Cherokee a dependent of the United States. Then, at age 72, an ill Chief Justice Marshall, stricken with pneumonia, ruled in favor of the Cherokee in *Worcester v. Georgia* in 1832. His ruling, which disturbed President Jackson, referred to the Cherokee as a sovereign nation that only the United States could deal with, not the state of Georgia.

During the 1830s and for the next decade, the Office of Indian Affairs supervised removals of Indian groups. The annexation of Texas expanded the western border of the United States beyond the Mississippi River. Born in Maryland, Samuel S. Hamilton supervised the Office of Indian Affairs for nearly a year: from September 30, 1830, to August 31, 1831. He had clerked for Thomas McKenney who was earlier in charge of the Indian Bureau. In his brief term, the distribution of annuity payments and depredation claims against various Indian groups increased. For the most part, Secretary of War John Eaton ran Indian affairs as he authorized the survey of Choctaw lands in Mississippi and pressured the tribe into removal. Eaton then worked to displace the Cherokees, Chickasaws, and Creeks to the West.

Creation of Commissioner of Indian Affairs

In 1832 Congress officially acknowledged the Bureau of Indian Affairs and passed a law on July 9 to create the position of commissioner of Indian Affairs. Congress empowered the president to appoint this position. As indicated in *United States Statutes at Large*, the law stated that the new official "shall, under the direction of the Secretary of War, and agreeably to such regulations as the President . . . have the direction and management of all Indian affairs, and of all matters arising out of Indian relations, and shall receive a salary of three thousand dollars per annum" (564).

Following Hamilton, a successful lawyer from New York, Elbert Herring, served as head of the Indian Office beginning on July 10, 1832. Herring had no previous experience with Indians. Secretary of War Lewis Cass persuaded Andrew Jackson to appoint his friend Herring to direct the Indian Bureau. Herring accepted the pro-removal argument of transporting Indians to the West and quickly gained Jackson's support. Herring understood the Jackson-Cass argument that the only way for the Indians to survive was if they were removed west of the Mississippi. They would not be able to survive the advancing settler expansion that had crossed the Appalachians into the Ohio Country and into the southern region. Corrupt traders providing liquor to Indians added to the woes of the Indian Office.

Herring proved to be inefficient in his job and served as Cass's puppet. For the next five years more treaties were negotiated and ratified, with these agreements affecting more Indian nations in the East, South, and the Ohio Country that now included Michigan. Herring allowed unfair practices in treaty negotiations such as "chief making" in which federal officials negotiated with Indians who were not the true leaders of their people. Increased business in the BIA called for a reorganization of the office and an amendment to the Trade and Intercourse Act of 1802. Cass pushed legislation through Congress in 1834, calling for the Indian Service Reorganization Act and a new trade and intercourse act.

BIA Organization of Indian Agents

On June 30, 1834, Congress passed a law to organize the department of Indian Affairs. As indicated in the statute, the double responsibilities of territorial governor and superintendent of Indian affairs ended for the territories of Florida, Arkansas, and Michigan. Superintendents of Indian affairs became separate "with general supervision and control over the official conduct and accounts of all officers and persons employed by the government in the Indian department." In addition the president appointed Indian agents for terms of four years with two agents for the western territory, an agent for the Chickasaw, an agent for the Eastern Cherokee, an agent for the Florida Indians, an agent for the Indians in Indiana, an agent placed at Chicago, an agent at Rock Island, an agent at Prairie du Chien, an agent for Michilimackinac and the Sault Sainte Marie, an agent for the Saint Peter's, and an agent for the Upper Missouri (735–738).

Although Commissioner Herring disliked Indian cultures, he favored Richard Johnson's Choctaw Academy, located in Kentucky. Johnson added educational curriculum to the industrial courses in 1833 with the idea that the academy would produce Indian teachers that would introduce a civilized culture to its students. Herring's support of the school failed to win the support of an impatient Cass who disliked the Indian commissioner and convinced Jackson to demote him and name him as a paymaster for the War Department in 1836.

On July 4, 1836, Jackson appointed Carry Allen Harris to be commissioner of Indian Affairs. A fellow Tennessean, Harris joined his father-in-law in the founding of the *Nashville Republican*. He kept up with politics and moved his family to Washington where he gained the favoritism of Jackson. Interestingly, President Martin Van Buren retained Harris as commissioner when the new president entered the White House in March 1837. As commissioner, Harris conducted the first review of the history of Indian affairs with the United States. He realized that the Indian policy called for removal of eastern Indians to the West, the founding of a territorial government for the relocated Indian nations, and a plan to "civilize" the indigenous people. The commissioner worked ardently to remove the southern Indian nations, particularly the Cherokees, from their lands in

Tennessee, North Carolina, Georgia, and Alabama. During this turmoil the Second Seminole War broke out in 1835, and Harris called for the removal of the Seminoles from Florida to the West. Under Harris the BIA followed the "civilization" plan and constructed local schools for the removed tribes so that educators and missionaries could teach the farm vocation to Indian youths. In October 1838, Van Buren received firm evidence of a business scheme allowing Harris to gain wealth from Indian allotments in the South. The Harris scandal discredited the Indian Office, and an embarrassed Van Buren called for Harris's resignation.

During this time American settlers continued to push westward as many entered a land called Texas. Held by the Mexican government, Texas won its independence in its revenge—"Remember the Alamo!" From 1836 to 1845, Texas enjoyed its independence. For the first time, Plains Indians became the major concern in Indian affairs for the United States when Texas entered the union in 1845 as the 28th state. Kiowa, Apache, and Comanche—noted Indian warrior nations—changed the course of Indian affairs and how the Indian Office responded. The warrior nations' mobile culture and hunting-oriented economy were unlike what American officials had seen before.

The first 25 years of the Indian Office involved a federal policy of peaceful diplomacy and obtaining Indian lands by means of purchasing them. Without a treasury the United States could ill afford a war of any expense against Indians. As a result, the early treaty negotiations called for the recognition of sovereignty of the United States as well as treatment of the Indian nations as equal sovereign nations.

Conclusion

The Bureau of Indian Affairs found itself supervising a very large variety of issues with Indian communities. Ironically the BIA numbered a mere 108 employees in 1852 (Taylor 1959, 98). Trade, new boundaries, and settlers crossing into Indian lands were among the earliest activities for the Indian Office to supervise. This general situation became more complicated and complex as more Native nations came into contact with the United States. It became evident that the United States had a continual relationship with all Indian nations generally speaking, although some Indian groups were friendlier than others. American westward expansion acted as a catalyst in increasing the urgency of government-Indian relations. New territories developed into new states. By the end of Indian treaty making in 1871, only about a dozen territories had not been named states.

Furthermore, Indian affairs increased as westward expansion pushed across the Appalachian Mountains into the Ohio Country and the Old South. American settlers came into contact with more Indians from different Indian nations. This movement meant also that officials appointed to the Indian commissioner position began to come from other parts of the country and not just from the New England cities. Individuals such as Thomas McKenney; William Clark, the adventurer-explorer from Virginia; and others who had experience with Indians became a valuable asset as westward expansion continued to push the Indian nations in a domino fashion with more treaties being negotiated.

References

"Act Creates the Commissioner of Indian Affairs." July 9, 1832. *United States Statutes at Large*, 564.

"An Act Creating the Secretary of War." August 7, 1789. *United States Statutes at Large*, 49.

Fitzpatrick, John C., ed. *The Writings of George Washington from the Original Manuscript Sources*, Volume 27. Washington, DC: U.S. General Printing Office, 1938.

Gallaher, Ruth A. "The Indian Agent in the United States before 1850." *Iowa Journal of History and Politics* 14, no. 1 (January 1916): 3–55.

"Indian Civilization Act," March 3, 1819. U.S. Statutes at Large, 3:516–17.

Jacobs, Wilbur. *Wilderness Politics and Indian Gifts: The Northern Colonial Frontier, 1748–1763*. Lincoln: University of Nebraska Press, 1966.

Journals of the Continental Congress. Volume 25. Washington, DC: Government Printing Office, 1922.

Journals of the Continental Congress. Volume 32. Washington, DC: Government Printing Office, 1936.

Kappler, Charles J., ed. *Indian Affairs: Laws and Treaties*, Volume 2. Washington, DC: Government Printing Office, 1904.

Kvasnicka, Robert M. and Herman J. Viola, eds. *The Commissioners of Indian Affairs*. Lincoln: University of Nebraska Press, 1979.

McKenney, Thomas and James Hall. *McKenney and Hall's History of the Indian Tribes of North America, with Biographical Sketches and Anecdotes of the Principal Chiefs. Embellished with One Hundred and Twenty Portraits from the Indian Gallery in the Department of War, at Washington*. Cincinnati, OH: Cincinnati Digital Press, 2002. Originally published by E. C. Biddle, 1836–1844.

Meriwether, Robert L., ed. *The Papers of John C. Calhoun*, Volume 5. Columbia: University of South Carolina Press, 1968.

Merrell, James. "Indians and the New Republic." In *The Blackwell Encyclopedia of the American Revolution*, ed. Jack P. Greene and J. R. Pole. Cambridge, MA: Blackwell Reference, 1991.

"Organization of the Department of Indian Affairs Act." June 30, 1834. *U.S. Statutes at Large*, 4: 735–738.

Prucha, Francis P. *American Indian Policy in the Formative Years*. Lincoln: University of Nebraska Press, 1962.

Richardson, James D., comp. *A Compilation of the Messages and Papers of the Presidents*, Volume 1. New York: Bureau of National Literature, 1897.

Taylor, Theodore. *The Bureau of Indian Affairs*. Boulder, CO: Westview Press, 1984.

Taylor, Theodore. "The Regional Organization of the Bureau of Indian Affairs." PhD diss., Harvard University, 1959.

"Trade and Intercourse Act." March 30, 1802. *U.S. Statutes at Large*, 2: 139–146.

TWO

The BIA in the Department of the Interior and Grant's Peace Policy

The rapid expansion of the United States spreading west of the Mississippi River increased the need to cultivate Indian relations. By 1840, 26 more states had joined the union, and more settlers embracing Manifest Destiny pursued their dreams of building new homes and developing the land. On the other side of the frontier, the Indian nations felt the sting of westward expansion again. Indian Country at this time consisted of the present states of Oklahoma, Kansas, Nebraska, and beyond. The Bureau of Indian Affairs had the multiple duties of supervising Indian removal and negotiating contracts with independent companies as well as working with the army, which escorted Native removal parties to their newly reserved homelands.

In 1838 Thomas Hartley Crawford moved into his new office as commissioner of Indian Affairs, and he served until 1845. From the elite class in Chambersburg, Pennsylvania, Crawford became a lawyer and entered politics. He advocated Indian removal legislation in Congress, and Andrew Jackson supported his friend Crawford to head the BIA. Crawford had helped to investigate fraud in Indian affairs, which involved opportunists charging high rates for goods and equipment to move Indian groups westward.

Simultaneously the commissioner developed a plan to introduce manual training schools among Native communities, located near farms, to learn from white families. His civilization plan focused more on Native women as a means to change the cultural traditions. Like so many of his predecessors, Crawford worked to stop the illicit liquor trade to make the Indians feel "that the Government was their best friend" (Commissioner of Indian Affairs 1838, 441–443).

Among Native people, President Andrew Jackson is most closely identified with the Indian Removal Act of 1830, which forced at least 100,000 Indians off their traditional homelands. (Library of Congress)

BIA Responsibility in the Southwest

While the Indian Office personnel realized the increasing problem of supervising Indian affairs from a greater geographic distance, the United States entered a war with Mexico. The Mexicans had won their freedom from Spain in 1821, and conflicting Mexican and American interests soon spurred a war that lasted two years, from 1846 to 1848. The hailed hero Sam Houston and his men of mostly volunteers defeated the Mexican General Antonio Lopez de Santa Anna on April 21, 1836. The Treaty of Guadalupe Hidalgo on February 2, 1848, called for Mexico ceding 525 million square miles of present-day California and the Southwest to the United States in exchange for $15 million.

For the Indian Office, the victory meant added responsibility for more than 100 more Indian nations. Commissioner Crawford and others who succeeded him encountered a dilemma as some Indian nations were residing in permanent settlements, and others were living a nomadic life in pursuit of the buffalo and other wild game. Systematically the Indian Office began its procedure of getting Native people to recognize the United States and to recognize the president as their symbolic father in the White House. Crawford moved next to establish boundaries acknowledged by the Indian nations and the United States. In addition the secretary of war authorized military officials to maintain peace while Crawford deployed agents to supervise and solve daily problems on reservations. Crawford took the next step of calling for further treaty negotiations to establish reservations and smaller areas called *rancherias* for Indians in Southern California.

In 1845 President James Polk appointed William Medill to replace Crawford as Indian commissioner as a political favor to Ohioan politicians and supporters of Van Buren. Medill had absolutely no knowledge of or experience with Indians. To make up for his deficiency, Medill studied the activities of previous commissioners, especially Crawford's work. Within weeks, Medill convinced himself of the need to civilize Indians for assimilation.

At the same time, Medill faced new problems of significant proportion with the addition of Texas; the establishment of the Oregon boundary; and the annexation of the Southwest, including California. These major additions involved more Native communities and created more reservations. Much of Indian affairs had moved further west, convincing Medill that conditions dictated necessary changes in the bureau. In August 1846, Medill made public his views on reforming the Indian Bureau when the House of Representatives requested the War Department make changes in the supervision of Indian affairs. Medill noted to Secretary William L. Marcy that most of the Indian activities occurred in the West. Specifically, Medill recommended improved management, and especially the hiring of better personnel, and he wanted tighter control on Indian trade. Monies paid to Indians, according to the commissioner, too quickly found its way into the hands of traders who gave whiskey to the Indians. In response, Congress passed the Indian Intercourse Act on March 3, 1847. The well-intended law aimed to provide better regulation to stop the liquor trade to Indians, and it called for the distribution of annuities to the heads of families rather than to tribal chiefs (*Statutes at Large* 9, 203–204).

In 1847 the Office of Indian Affairs was officially renamed the Bureau of Indian Affairs. By this year, the federal government paid over a million dollars annually to Indians. Critics in Congress and outside of its halls claimed that Medill wielded too much power, which did not stop him from preparing a new plan that called for creating two large areas set aside for Indians.

As settlers pushed westward with signs on their wagons, "Oregon or Bust," the California and Oregon Trails became popular routes. The Williamette Valley became the final destination for many pioneers. The increasing number of settlers crossing the West acted as a catalyst in intensifying Indian-white relations and provoking discussions of Indian removal. Medill envisioned a northern and a southern region reserved for Indians.

In 1848 a greater catalyst occurred that increased westward movement to California. Miners working for James Marshall in the American River discovered gold on January 24, 1848, at Sutter's Mill in Coloma, California.

This sudden event changed the course of American history and added to the woes of the Office of Indian Affairs. As crazed men found more gold, mining camps sprang up everywhere in the area. The gold rush of 1849 flooded 300,000 people from the rest of the nation and the world to California. One year later, California transitioned from its military government to become the 31st state on September 9, 1850. All of the whirlwind activities pressured Native communities living in the region as well as the Indian Office, which had to send more officials westward to solve problems.

The presidential election of 1848 brought an old war hero to the White House, General Zachery Taylor. Elected as the 12th president, "Old Rough and Ready" was too used to his military commanding style and viewed himself above politics. Taylor named a new commissioner of Indian Affairs, Orlando Brown. Ironically, Brown did less as the commissioner than Medill who had started out knowing nothing about Indians. Brown lasted as commissioner for two years.

The Department of the Interior

The westward expansion of the United States involved the accumulation of much more land than expected and natural resources that needed managerial attention. On March 3, 1849, Congress created the Department of the Interior and moved the newly named Bureau of Indian Affairs under its jurisdiction. Section 5 of the law stated: "That the Secretary of the Interior shall exercise the supervisory and appellate powers now exercised by the Secretary of the War Department, in relation to all the acts of the Commissioner of Indian Affairs" (*Statutes at Large* 9:395). President Taylor named a Whig politician, Thomas Ewing, as the first secretary of the interior on March 8, 1849. The rationale behind the move of the Indian Bureau was that the commissioner of Indian Affairs needed to be in direct communication with other federal officials who ruled over natural resources like water, federal land management, territorial affairs, and wildlife conservation.

Taylor's 16 months in office proved to be short lived with his sudden death from gastroenteritis on July 9, 1850. Luke Lea of Tennessee became the new commissioner, and he served from 1850 to 1853. Lea believed that Indians could and should be assimilated. For three years and more, Indian war raged in Texas and New Mexico, settlers complained to Lea, and gold seekers encroached on Indian lands in California. For most of the rest of the decade, George W. Manypenny served as Indian commissioner from 1853 to 1857. Manypenny would leave a legacy as a proactive commissioner.

First BIA Manual and the Inside of the Office

In 1850, Chief Clerk Charles E. Mix in the bureau wrote the first BIA manual for procedures and supervision of federal-Indian policy. Amidst chaos in the bureau with the commissioner traveling, Congress gave special authorization to develop order in the Indian Office. Mix compiled rules, regulations, and additional helpful information for the use of BIA employees. Clerk Mix, who would become Indian commissioner in 1858, produced an 80-page document published as *Office Copy of the Laws, Regulations, Etc. of the Indian Bureau, 1850* (Mix 1850).

BIA responsibilities increased when the U.S. government completed the Gadsden Purchase in 1854 for $10 million. Ambassador James Gadsden negotiated the agreement that extended the southern extreme portions of Arizona and New Mexico, which were one area at the time, for nearly 30,000 square miles. This addition complicated Indian affairs, which increased greatly when Native groups like the Comanche and Apache raided into Mexico.

While William Dole served as commissioner of Indian Affairs from 1861 to 1865, a wing of the Patent Office building housed the Indian Bureau. Employees described the building as something of an updated structure for its time with central heating that worked only sometimes. This irregularity compelled the two to three clerks to push desks and cabinets to block the heat outlets, thus allowing them to use the fireplaces. The clerks were among the first females working for the federal government. They labored six-hour days, reviewing reports from Indian agents in the field, preparing cost estimates for the congressmen, ordering goods for distribution to the Indian nations, and writing drafts of treaties that were sent for approval by the leaders of the Indian nations (Mix 1850).

From 1850 to 1860, the U.S. government made numerous treaties with the Native communities in California. However, Californians rallied to stop the ratification of these agreements by Congress. Outside of California, the United States made at least 52 treaties with Indian nations while Manypenny served as commissioner of Indian Affairs, resulting in the cession of roughly 174 million acres of Indian land. The advent of the railroad in the West had already followed the success of rail shipping east of the Mississippi for decades. In this light, Manypenny served the good of the United States instead of Indian welfare by making more Native land available for white settlements, ranches, and mines with the westward coming of the railroad development.

The westward movement of settlers, miners, and cattlemen created a corridor through the central plains of the nation. This pathway cut through Indian Territory, and Congress passed the Kansas-Nebraska Act of 1854 with plans for the territorial preparations of Kansas and Nebraska. Congressmen viewed Indians in the two regions as being in the way of progress and schemed to remove the tribes to Indian Territory, which now consisted of the present-day state of Oklahoma. Originally conceived to construct a railroad to connect in Chicago, the measure also repealed the Missouri Compromise of 1820 and added to the division of the nation over slavery.

In the new Indian Territory, the Chickasaw established a constitutional government in 1855. Their government would last until the Curtis Act of 1898 eliminated it. In 1860, the nearby Choctaws started their own constitutional government. Their government had a principal chief, three district chiefs, a legislature, and a court. Like the Chickasaws, the Choctaw government ended with the passage of the Curtis Act in 1898. The Bureau of Indian Affairs under Commissioner Alfred Barton Greenwood supported the Chickasaw and Choctaw as a part of the civilization plan.

The Bureau during the Civil War

South Carolina's attack on Fort Sumter in 1861 and the outbreak of the Civil War muddled Indian affairs for the bureau, incoming Commissioner William Dole, Congress, and Indians. The spread of fighting eventually involved the Indian nations.

In 1861, Colonel James Carleton led the California Volunteer Infantry Regiment; and in the following year, he defeated Confederate forces in two battles in New Mexico. Carleton remained in the area to take charge of the New Mexico department. Carleton planned to force the Mescalero Apaches and the Navajos onto one reservation. The Bosque Redondo was constructed as a reservation of 40 square miles. As many as 8,000 Navajos surrendered to the United States and 53 groups made the "Long Walk" of 300 to 400 miles over 18 days or less to Bosque Redondo in 1864. Two hundred Navajos died. The U.S. military proved to be more of a problem for Commissioner Dole. Carleton's forced Long Walk and the tribal rivalries at the Bosque Redondo caused trouble. Living conditions at the 40-square mile reservation worsened when crops failed, a blow to attempts to teach the Indians agriculture. Poor soil and Indian reluctance to farm as prisoners of war added to the failure.

America's Largest Mass Execution

Responsibilities of the Indian Bureau did not involve war but rather picking up the pieces after the fighting. In the early years, the Union was on the verge of losing the Civil War, and the federal government failed in its promised treaty annuities to the Dakota from two agreements signed in 1851. Agent Thomas J. Galbraith ordered troops to stop the Dakota from breaking into a food warehouse at the Lower Agency. The Dakota went hungry, and starvation compelled Dakota warriors to leave the reservation without the agent's permission to raid the livestock of German settlers.

Governor Alexander Ramsey assured Minnesota settlers that military assistance would respond, and he turned to his good friend and former Governor Henry Sibley to raise a militia of 1,500 men. After several attacks and battles, the militia forced the final defeat of Little Crow at the Battle of Wood Lake on September 23, 1862. The Minnesota legislature authorized bounties put on the Dakota, and the scalp of Little Crow brought an additional $500.

Ramsey and other Minnesota officials charged 303 Dakota with the attacks on the settlements and submitted a list of the alleged guilty to President Abraham Lincoln. Lincoln conferred with Commissioner Dole who wanted only the guilty Indians to be punished. Dole's view supported Lincoln's inclination to reduce the list by over 100. President Lincoln compromised with Minnesota officials to reduce the list to 39 Dakota to be hung, and he also agreed to provide Minnesota with $2 million. In the last hour, one Dakota received a reprieve from execution. At 10:00 A.M. on December 26, officials marched the 38 Dakota to the gallows. The prisoners walked to their appointment with death without any resistance as a military official placed white hoods over their heads. The rope was cut that released the trapdoor underneath all of the prisoners as they yelled out to each other that they were there for their friends. In their moments of dying, several of the Indians managed to hold the hand of the friend next to them. Others kept trying to reach out for the other person's hand. An estimated 3,000 revengeful and curious people gathered at Mankato, Minnesota, to watch the largest mass execution in U.S. history. This ended the Minnesota War of 1862, also called the Little Crow War, but not the ill feelings toward Indians. Almost half a year later, Nathan Lampson, a farmer, shot and killed Little Crow while he and his teenage son picked raspberries. The killer received an extra $500 bounty after town officials identified the dead Indian as Little Crow. Anti-Indian citizens hauled Little Crow's body to Hutchinson, the

As punishment for their role in the Minnesota Dakota Sioux uprising, 38 Dakota Indians are executed in Mankato in December 1862, at the largest public execution in U.S. history. (Library of Congress)

nearest town, where citizens mutilated it, and then they dragged the body down Main Street while some people stuffed firecrackers in his ears, and dogs bit at his head. The crowd hauled Little Crow's body to an alley where garbage was thrown.

Chief Joseph

A small amount of gold discovered at Pierce, Idaho, in 1860 earned little notice until three years later. In 1863 a small group of prospectors discovered gold on the Nez Perce Reservation in Idaho. The gold rush to Idaho resulted in the sudden town of Lewiston. American officials negotiated the Treaty of 1863 with the Nez Perce. The agreement, also known as the Thief Treaty, divided the reserved land into three parts and reduced the Nez Perce land holding to 700,000 acres, about one-tenth of the original size. All of the chiefs left the council, except for Lawyer who signed the treaty with 51 other tribal members.

Indian Commissioner William Dole realized that his office needed to concentrate on working with the Nez Perce and other western Indian nations by making treaties with them. During Dole's tenure in office, an estimated 50 treaties were negotiated, but Congress only ratified about half of them. With help from Senator James Doolittle, Commissioner Dole started a policy of placing several tribes on large reservations in an effort to isolate them from mainstream opportunists. Indians had to have permission from the Indian agent or superintendent to leave their reservations. Furthermore, Dole believed in education as the key to civilize Indians, and he allowed the construction of schools. During these years, the bureau oversaw 40 schools supported by several religious groups (Kersey 1979).

Sand Creek

Dole's ousting from the BIA resulted from a military action that has become infamous. Colonel John M. Chivington, a former Methodist minister, led a force of Colorado volunteers in a surprise attack on the peaceful Cheyennes and Arapahoes under the leadership of the Peace Chief Black Kettle. For this savage attack on peaceful Indians, Congress initially bestowed the highest military medal, the Medal of Honor, on 23 soldiers who murdered men, women, and children at Sand Creek.

This brutal attack became known as the Sand Creek Massacre of 1864. Some congress men wanted the immediate removal of army officers, agents, and politicians who were responsible for aiding this attack. Dole was among those blamed, and he was forced to resign as commissioner (Kersey 1979). As more information came later, some congressmen had a different impression of the Sand Creek affair. At the time, all of the corruption relating to Indian affairs fell on the shoulders of Dole.

Congress took further action. In March 1865, Congress formed a special joint committee with Senator Doolittle in charge to investigate the living conditions of Indians on reservations in the West. The Doolittle Committee published its report in 1867, and it also blamed Dole for many of the problems on reservations.

In Indian Territory, the BIA and the rest of the federal government virtually ignored the Indian nations. Consumed with the fighting east of the Mississippi, the federal officials left the Indian nations vulnerable to pressure from the Confederacy. Ironically, the Southern states did not previously want the Indians—the Cherokee, Chickasaw, Choctaw, Creek, and Seminole—within their borders, but now the Confederate government wanted them as allies to fight the North. The Confederacy sent a former Arkansas newspaper editor, Albert Pike; and Commander Douglas Cooper to negotiate with the former five Southern tribes. The decision to fight for the South or North or even to remain neutral divided the tribes. Interestingly Colonel Cooper and his Southern soldiers fought the first battle of the Civil War in Indian Territory against a neutral group of Creek Indians led by Opothleyahola. They fought three battles with the Creeks, winning the first two but losing the last one that forced survivors to find their way to Kansas during the winter with no relief given to them by Union troops.

Chastising Indian Territory

The end of the Civil War produced serious repercussions for the five Indian nations. Newly appointed Commissioner Dennis Cooley had to decide how to deal with the five tribes for siding with the South against Union troops. In August 1865, Cooley chaired a peace commission to bring the leaders of the five nations to the negotiating table. Cooley informed others on the committee that "The President is willing to grant them peace; but wants land for other Indians, and a civil government for the whole Territory" (Kvasnicka and Viola 1979, 103). Cooley referred to President Andrew Johnson, who knew very little about Indians and had considerable political and monetary problems while reconstructing the nation.

The Treaties of 1866 became measures for punishing the five tribes for fighting with the Confederacy, although Cooley and his commission neglected to consider that the federal government had offered no assistance to Opothleyahola and the loyal Indians. The five tribes signed four treaties with the Choctaw and Chickasaw signing one agreement together. Each tribe agreed to peace with the United States. All four treaties abolished slavery and granted tribal citizenship to the freedmen with tribal rights as members. Government officials forced on the Indian nations rights of way for railroads to be constructed across Indian Territory (Gibson 1965, 213).

These treaties forced leaders of the five Native nations to agree to unfair large land reductions to make room to receive other Indians from the West. The Cooley Commission forced the Seminoles to sell their entire reservation of 2.17 million acres to the United States for 15¢ per acre. In return the Seminoles bought 200,000 acres on the western edge of the Creek Reservation for 50¢ per acre. The Muscogee Creek suffered less when the United States seized the western half of their reservation in exchange for payment of 30¢ per acre for 3.25 million acres. Together the Choctaw and Chickasaw received $300,000 for surrendering the southwestern portion of their lands that became the Leased District for displaced Southern Plains tribes. The Cherokee ceded their Neutral Lands, located in southeast Kansas, plus the Cherokee Strip (Gibson 1965, 214).

Taking advantage of the tribes for fighting for the South in the Civil War, Cooley implemented his policy of placing tribes on smaller reservations, thereby creating space for more reservations and more western tribes to be removed to them. As the entire United States slogged through Reconstruction, Cooley became frustrated with Congress for not supporting the Bureau of Indian Affairs. His annual report for 1866 demonstrated his feeling of being overwhelmed as he stated:

> It does not seem a great task to attend to the business of directing the management of about three hundred thousand Indians; but when it is considered that those Indians are scattered over a continent, and divided into more than two hundred tribes, in charge of fourteen superintendents and some seventy agents, whose frequent reports and quarterly accounts are to be examined and adjusted; that no general rules can be adopted for the guidance of those officers, for the reason that the people under their charge are so different in habits, customs, manners, and organization, . . . and that this office is called upon to protect the Indian, . . . from abuse by unscrupulous whites, while at the same time it must concede every reasonable privilege to the spirit of enterprise and adventure which is pouring its hardy population into the western country; when these things are considered, the task assigned to this bureau will not seem so light as it is sometimes thought. (Commissioner of Indian Affairs 1866, 1–2)

The start of Reconstruction at the end of the war allowed the government to rebuild itself and to reexamine various parts, including the Bureau of Indian Affairs.

The Doolittle Report

On March 3, 1865, Congress passed a joint resolution to investigate Indians living on reservations. Senator James Doolittle of Wisconsin chaired a joint special committee of Congress to conduct the report "Conditions of the Indian Tribes." The Doolittle Committee concluded that the Indian population on all reservations except in the Indian Territory was rapidly decreasing: "By disease; by intemperance; by wars, among themselves and with the whites" (Senate 1867, 3–10).

The Doolittle report began to uncover many problems caused by non-Indians for Indians. The pressure of white settlement produced opportunists who exploited any situation for their own personal gain, and the bureau remained responsible to solve the problems on a daily basis. This report revealed significant corruption in the Indian Office that provoked public and congressional scrutiny.

War Department or the Interior Department?

The Doolittle Committee also scrutinized the best administrative location for the BIA. Should Indian affairs be in the War Department or the Department of the Interior? This became the burning question in Washington for the next decade. Each department lobbied for the BIA. In the report, the committee observed that "Military men generally, are united in recommending that change needs to be made, while civilians, teachers, missionaries, agents and superintendents, and those not in the regular army generally oppose it [in the War Department]." One of the strongest arguments made for keeping the BIA in the Interior Department came in this statement of the report, "that the making of treaties and the disposition of the lands and funds of the Indians is of necessity intimately connected with our public land system, and, with all its important land questions, would seem to fall naturally under the jurisdiction of the Interior Department" (Senate 1867, 3–10).

Reconstruction meant less money for all federal departments including the Indian Bureau. Recovering from the war represented one of the biggest challenges in the history of the United States and made Native people more vulnerable as the bureau lacked the support to carry out its responsibilities and daily operations.

Indian Peace Commission

The assassination of President Lincoln caused considerable confusion. Vice President Andrew Johnson became the nation's 17th president. Turmoil plagued his presidency from 1865 to 1869, and Indian affairs became a matter of trying to sustain peace on the western frontier. Rather than wage expensive wars with the Plains tribes, the federal government opted to try a peaceful approach. On July 20, 1867, Congress authorized the creation of an Indian Peace Commission. The commission consisted of Indian Commissioner Nathaniel Taylor; John B. Henderson, chairman of the Committee of Indian Affairs of the Senate; S. F. Tappan and John B. Sanborn; plus three unnamed officers of the army not below the rank of brigadier general. The federal government sought to deal with hostile Indians "to . . . ascertain the alleged reasons for their acts of hostility, and in their discretion, under the direction of the President, to make and conclude with said bands or tribes such treaty stipulations, . . . [and] insure civilization for the Indians and peace and safety for the whites" (*Statutes at Large* 15, 17–18).

The Peace Commission acted swiftly and made an initial report on January 7, 1868. The findings proved to be less than promising for peace but did not blame the Indians entirely. After exploring the causes of Indian hostilities, the Commission reported,

We have done the best we could under the circumstances, . . . The best possible way then to avoid war is to do no act of injustice. . . . But, it is said our wars with them have been almost constant. Have we been uniformly unjust? We answer, unhesitatingly, yes! . . . Nobody pays any attention to Indian matters. This is a deplorable fact. Members of Congress understand the negro question, and talk learnedly of finance, and other problems of political economy, but when the progress of settlement reaches the Indian's home, the only question consider is "how best to get his lands." (House 1868, 15–17)

Plains Indian Wars

The U.S. military and western Indian groups engaged in a considerable amount of fighting throughout 1867 on the southern plains, central region, and northern plains. The Comanche on the southern plains raided regularly with their attacks on settlements in Texas. On July 2, the Cheyenne and Sioux ambushed and killed a second U.S. Cavalry force of 11 soldiers in Kansas, known as the Kidder Massacre. Sioux and Cheyenne engaged soldiers in the Hayfield fight on August 1 in Montana Territory. The next day Red Cloud and Crazy Horse led Sioux warriors against soldiers in the battle known as the Wagon Box Fight. On August 22, Indians attacked the 18th Kansas Volunteer Cavalry in the Battle of Beaver Creek. In September, Paiute, Pit River, and Modoc warriors engaged an army force in the Battle of Infernal Caverns. During September 17–19, Roman Nose led Northern Cheyenne warriors in an attack on scouts for the U.S. 9th Calvary force in the Battle of Beecher Island. These outbreaks were only the beginning of widespread Indian wars that lasted into the next decade.

Despite the continuing violence, the Peace Commission continued to operate and experienced major success in holding an important council with the Kiowa, Comanche, Plains Apache, Southern Cheyenne, and

Southern Arapaho at Medicine Lodge Creek in Kansas during October 1867. In meeting with nearly 10,000 Indians, the Peace Commission held the largest treaty council in the West. After several days of talk, the commissioners made three agreements with the most powerful tribes on the southern and central plains. Under these agreements, the Kiowa and Comanche surrendered 60,000 square miles in return for three million acres in Southwest Indian Territory, lying mostly between the North Fork of the Red River and the North Canadian River. In the second treaty, the Kiowa-Apache, also known as the Plains Apache, were made a part of the first treaty. Although they did not request them, the Peace Commission added that the tribes would receive houses, barns, and schools of about $30,000. However, the Indians wanted annuities of food, clothing, equipment, and guns with ammunition for hunting.

On October 9, 1868, the Indian Peace Commission announced its resolutions and reversed its earlier conclusions that hostilities were not entirely the fault of Indians. In their resolutions, the commission stated, "That the recent outrages and depredations committed by the Indians of the plains justify the government in abrogating . . . the treaties made in October 1867, at Medicine Lodge Creek" (House 1868, 831–832). So much war provoked the Peace Commission to argue that the Bureau of Indian Affairs should be moved back to the War Department. Secretary of War J. M. Schofield pushed strongly for this transfer and rationalized, "But if the army must be kept there for the protection of railroads and frontier settlements, why not require the army officers to act as Indian agents, and thus save all the expense of the civilians so employed" (House 1868, xvii–xviii).

In his annual report for 1868, BIA Commissioner Nathaniel Taylor firmly argued 11 main points for not transferring the Indian Bureau to the War Department. Taylor pointed out "1. That the prompt, efficient, and successful management and direction of our Indian affairs is too large, onerous, and important a burden to be added to the existing duties of the Secretary of War." Taylor stated that "2. The 'transfer,' in my judgment, will create a necessity for maintaining a large standing army in the field." The commissioner said "3. Our true policy towards the Indian tribes is peace, and the proposed transfer is tantamount, in my judgment, to perpetual war." The military presence in the West created the prelude to war, thereby defeating the peaceful intentions of the Peace Commission. Taylor further argued "4. Military management of Indian affairs has been tried for seventeen years and has proved a failure, and must, in my judgment, in the very nature of things, always prove a failure." Regarding the results of the transfer, the commissioner argued "5. It is inhuman and unchristian, in my opinion, leaving the question of economy out of the view, to destroy a whole race by such demoralized and disease as military government is sure to entail upon our tribes." Add to this view, he said "6. The conduct of Indian affairs is, in my judgment, incompatible with the nature and objects of the military department." From the view of the Indians, Taylor believed that "7. The transfer to the War Department will be offensive to the Indians, and in the same proportion injurious to the whites." He added "8. In the report, 7th January last, of the peace commission, after full examination of the whole question, the commission unanimously recommended that the Indian affairs should be placed, not in the War Department, but upon the footing of an independent department or bureau." In the care and supervision of Indian affairs, Commissioner Taylor said "9. The methods of military management are utterly irreconcilable with the relation of guardian and ward." He believed that "10. The transfer will in my opinion entail upon the treasury a large increase of annual expenditure." Finally the commissioner stated that "11. The presence in peaceful times of a large military establishment in a republic always endangers the supremacy of civil authority and the liberties of the people" (House 1868, 467–474).

With wars continuing in the West between Indian tribes and the U.S. military, the movement for a peace policy continued, despite continual criticism that it was not feasible at the time. On April 10, 1869, Congress passed the Indian Appropriation Act for that year, and section four of the law added to the peace policy. The law created the Board of Indian Commissioners. The board consisted of a group of unpaid philanthropists to be appointed to assist in advising the secretary of the interior in Indian Affairs.

First Indian Commissioner of Indian Affairs

On March 4, 1869, war hero Ulysses S. Grant entered the White House. While the rest of his presidency would be riddled with fraud, he wanted the Indian peace policy to work. To assist in this effort, Grant appointed the first American Indian to be commissioner of Indian Affairs, Ely Samuel Parker, a full-blooded Seneca from his people's reservation in upper New York. Parker's family had a history of loyalty to the United States. His father, William Parker, fought for the United States in the War of 1812 and was wounded. Parker had attended a missionary school. Further education led him to obtain a law degree. But due to racial prejudice, Ely Parker was banned from taking the bar exam. This barrier detoured him to earn an engineering degree, and he then worked on the Erie Canal and the Albermarle and Chesapeake Canal. Parker was elected leader of the Iroquois Nation in

Brigadier-General Ely S. Parker, 1863. He was a Seneca Indian, a lawyer, engineer, and appointed by President Grant as the first Indian to serve as the commissioner of Indian Affairs, 1869–1871. (Parker, Arthur C. *The Life of General Ely S. Parker*, Buffalo Historical Society, 1919)

1853. He experienced discrimination again when Secretary of War William H. Seward disallowed him from joining the Union Army. But with Grant's influence, Parker joined the army and enlisted as a captain in 1863.

For his loyalty to General Ulysses S. Grant and his expertise, Ely Parker served as the advisor to the general on Indian Affairs from 1865 to 1871. He was named officially as commissioner of Indian Affairs in 1869 and served for two years with Grant as president.

Grant's Peace Policy

Commissioner Parker advocated assimilation for Native people as he worked to help establish Grant's "Peace Policy." The Peace Policy changed the course of federal-Indian relations. And the Civil War had caused considerable destruction to the United States, costing over $6 billion. Grant became convinced that peaceful negotiation with Indians would be less costly, and there was no money in the U.S. Treasury. Both President Grant and Commissioner Parker gave instructions to the Board of Indian Commissioners. The board consisted of William Welsh of Philadelphia, John V. Farwell from Chicago, George H. Stuart of Philadelphia, Robert Campbell from St. Louis, William D. Dodge of New York, E. S. Tobey from Boston, Felix R. Brunot of Pittsburg, Nathan Bishop from New York, and Henry S. Lane from Indiana. Parker requested that the board determine "what should be the legal status of the Indians; a definition of their rights and obligations under the laws of the United States, of the States and territories and treaty stipulations; whether any more treaties shall be stipulated with the Indians, and if not, what legislation is necessary for those with whom there are existing treaty stipulations, and what for those with whom no such stipulations exist; should Indians be placed upon reservation and what is the best method to accomplish this object[ive]" (Commissioner of Indian Affairs 1869, 3–5).

The Board of Indian Commissioners submitted their first report on November 23, 1869. The board members took their job seriously, and they pointed out the impact of the failures of past policies on the Indian population. Using testimonies from some of the highest military officers, the board surmised that

> the first aggressions have been made by the white man, and the assertion is supported by every civilian of reputation who has studied the subject. In addition to the class of robbers and outlaws who find impunity in their nefarious pursuits upon the frontiers, there is a large class of professedly reputable men who use every means in their power to bring on Indian wars, for the sake of profit to be realized from the presence of troops and the expenditure of government funds in their midst. (Board of Indian Commissioners 1869, 5–11)

In his book *Our Red Brothers and the Peace Policy of President Ulysses S. Grant,* former Indian agent Lawrie Tatum, a stout Quaker, wrote that the peace policy that "commenced in 1869, has proved a great blessing to them [Indians], to the government, and to people of the nation" (Tatum [1899] 1970, 1). He believed earnestly that a better day would come for Native people.

Missionaries in Federal-Indian Affairs

Grant altered his peace policy from using concerned civilians to making missionaries a part of the peace effort. In his second annual message to Congress on December 5, 1870, the president laid out his plan. Grant selected religious groups, and they named their own agents to work among the Indians on reservations. Grant warned, "The Government watches over the official acts of these [missionary] agents, and requires of them as strict an accountability as if they were appointed in any other manner. I entertain the confident hope that the policy now pursued within a few years bring all the Indians upon reservations, where they will live in houses, and have schoolhouses and churches, and will be pursuing peaceful and self-sustaining avocation, and where they may be visited by the law-abiding white man with the same impunity that he now visits the civilized white settlements" (Richardson 1897, 109–110).

The introduction of Christian denominations among the Indians represented an intrusion of a different type: religious ideology. However, this was not the first time as missionaries had worked among Indian communities during the early 1800s with some success. Grant's desire for missionaries and civilians represented something new and demonstrated the Indian Office's narrow approach of carrying out the Indian civilization plan. The challenge proved to be the imbedded Native cultural beliefs within the Indian communities, grounding their identities with the earth and the supernatural, and defining their worldview.

Missionary schools would have some success among the Indian communities, even to the extent that Indians would run the schools themselves. Interestingly Indians would often end up incorporating Christian beliefs into their own religious views. To Native people, no contradiction existed when a majority of Indians practiced both Christianity and traditional beliefs. Their ability to incorporate a second belief system represented a means of survival as the government asserted increasing control over their lives.

The government became increasingly aware that an independent organization was needed to work to bring peace to U.S.-Indian relations. Government officials considered several factors. It would seem that an independent organization could not hurt, considering that neither the War Department nor the Bureau of Indian Affairs was capable of achieving peace. Since the Indian Bureau was most responsible for attempting peace, the Board of Peace Commissioners singled out the bureau for being unable to do its job. Finally, the creation of the Board of Peace Commissioners brought more civilians into the realm of Indian affairs as well as other interests such as missionaries who started boarding schools and wanted to Christianize Indian students. The introduction of civilians in these peace efforts enabled a greater nonmilitary supervision of Indian affairs and strove to obtain the assistance from civilians who knew Indians and wanted to assimilate them.

Indian Police on Reservations

As the military moved western tribal groups to reservations, Indian agents began to realize that they needed help to keep order among Native people. The Southeastern groups, often called the Five Civilized Tribes, developed light horsemen police to keep tribal law and order among their nations in Indian Territory. Following the Civil War, the Cherokees introduced the light horsemen first and the Choctaw, Chickasaw, Creek, and Seminole followed. They began to develop tribal courts to sustain tribal laws. The Lighthorsemen and tribal courts came to an end when a federal court system was introduced in the 1890s, and the Curtis Act of 1898 dissolved the Indian legal systems.

The Lighthorsemen only had jurisdiction over their own tribal members and not non-Indians, including African Americans. Judge Isaac Parker, also known as the Hanging Judge of Fort Smith, Arkansas, presided over the U.S. District Court of the Western District of Arkansas for over 20 years. His court's jurisdiction included white men and African Americans in Indian Territory from May 4, 1875 to 1889.

During this same time, the Board of Indian Commissioners appointed by President Grant noted that the tribes needed law and order among themselves on the reservations. The board noted in 1871 that tribes needed to be taught "civilized law" as a part of the civilization process. The young new Indian agent John Clum, who arrived among the Apache at San Carlos Reservation in August 1874, realized that he needed a law enforcement organization and made this known to the Office of Indian Affairs. Similar conditions existed among agents on reservations of the Pawnee, Klamath, Modoc, Navajo, Blackfeet, Ojibwa, and Oglala Sioux in the 1860s and 1870s (Hagan 1980, 25).

In his first year of learning on the job in 1877, Commissioner Ezra Hayt recommended to Congress the creation of an Indian police force on reservations, noting that one existed on Canadian Indian reserves. Realizing that no more Indian treaties were going to be made and accepting Hayt's suggestion, on May 27, 1878, Congress authorized $30,000 for salaries for 430 privates at $5 per month and 50 officers at $8 per month to maintain order and stop liquor activities on several reservations. Hayt had 30 reservations under control in several months, and Congress increased the funding to double the number of Indian police. Forty agencies had Indian police by 1880, and 29 agencies had Indian police in 1890 due to the decrease of hostilities on reservations and ending of Indian wars (Prucha 1984, 196).

Conclusion

The national completeness of the physical expansion of the United States included the hundreds of thousands of gold rushers of 1849 and the annexation of Texas, California, and the Southwest. All of this shifted Indian affairs heavily to the West. In response, Congress created the Department of the Interior and relocated the newly named Bureau of Indian Affairs under the department.

The Civil War divided the country and forced different points of view on the war, on the rebuilding of the United States, and on Indian affairs. Peace or war represented one significant question, and Native people who chose to fight in defense of their homelands on the plains decided this answer. The federal government and the public continued to debate whether the BIA should remain in the Department of the Interior or be moved back to its original place in the War Department. Native loyalty to the U.S. at Sand Creek and Washita sparked an American protest of military actions against Native people. This ill feeling among the public made the job for the bureau and missionaries much harder as the Grant administration allowed this to happen with his peace policy failing. Indian wars and the aftermath and continual service to eastern tribes placed on reservations increased the number of bureau personnel from 108 in 1852 to 1,725 in 1888, indicating the increased responsibility for services to Native people (Taylor 1959, 98).

References

"Act Creating the Department of the Interior." March 3, 1849. *United States Statutes at Large*, 9:395.

Board of Indian Commissioners Annual Report, 1869.

Commissioner of Indian Affairs Annual Report, 1838.

Commissioner of Indian Affairs Annual Report, 1866.

Commissioner of Indian Affairs Annual Report, 1869.

"Commissioner of Indian Affairs Nathaniel Taylor on Transfer of the Indian Bureau." November 23, 1868. *House Executive Document* no. 1. 40th Congress. 3rd Session. Serial 1366.

"Creation of an Indian Peace Commission Act." July 20, 1867. *United States Statutes at Large*, 15.

Gibson, Arrell M. *Oklahoma: A History of Five Centuries*. Norman, OK: Harlow Publishing, 1965.

Hagan, William T. *Indian Police and Judges: Experiments in Acculturation and Control*. Lincoln: University of Nebraska Press, 1980.

Kersey, Harry. "William P. Dole, 1861–1865." In *The Commissioners of Indian Affairs, 1824–1977*, ed. Robert M. Kvasnicka and Herman J. Viola. Lincoln: University of Nebraska Press, 1979.

Kvasnicka, Robert M. and Herman J. Viola, eds. *The Commissioners of Indian Affairs, 1824–1977*. Lincoln: University of Nebraska Press, 1979.

Mix, Charles E. *Office Copy of the Laws, Regulations, Etc. of the Indian Bureau, 1850*. Washington, DC: Gideon & Co., 1850.

Prucha, Francis P. *The Great Father: The United States Government and the American Indians*. Lincoln: University of Nebraska Press, 1984.

"Regulations Regarding Liquor and Annuities Act." March 3, 1847. *United States Statutes at Large*, 9.

"Report of the Doolittle Committee." January 26, 1867. *Senate Report* no. 156. 39th Congress. 2nd Session. Serial 1279.

"Report of the Indian Peace Commission." January 7, 1868. *House Executive Document* no. 97. 40th Congress. 2nd Session. Serial 1337.

"Resolution of the Indian Peace Commission." October 9, 1868. *House Executive Document* no. 1. 40th Congress. 3rd Session. Serial 1366.

Richardson, James D., comp. *A Compilation of the Messages and Papers of the Presidents*, Volume 7. New York: Bureau of National Literature, 1897.

"Secretary of War J. M. Schofield on Transfer of the BIA." November 20, 1868. *House Executive Document* no. 1. 40th Congress. 3rd Session. Serial 1367.

Tatum, Lawrie. *Our Red Brothers and the Peace Policy of President Ulysses S. Grant*. Lincoln: University of Nebraska Press, 1970. Originally published John C. Winston & Co., 1899.

Taylor, Theodore. "The Regional Organization of the Bureau of Indian Affairs." PhD diss., Harvard University, 1959.

THREE

The Reform Years and the Indian Problem

Following the Civil War, the entire country welcomed peace amidst the massive ruination left behind. Restoration of peace coincided with significant governmental change; in the Indian Service, personnel sought to improve conditions in Indian Country. This reform effort focused on the so-called Indian Problem, a longtime concern that proliferated as more tribal communities became involved. Poverty and poor health conditions complicated conditions on reservations more than Interior Secretary James Harlan and Indian Commissioner Dennis Cooley realized. The Reconstruction years witnessed widespread suffering, especially in the South, which looked toward the Union government for a helping hand. Such suffering was particularly acute for the native population, as a large portion had recently been displaced before the war. Like the North and the South reconstructing their communities east of the Mississippi, the tribal nations found themselves rebuilding their communities on reserved areas in the West. In addition, western tribal nations began to encounter newly arrived settlers encroaching on their lands, thereby pressing the BIA to carry out its trust responsibilities based on signed treaties.

Indian Reform

Reform means a change for the better. In the case of the American Indian, many people clustered and worked independently to form a movement to help Native people recover on their reservations. These reformers began to call themselves "Friends of the Indian." They hoped to work with the Indian Bureau to improve Native living conditions and to persuade the president and Congress to enact laws to bring about the assimilation and civilization of Indians.

Secretary of the Interior Carl Schurz, 1876–1881, played a prominent role in the supervision of Indian affairs, often overruling the Indian commissioner. He kept the BIA in the Interior Department when many critics wanted it transferred to the War Department. (U.S. Geological Survey)

The origins of the reform movement derived from Christian denominations, humanitarians, legal groups, women's organizations, and American guilt. These individuals and groups realized that the indigenous people were the victims of American colonization as the United States added to its total land area consisting of 41 states and 8 territories.

Indian reform also involved cleaning up the corruption in the supervision of Native affairs. Because the Indian Service was composed largely through political patronage, the appointment of unqualified individuals to leadership positions was far too common, the reformers argued. Dishonest politicians out for personal gain helped corrupt the Indian Affairs Office into becoming the worst office in the Department of the Interior. During his time as secretary of the Interior from 1877 to 1881, Carl Schurz set out to change this reputation.

The Indian Problem

The Indian Problem to which reformers referred when they debated the future of the American Indian dated back to the early years of Washington and Jefferson and was multifaceted. The problems and challenges that arose in the intervening years only heightened the so-called Indian Problem. Indeed it was a problem for both Indians and non-Indians. The problem, in the eyes of most non-Indians, was that Native people had not assimilated, had not been civilized, had not been converted overall to Christianity, and lived in squalor conditions on reservations. Furthermore, the fact that less than 238,000 Indians remained suggested that Native people were a vanishing race compared to over 50 million Americans.

Missionaries believed that Indians needed to be Christianized to become a part of the growing American civilization. This perspective overlapped with the view of some early important officials that believed Indians could adopt the white man's culture. Idealist Jeffersonians were convinced that Indians needed to learn agriculture and gradually become a part of the effort to build the United States side by side with white settlers. Both points of view purported the same ideal of making Indians a part of America by Christianizing and civilizing them.

An important part of the Indian Problem involved Indian legal rights and where Indians stood as individuals and as tribal communities or groups. As individuals, all Indians were not U.S. citizens until a law was passed in 1924 for this purpose. Simultaneously, tribal groups had rights as sovereign nations with laws of their own. Tribal laws proved significant as long as the tribes remained in power. This changed, however, with the military decline of the tribal nations, making the Native nations increasingly vulnerable to U.S. laws. If Native people were to become civilized and assimilate, then they would come under the U.S. Constitution.

Christians and other humanitarians considered the living conditions of Indians to be a problem, especially for assimilation, but removalists did not always concur. Some individuals called opportunists wanted Indians removed from their lands for availability, and they did not care about the Indian Problem. These views put many Christians and humanitarians on one side and removalists on the other. Among the removalists were opportunists who took advantage of the displacement of Native groups to reservations. Simultaneously, assimilation was not necessarily the objective of most Native people. They did not see the urgent need to assimilate as white Americans did. Yet the idea of assimilation dates back to the views of Washington and Jefferson. In his third annual message to Congress, President Washington stated his idealized plan for Native people to become a part of the new United States. On October 23, 1791, President Washington stated: "It is sincerely to be desired that all need of coercion in the future may cease and that an intimate intercourse may succeed, calculated to advance the happiness of the Indians and to attach them firmly to the United States" (Richardson 1897, 96–97).

At this early stage of his administration, Washington strove to make sure that the Indians remained allied with the United States as Indians would help defeat the British. Yet Washington implanted the idea in the federal government to make Indians a part of the United States.

In 1803 President Jefferson offered his view on trade with Indians in order to make a better life for them. Jefferson believed that Native people had to change their old ways and learn to use the goods and tools of settlers. In this special message to Congress, Jefferson argued that U.S. officials must "encourage them to abandon hunting, to apply to the raising stock, to agriculture, and domestic manufacture, and thereby proved to themselves, that less land and labor will maintain them in this better than in their former mode of living" (Richardson 1897, 340–341). Although Jefferson did not allude to an Indian Problem and specifically mention assimilation, it was well known that he believed that Native people could become a part of the United States.

Jefferson proposed that Indians needed time with assistance to learn how to become yeoman farmers, thus solving the problem. But they needed to take up white ways from white men, which unfortunately included those who traded whiskey to them and other opportunists. As the government negotiated more treaties for land, the idea of removing Indians to a safe area so they could become civilized via missionaries and Indian agents gained supporters. Congress passed a law on April 16, 1818, for the appointment of 16 agents to live among certain Indian groups in the Great Lakes region as well as in the South.

On January 27, 1825, President James Monroe reinforced the idea of Indians being removed to a safe area. He called for a systematic program of Indian civilization, but this caused other concerns since Native people were outside of the U.S. Constitution and were not U.S. citizens. Some of the concerns involved Indian legal rights since they possessed treaties signed with the United States, and Native people were officially members of foreign nations (Richardson 1897, 2:280–283).

U.S.-Indian treaties up to that time represented Indian tribes as sovereign nations. In the landmark court case *Worcester v. Georgia* in 1832, Chief Justice John Marshall ruled in favor of the Cherokee Nation. He ruled that Georgia had violated federal jurisdiction by sending state authorities onto Cherokee land to arrest 11 missionaries who had not applied for a state license to do missionary work among the Cherokee. In chastising Georgia, Marshall, in effect, recognized the Cherokee as an independent nation, thereby setting a historical precedent of tribal sovereignty for all Indian nations today. Missionaries proved to be the earliest nongovernment people who wanted to help the Indians in their fallen plight. At the same time, missionaries had a larger purpose of converting Indians to their religions to save the souls of the indigenous. Lutherans and Quakers were among the earliest denominations to work among the Northeast Native groups. The Dutch Reformed

Church was active as well, and the Catholics had succeeded in winning many Potawatomi converts. In the South, Methodists and Baptists sent missionaries to convert the Creeks, Choctaws, and Cherokees.

Humanitarians and Bishop Whipple

Humanitarians represented another important group that wanted to solve the Indian Problem. Largely easterners, they believed that the Indians deserved better living conditions. They worked to improve the situation on reservations and lobbied the government to do more for the Indians. They also believed Native people had been mistreated by both the federal government and opportunists, and both had taken advantage of Native people.

On March 28, 1853, President Millard Fillmore appointed George W. Manypenny to be Indian commissioner. Manypenny focused his efforts to supervise the negotiation of 52 treaties with the Indian tribes, the most of any Indian commissioner. At the same time, he believed that the Native population could become civilized. Manypenny served for four years—until March 1857—but this would not be the end of his involvement in federal-Indian relations.

In 1862 during the Civil War, the outbreak of the Dakota War, also known as the Minnesota War, captured national attention. As described earlier, this war resulted in the largest mass execution in American history. Bishop Henry Whipple, who had advocated assistance to the Dakota Sioux, faced severe criticism when the Indians attacked German settlements. Outside of the activities of the BIA, Bishop Whipple tried to solve the Indian Problem in Minnesota. While Minnesotans hunted the Dakotas with bounties placed on them, Whipple tried to stop the execution of the 38 Indians named guilty for the attacks. His most stern opponent was former Governor Henry Sibley, his cousin. Whipple continued to work among the Dakota and then concluded his missionary work among the Ojibwa in Minnesota.

In 1865, the first conflict between Utes and settlers began a series of battles that became known as the Ute War. The war lasted until 1868 and was briefly reignited in 1879. The Indians rose up as a response to settler encroachment on their homeland and the resulting scarcity of food. Led by Black Hawk, the Ute warrior, Paiutes and Navajos joined in a loose alliance to fight Mormon settlers. With both sides weary, the Indians and the United States struck a peace treaty in 1868. The government sent Indian agent Nathan Meeker to supervise the Utes in agriculture on the Ute White River Reservation in 1878. Attempting to change hunters into farmers caused a major problem. Meeker ordered the plowing of a Ute horse racetrack that provoked the Utes who then massacred Meeker and 10 men employed by the Indian agent. The Utes proceeded to burn the agency to the ground. Citizens of Colorado publically declared "The Utes Must Go." With the death of the noted Ouray, the Ute leader, the Utes subsided. The Ute Commission was created to bring a final resolution in 1879. The Ute Agreement resulted at the wish of the people of Colorado, and the U.S. military moved the Utes to the Uintah reservation in Utah. In 1886 the BIA, under John D. Atkins, consolidated the Uintah and Ouray Reservations.

Friends of the Indian and the Act of 1871

On March 3, 1871, Congress made a regular appropriation of funding, this time $1,500 to support the Yankton Sioux, but a rider was added to the legislation. The rider to this harmless act for funding held great implications. The law stated: "That hereafter no Indian nation or tribe within the territory of the United States shall be acknowledged or recognized as an independent nation, tribe, or power with whom the United States may contract by treaty: *Provided, further*, That nothing herein contained shall be construed to invalidate or impair the obligation of any treaty heretofore lawfully made and ratified with any such Indian nation or tribe" (*Statutes at Large* 16:566).

The Friends of the Indian sharply criticized the federal government for breaking its treaties to the Indian tribes. As stated in the law, the act did not dissolve treaties, but it halted further treaty making with Indian tribes. That the U.S. government would not recognize the independence of any Indian tribe or nation was a blow to tribal sovereignty. Only a sovereign can make a treaty with another sovereign, according to the principle of international law. Ironically, the U.S. government continued to make 5 non-treaty called agreements with Indian tribes after 1871 until 1883 (Kappler 1904, 1027–1074).

The act of Congress took some supervision of Indian affairs out of the hands of the Indian Bureau. Whereas much of Indian affairs involved war, the government considered other approaches for dealing with Indians. To solve the Indian Problem, President Grant looked toward missionaries. After his election, Grant met with a committee of Friends, also called Quakers. The Indian agent Lawrie Tatum, formerly a farmer from Iowa and a Quaker, recalled that the president listened to the group for a considerable length of time. Then President Grant replied, "Gentlemen, your advice is good. I accept it. Now give me the names of some Friends for Indian agents and I will appoint them. If you can make Quakers out of the Indians it will take the fight out of them. Let us have peace" (Tatum 1970, 17).

This agreement resulted in yearly meetings of the Orthodox Friends, who formed an executive committee to appoint teachers and other important employees to work on reservations. These Indian groups included the Southern Cheyenne and Arapahoe, Kiowa, Comanche, and Apache. Other Indians included the Waco, Caddo, Wichita, and Kuchie (Tatum 1970, 18). Before anyone from Washington informed him, Lawrie Tatum saw his name in a newspaper assigning him to work at the Wichita and Comanche Agency in Indian Territory.

The majority of Indian bureaucrats like Commissioner Francis Walker believed that the end was near for Native people. In his annual report for 1872, Walker spoke frankly about their doomed future. He wrote, "[Their defeat], indeed, the only hope of salvation for the aborigines of the continent. If they stand up against the progress of civilization and industry, they must be relentlessly crushed. . . . They must yield or perish" (House 1872, 391–399).

Following President Grant's lead, Commissioner Walker worked with religious groups, assigning them to certain Indian groups. Walker made the first assignment to the Quakers in 1869. Almost all of the previous Indian agents were army officers. The Indian Bureau assigned several religious associations to work with the Indian groups. The BIA assigned the Friends or Hicksite to work with the Omaha, Winnebago, Pawnee, Otoe, and Santee Sioux, all located in Nebraska. The Friends known as Orthodox worked with the Potawatomi, Kaw, Kickapoo, Osage, Sac and Fox, Shawnee, Wichita, and Kiowa in Indian Territory.

The BIA assigned the Baptists to work with the Cherokee and Creek in Indian Territory, plus the Walker River Paiute and Paiute in Nevada. The Presbyterians worked with the Choctaw and Seminole in Indian Territory, and the Navajo, Mescalero Apache, Southern Apache in New Mexico as well as the Moquis Pueblo in Arizona Territory and the Nez Perce in Idaho Territory. The BIA assigned the Christians to work with the Pueblo in New Mexico and Neeah Bay Indians in Washington Territory. The Methodists worked with the Hoopa Valley, Round Valley, and Tule River in California as well as the Yakima, Skokomish, and Quinaielt in Washington Territory. This assignment also included the Warm Springs, Siletz, and Klamath in Oregon; and the Blackfeet, Crow, and Milk River Indians in Montana Territory. Catholics were assigned the Tulalip and Colville in Washington, Umatilla in Oregon, Flathead in Montana Territory, and Grand River and Devil's Lake Indians in Dakota Territory. The Reformed Dutch worked with the Colorado River Indians, Pima and Maricopa, Camp Grant, Camp Verde, and White Mountain or Camp Apache in Arizona Territory.

Walker assigned the Congregationals to the Ojibwa of Lake Superior in Wisconsin and the Ojibwa of the Mississippi in Minnesota. He assigned the Protestant Episcopalians to work with the Fort Berthold, Cheyenne River, Yankton, and Red Cloud in Dakota Territory and the Shoshone in Wyoming Territory. The Unitarians went to work among the Los Pinos and White River in Colorado. The Lutherans received authorization to work with the Sac and Fox in Iowa. Last, the BIA assigned the American Board of Commissioners for Foreign Missions to do missionary work among the Sisseton in Dakota Territory (House 1872, 391–399).

While missionaries wanted parcels of Indian land for schools for Native children, prospectors had a much greater interest. Colonel George Custer's military expedition in 1874 to the Black Hills to study the situation regarding Indians and the rumor of gold led to more Indian confrontations. The local groups responded to protect their sacred Black Hills as miners rushed to the area much like what had happened in the California gold rush of 1849 and the Colorado gold rush of 1858. More complicated than ever, miners, missionaries, settlers, and the military became involved with Indians in the West.

General George Crook pursued his campaign in the Yellowstone River country to defeat the Lakota Sioux and Cheyenne. In the early months of 1876, he marched a force of 970 cavalry, infantry mounted on mules, 80 teamsters including miners, and roughly 260 Crow and Shoshone scouts (traditional enemies of the Sioux and Cheyenne). A late blizzard in March forced Crook to wait out the weather. In the early morning of June 17, Crook's weary soldiers heard gunshots where his scouts had engaged the Lakota and Cheyenne on Rosebud Creek in Montana Territory. Crazy Horse led as many as 1,500 warriors against Crook in the Battle of Rosebud. By early afternoon, the Sioux and Cheyenne lost 21 warriors with 63 wounded, and Crook had 32 dead and another 21 wounded. Crook had to withdraw his force to recover.

For the next several days, Custer and the Seventh Cavalry continued the pursuit of the Sioux and Cheyenne. Custer and his men caught up with the Sioux and Cheyenne camped along the Little Bighorn River on June 25. Hoping to take the Indians by surprise, Custer divided his force into three parts with Captain Marcus Reno and Captain Frederick Benteen in charge. The Indians overwhelmed Custer and his soldiers, while Benteen and Reno managed to hold on for the next day until the Indians left at the advice of Sitting Bull. In all, the U.S. military engaged the Lakota Sioux and Cheyenne in eight major battles. Such violence complicated Indian affairs for the Indian Office as it caused an overlap with the War Department and created the impression that the army was in charge.

Sioux Commission

The final defeat of the Sioux and Cheyenne led to the federal government creating the Sioux Commission. Former Indian Commissioner George Manypenny was appointed chairman of the Sioux Commission. Other members included former Lieutenant Governor H. C. Bullis of Iowa, A. G. Boone of Colorado, former Dakota Territory Governor Newton Edmunds of Dakota, Bishop Henry Whipple of Minnesota, A. S. Gaylord of Michigan, assistant attorney general of the Interior Department, Reverend Samuel D. Hinman, and Dr. M. Daniels; Hinman served as the interpreter. After negotiations with the Sioux started in fall 1876, the Commission talked some Native leaders into signing away the Black Hills to the U.S., but the commissioners ignored article 12 of the 1868 treaty to obtain three-fourths of all the males's signatures.

From October 17, 1882, to January 3, 1883, the commission now headed by Newton Edmunds negotiated the agreement with the Oglala Sioux, allowing the United States to receive a strip of land along the western border of Dakota Territory that was 50 miles wide, including all land west of the Cheyenne and Belle Fourche Rivers consisting of 11 million acres. The Oglala Sioux received 5 specific reservations named in the agreement: Standing Rock, Cheyenne River, Crow Creek, Rosebud, and Pine Ridge with each family head to receive 320 acres and 80 acres per minor child (Prucha 1976, 171–175 and Kappler 1904, 1065–1068). This negotiated agreement was the last to be made with the Lakota Sioux, one of the major Indian nations on the plains.

War Department or Interior Department

The failure of Grant's Peace Policy, due to the increased warfare with the western tribes, generated a movement seeking to return the Bureau of Indian Affairs to the War Department. Military men like Lieutenant Colonel Elwell Otis advocated for the BIA to be in the War Department to allow the military to handle the resisting Indians. A Harvard Law School graduate, Otis had distinguished himself by fighting at Fredericksburg, Chancellorsburg, and Gettysburg and afterwards he was transferred to the West to fight Indians. He fought in the post-Little Bighorn campaign that influenced his political view.

In 1878, Elwell S. Otis published his pro-military book, *The Indian Question*. Otis wrote, "The transfer of the Indian Bureau to a peace department, and the substitution of the olive branch for the emblems of force, did not bring promised results. The practice of furnishing subsistence was adopted, and yet this ungrateful people would not appreciate the efforts put forth for its preservation . . . two opinions upon the possibility of Indian advancement have been reached. One, that the Indian is incapable of civilization, and the other, that the responsibility for a failure to civilize him rests upon the Government. . . . Paradoxical as it may seem, the white man has been the chief obstacle in the way of Indian civilization. The benevolent measures attempted by the Government for their advancement have been almost uniformly thwarted by the agencies employed to carry them out" (Otis 1878, 1998–1999).

Our Indian Wards

In response to Otis's *The Indian Question*, former Indian Commissioner George Manypenny published his own book, *Our Indian Wards*, in 1880. In the introduction, Manypenny wrote, "It can not be denied, that from the period when the first infant settlements were made upon the Atlantic sea-board by European colonists, until the present time, there have been constant, persistent, and unceasing efforts on the part of the white man to drive the Indian from his hunting ground and his home. When the encroachments of the former became unbearable, they were forcibly resisted by the latter. This was the only mode left to the Indian by which to redress his wrongs, since he had no standing in the civil tribunals of the colonies, and even to this day we have practically denied him the benefit of our courts" (Manypenny 1880, vii–viii). Manypenny believed that the Indian Office should play a direct role in supervising Indian affairs, while military officials wanted the Indian Bureau transferred to the military.

Commissioner of Indian Affairs George Manypenny. (Courtesy of the U.S. Department of the Interior)

The increasing resistance of Indians in the West, like the Ponca, was seen by many as buttressing the military's arguments. A group of Poncas under Standing Bear attempted to leave Indian Territory to return to their homeland in present-day Nebraska. On their way home, General George Crook intercepted the Ponca and arrested them to return them back to Indian Territory. This action went to court before Judge Elmer S. Dundy. After hearing both sides and the earnest plea from Standing Bear to return his little daughter's body and his people to their homeland, Judge Dundy ruled in favor of the Indians on May 12, 1879. He concluded, "That an Indian is a 'person' within the meaning of the laws of the United States, and has, therefore, the right to sue out a writ of habeas corpus in a federal court, or before a federal judge, in all cases where he may be confined or in custody under color of authority of the United States, or where he is restrained of liberty in violation of the constitution or laws of the United States" (*Federal Cases* 695, 697, 700–701).

The legal rights of Indians rested outside of U.S. law until this case. As tribal groups, tribal sovereignty had been upheld in *Worcester v. Georgia* (1832). Yet the *Standing Bear* ruling recognized Indians as persons within the United States, subject to U.S. laws. But within U.S. law, Indians were wards of the state. Therein lay the responsibility of the federal government and the BIA. In sum, Commissioner Manypenny described, "That a better and brighter day may speedily come to the despised Indian, should be the aspiration and prayer of every man and woman in our broad land, and all should earnestly and faithfully labor for such reforms as will secure exact justice in our dealings with, and thus assure the civilization of, our Indian Wards" (Manypenny 1880, xxvi).

Boston Indian Citizenship Association

The Standing Bear case encouraged a small group of easterners interested in the law to argue on behalf of Indian legal rights. These reformers included Massachusetts Republican Governor John D. Long, Senator Henry L. Dawes, and Helen Hunt Jackson. While Standing Bear spoke in Boston after his trial, Jackson listened in the audience and became an ardent reformer to help Native people. Dawes had been in Congress since 1857 and became interested in Indian affairs following Grant's Peace Policy in 1869. He actively supported educating Indians and promoted the idea of allotment to his colleagues in Congress. As governor, Long supported Indian reform until he was appointed secretary of the Navy in 1897.

The association of reformers became formally organized in late 1879. The main goal of the Boston organization focused on Indian equality in the courts and rights as potential citizens. These eastern reformers started as critics of the BIA, and the government in general, but soon learned that it was to their advantage to try to work within the federal system. Jackson and Dawes soon played major roles in the Indian reform movement with the latter pushing for allotment in severalty. Dawes and the rest of the association as well as the Indian Rights Association wanted to extend the allotment bill to reservations and to create courts of law for them (Mardock 1971, 198, 224).

Women's National Indian Association

In 1879, Mary Bonney and Melia Stone Quinton led a group of women to organize the Women's National Indian Association (WNIA). These concerned women made efforts to stop the encroachment of white settlers on Indian lands. They lobbied for the government to uphold its treaties with Indian tribes and started a petition to demonstrate how many people wanted this to happen. The organization circulated the petition in 15 states and presented it to President Rutherford B. Hayes and the House of Representatives in 1880. Hayes and Congress knew that it was impossible to stop settler encroachment. And the women's efforts did not stop.

A branch of the WNIA became well known on its own merits in 1881. Known as the Connecticut Indian Association, this group organized in Hartford. Its true origin began in October 1880 with Harriet Beecher Stowe serving as vice president. Her involvement gave recognized status among humanitarians and the Board of Indian Commissioners. The Connecticut association rallied support for Native people and increased the number of easterners in support of Indian reform. Stowe and others alerted and informed the public of Indian living conditions on reservations and made the Indian Problem a national issue.

The mission of the Women's National Indian Association focused on the Christianization and assimilation of Indians. The WNIA supported missions and produced several publications to influence the making of federal-Indian policy, including the Dawes Act of 1887. By the end of the century, the Women's National Indian Association had grown to 60 branch organizations in 27 states (Prucha 1976, 134–138, 146–148). The national organization then changed its name to the National Indian Association, and it continued its work until 1951.

A Century of Dishonor

The year 1881 proved to be a turning point in Indian reform when an eastern humanitarian published the book *A Century of Dishonor*. In this revealing account, Helen Hunt Jackson criticized the U.S. government for its insufficient policies regarding Indians. After hearing Standing Bear speak

A CENTURY OF DISHONOR

A SKETCH

OF THE UNITED STATES GOVERNMENT'S DEALINGS
WITH SOME OF THE INDIAN TRIBES

BY HELEN JACKSON (H. H.),

AUTHOR OF "RAMONA," "VERSES," "BITS OF TRAVEL," "BITS OF TRAVEL AT HOME,"
"BITS OF TALK ABOUT HOME MATTERS," "BITS OF TALK FOR YOUNG FOLKS,"
"NELLY'S SILVER MINE," H. H.'s CAT STORIES, ETC.

*"Every human being born upon our continent, or who comes here from any quarter
of the world, whether savage or civilized, can go to our courts for protection—except
those who belong to the tribes who once owned this country. The cannibal from the
islands of the Pacific, the worst criminals from Europe, Asia, or Africa, can appeal
to the law and courts for their rights of person and property—all, save our native
Indians, who, above all, should be protected from wrong"*
GOV. HORATIO SEYMOUR

NEW EDITION, ENLARGED BY THE ADDITION OF THE REPORT OF
THE NEEDS OF THE MISSION INDIANS OF CALIFORNIA

BOSTON
ROBERTS BROTHERS
1889

The title page of Helen Hunt Jackson's *A Century of Dishonor*, 1881. (Library of Congress)

in Boston about what his people had endured in their removal to Indian Territory, Jackson became an activist for Indian reform. She blamed the mainstream society for its mistreatment of Indians, but the federal government took the blunt of Jackson's exposé. In fact, Jackson sent everyone in Congress a copy of her book. Jackson's book influenced Congress to create a commission to examine past policies and to offer new approaches to improve the living conditions of Native people.

In the conclusion, Jackson reminded readers that U.S.-Indian relations had a long, dark history. She wrote, "It makes little difference, however, where one opens the record of the history of the Indians; every page and every year has its dark stain. The story of one tribe is the story of all, varied only by differences of time and place; but neither time nor place makes any difference in the main facts. Colorado is as greedy and just in 1880 as was Georgia in 1830, and Ohio in 1795; and the United States Government breaks promises now as deftly as then, and with an added ingenuity from

long practice." Jackson added, "The history of the Government connec-
tions with the Indians is a shameful record of broken treaties and unful-
filled promises" (Jackson [1881] 1964, 337–339). Jackson was the leading
woman reformer to speak on behalf of the Indians.

Indian Rights Association

On December 15, 1882, a social activist group met in Philadelphia under
the leadership of Herbert Welsh and formed the Indian Rights Association.
Welsh and cofounder Henry Spackman Pancoast opened a second office
two years later in Washington to lobby Congress and serve as a liaison
to the Board of Indian Commissioners and the Bureau of Indian Affairs.
Indian legal rights became a heated issue on reservations and in federal
courts. According to the law, both Indians and the United States were to
uphold the treaties signed between them. Yet the American judicial system
and lawmaking branch began to test tribal sovereignty and Indian rights.

The association mainly consisted of five active members: Herbert Welsh,
Matthew Sniffen, Lawrence E. Lindley, Charles C. Painter, and Samuel M.
Brosius. The members acted as lobbyists in Washington. They observed the
activities of Indian agents and kept updated on Indian living conditions and
improvements. In 1884 the association lobbied Congress to spend surplus
funds to educate Plains Indians. Their formal petition reminded Congress
that some reservations still had no schools. Congress moved much slower
than the association wanted, and the active Connecticut Indian Association
stepped forward with funds to go along with federal funding to construct
homes for married students and to assist others in attending professional
schools (Mardock 1971, 204).

Ex Parte Crow Dog

On December 17, 1883, the Supreme Court handed down one of its most important court decisions regarding Indian legal rights. On the Lakota Sioux
reservation, Crow Dog shot to death Spotted Tail, a Brule Sioux leader.
In the traditional justice system of the Lakota Sioux, Crow Dog paid the
demanded tribute of $600, eight horses, and a blanket to the Spotted Tail
family, and both sides considered the issue settled.

Nonetheless, the chief clerk on the reservation who was also the acting
Indian agent ordered that Crow Dog be arrested and taken into custody.
Crow Dog remained in jail until a U.S. court convicted him of murder and
sentenced him to be hanged. The case went to the U.S. Supreme Court with

the final ruling made in 1883 that U.S. courts lacked jurisdiction over crimes committed that involved Indians in Indian Country, thus upholding tribal sovereignty. Justice Thomas Stanley Matthews wrote the decision for the Supreme Court. In response, Congress passed the Major Crimes Act two years later that defined 7 crimes that allowed federal courts to have jurisdiction in Indian Country, thus usurping a significant amount of tribal sovereignty (and in the following years Congress amended the law twice, increasing the number of crimes to 10 and 14). A year later, in 1886, *U.S. v. Kagama* challenged the Major Crimes Act. In this incident, Pactah Billy, a Klamath Indian, murdered another Klamath Lyouse on the Hoopa Valley Reservation in California in June 1885. Justice Samuel Freeman Miller ruled that the Major Crimes Act was in effect, thus Congress's plenary power proved to be the ruling factor, thereby upholding the Major Crimes Act (Echo-Hawk 2010, 166, 198, 200).

Lake Mohonk Conferences

Earlier in 1883, the first Lake Mohonk Conference of the Friends of the Indians was held in the Catskill Mountains of upper New York. Two brothers, Alfred and Albert Smiley, organized the conference and the subsequent annual meetings. Members of the Quaker religion, the Smileys wanted to help Native people to improve their lives. They invited other like-minded humanitarians to meet at the Lake Mohonk mountain lodge on the northwest lakeshore on 310 beautiful acres. Teachers, churchmen, businessmen, and bureaucrats were invited to the meetings, seemingly everyone except for American Indians. The first official meeting had two purposes: "To inform the people of the United States as to the most direct practicable way in which the Indian question may be solved" and "To stimulate the thoughtful and right-minded citizens of the country to take immediate steps toward the solution of the problem" (Lake Mohonk Conference 1884, 3–4).

The Mohonk meetings resulted in annual reports that involved making recommendations to the Bureau of Indian Affairs in its supervision of reservations. Over the next 34 years, annual meetings were held to work toward the equality of American Indians as well as to encourage the appreciation of Indian arts and crafts.

Reservation Conditions

The so-called dark days on the plains began about 1880 and continued through the early decades of the 20th century. These times witnessed professional hunters working for railroad companies to supply food to construction crews. The once enormous herds of buffalo began to disappear from the plains during what became known as the reservation era when the military moved Indians onto reserved lands.

During the late 1800s, Richard Davis arrived in Indian Territory. Davis was not an agent, only a citizen who was considered a newcomer to the territory. He described Indians standing in a long line to receive rations at Anadarko in the southwestern part of Indian Territory. Anadarko consisted of a small town of six stores, a hotel, and a few frame houses with the agency nearby. Davis said:

> There are bluffs and bunches of timber around Anadarko, but the prairie stretches towards the west, and on it is the pen from which cattle are issued. The tepees and camp-fires sprang up over night, and . . . more Indians were driving in every minute, with the family in the wagon and the dogs under it . . . The men galloped off to the cattle-pen, and the women gathered in a long line in front of the agent's store to wait their turn for their rations. It was a curious line, with very young girls in it, very proud of the babies in beaded knapsacks on their backs—dirty, bright-eyed babies . . . and wrinkled, bent old squaws, . . . with coarse white hair, and hands worn a lost out of shape with work. Each of these had a tag . . . on which was printed the number in each family, and the amount of grain, flour, baking-powder, and soap to which the family was entitled. (Savage 1977, 114)

Reservations in the West were much like this one at Anadarko. Lining up to receive rations became a part of reservation life and the rather new culture forced on Native people. Once rulers of the plains, proud Indians were humbled, treated like beggars. Richard Davis described an Indian agent issuing underweight steers to feed 25 Indians for a period of two weeks. Davis saw the steers, and they tried to run. The steers "stumbled with the weakness of starvation" and had almost no meat on them to feed the Indians" (Savage 1977, 131).

Reservation life proved to be miserable. Becoming dependent on the federal government, the Indians could not forage for food and had to have permission from the Indian agent to even leave the reservation. On the northern plains, Indian agent Reuben Allen reported to Indian Commissioner Hiram Price the devastating conditions on the Blackfeet Reservation in Montana in 1884. Allen stated:

When I entered upon the duties of agent, I found the Indians in a deplorable condition. Their supplies had been limited and many of them were gradually dying of starvation. I visited a large number of their tents and cabins the second day after they had received their weekly rations . . . All bore marks of suffering from lack of food but the little children seemed to have suffered most . . . it did not seem possible for them to live long . . . so great was their destitution that the Indians stripped the bark from the saplings that grow along the creeks and ate the inner portions to appease their gnawing hunger. (Wissler 1971, 64)

Commissioner Price responded quickly and received a special appropriation to feed the Blackfeet Indians for the remaining months of the year (Ewers 1958, 294).

Conditions on reservations like this one represented most treaty lands. Indians were now prisoners of war. With authorization from the Grant administration, the Indian Office assigned agents to keep the Indians under control so that they would not escape to join hostile Indians.

Apache War in the Southwest

The Apaches caused considerable problems for the United States during the 1800s in the Southwest. From 1861 to 1863, the Apaches raided American and Mexican settlements in Arizona and in Mexico along the border. Apache leader Cochise was blamed for a raid on John Ward, a rancher, and Lieutenant George Bascom ordered his men to seize Cochise's relatives, but the famed Apache managed to escape, slashing his way through the tent where he was talking with Bascom. Bascom presumed that Cochise was guilty for the Ward attack and tried to capture the noted leader. Cochise and the Chiricahuas began taking prisoners of their own, while killing Mexicans along the Butterfield Overland mail route. In the end, both sides killed their hostages.

The Chiricahuas were joined in the hostilities by the Mimbreno Apaches led by Mangas Coloradas, Cochise's father-in-law. The White Mountain Apaches, who were likely the original culprits against Ward, the rancher, also joined. Bascom hung his Apache hostages, which included Cochise's brother. During the following months of 1861, the Apaches retaliated, killing about 150 whites and Mexicans.

From 1877 to 1880, the Apaches rose up again. Six years earlier, about 150 Western Apache under Chief Eskiminzin wanted peace and moved to

Camp Grant. Hatred for Apaches precipitated a vigilante mob of nearly 150 whites, Mexicans, and Papago (Tohono O'odam) mercenaries to slaughter 85 Apaches near Camp Grant on the morning of April 30, 1871. The mob raped Apache women and forced children into slavery. Apache raids continued, compelling the Tonto Basin Campaign led by General George Crook.

More than 20 clashes occurred between soldiers and Apaches. Of these, two particularly decisive clashes include a battle at Salt River Canyon on December 28 and the Battle of Skull Cave against the Yavapai on the same day in 1872. A third battle—at Turret Peak on March 27, 1873—broke the Apache and Yavapai resistance, and about 6,000 Apaches and Yavapais were placed on reservations in Arizona and New Mexico. However, this was not the end of the Apaches. Victorio led Membreno Apache raids from 1877 to 1880. Victorio and 80 warriors won a victory on September 4, 1879, and he led his warriors into Mexico and Texas, then back into New Mexico and Arizona. But at a two-day fight at the Battle of Tres Terrazas or Three Peaks, a force of 350 Mexicans and Tarahumars led by Colonel Joaquin Terraas killed more than half of Victorio's force. Terraas and his troops took many Apaches prisoner and killed Victorio.

In the summer of 1881, the aged Apache leader Nana led 40 warriors in two months of raids, killing 40 whites, covering more than 1,000 miles, winning 8 battles, and evading 1,400 soldiers before escaping to Mexico. Geronimo, who had fought with Cochise, led his people, the Chiricahua Apaches, in raids and clashes with the U.S. military from 1881 for the next several years. Other Apache warriors, Juh, Nachise (Cochise's son), and Chato joined in leading the Mescalero Apaches on raids.

Finally, Chato, Nachise, Loco, and Nana surrendered in March 1884. On September 4, 1886, the legendary Geronimo surrendered for the fourth and final time. With the defeat of the Apache in the Southwest, the Indian Bureau and reformers focused on improving conditions for Native people on their reservations.

The Ghost Dance

Local information reported that on January 1, 1889, Wovoka, a Paiute Indian, experienced a vision during a solar eclipse. Local Indians of Mason Valley in present-day Nevada knew about the talented young medicine maker who was blessed with the gift of prophecy. A neighbor named Ed Dyer described Wovoka as "a tall, well proportioned man with piercing eyes, regular features, a deep voice and a calm and dignified mien. He stood straight as a ramrod, spoke slowly, and by sheer projection of personality commanded the attention of any listener. He visibly stood out among his fellow Indians" (Lynch and Hittman 1997, 108).

In his vision, Wovoka said that he traveled to the spiritual world and stood in the presence of the Creator. The Creator showed Wovoka a bountiful land full of streams, green meadows, and wild game where everything was in harmony as it used to be. The Creator instructed Wovoka to return to earth and to teach all the people that he could that the time had come to stop fighting and to love one another. People should work hard, not steal or lie, and they should dance to celebrate the coming of the new earth.

The Ghost Dance began to spread throughout the West. This spiritual movement attracted Indians throughout 16 states and persuaded some 30 different tribes, which included the Kiowas, Caddoes, and Wichitas who learned about it from the Cheyennes. Osages, Otoes, Cherokees; and others learned from the Caddoes. On the northern plains the Crows, Northern Cheyennes, Arapahos, Shoshonis, and Lakotas took up the Dance of the Ghosts (Miller 1959, 36). To the south, the Southern Paiutes introduced the Ghost Dance to the Pai tribes of Arizona. First the Walapai took up the dance in May of 1889, who likely introduced it to western bands of the Pai, then eastern bands joined the movement as well as groups like the Havasupai and Chemehuevi (Dobyns and Euler 1967, 14–28).

Wounded Knee and Sitting Bull

In the following months Kicking Bird, a band leader of the Minneconjou Lakota Sioux, and Short Bull traveled to meet Wovoka to observe his teaching and powers over the weather and learn of his prophecy. They became believers in the Ghost Dance and brought this information about the spiritual movement to Sitting Bull. Alarmed at these events in the West, the federal government wanted Sitting Bull brought in.

In 1888 and 1889, John H. Oberly served as commissioner of Indian Affairs. As a former Indian school superintendent, he had experience in Indian affairs and education. Oberly received reports of the Ghost Dance permeating Indian Country, but reports of him being replaced prevented him from doing anything about it. His resignation on June 30 enabled the appointment of Thomas Jefferson Morgan as Indian commissioner who served until 1893. Morgan worked on a lengthy proposal, a "Supplemental Report on Indian Education," which he submitted to the Interior Secretary John Noble. He strove to educate Native youth, bring about Indian civilization, and support the Lake Mohonk conferences. Morgan disregarded the Ghost Dance as a military threat and wanted to work with reformers to change Native culture for assimilation (Board of Indian Commissioners 1890, 166; Commissioner of Indian Affairs 1891, 9).

The War Department was very much concerned and wanted to arrest Sitting Bull for fear that his influence would cause war to break out throughout the West. Sitting Bull and his Lakota Sioux band had surrendered eight years earlier after living in Canada. The noted leader lived in a cabin on the Standing Rock Reservation. Indian agent James McLaughlin became concerned about the growing intensity of the Ghost Dance. On December 10, General Nelsen Miles ordered General Thomas H. Ruger in charge of the Department of Dakota to arrest Sitting Bull. Ruger asked Colonel William F. Drum to carry out the order, and Drum worked with McLaughlin to devise a plan. On December 14, agent McLaughlin wrote a letter to Lieutenant Bullhead, a tribal policeman, containing instructions to gather other policemen with a plan to capture Sitting Bull and bring him to Fort Yates. McLaughlin had ordered the capturing of Sitting Bull at daybreak on December 15. A Lakota called Catch-the-Bear shot his rifle and hit Bullhead, who turned and shot Sitting Bull in the chest. Red Tomahawk, another policeman, immediately shot Sitting Bull in the head with his gun. Within minutes, Sitting Bull's people killed six policemen, and two more died from wounds, while seven of his followers were killed, and Sitting Bull's body was delivered to Fort Yates (Andersson 2008; DeMontravel 1986).

The death of Sitting Bull did not deter the Ghost Dance spiritual movement, which had become a craze among many Indians. Some ghost dancers went into a trance while dancing, claiming afterwards that they saw their relatives and other ancestors. Some of Sitting Bull's people joined the Ghost Dance movement, although the legendary leader had been skeptical. A Minneconjou Sioux leader, Big Foot, led a group of ghost dancers en route to the Pine Ridge agency. Intercepted by soldiers, the troops forced Big Foot and his followers to camp near Wounded Knee Creek.

On December 29, 1890, during a second search of the camp for weapons, a shot was fired and the U.S. army began shooting, killing between 150 and 370 Sioux men, women, and children. Soldiers pursued and killed those who attempted to escape. Wounded Knee represented the last major confrontation between Indians and the U.S. military. This confrontation ended all Indian wars. In response, reformers and the BIA worked together to improve reservation conditions throughout Indian Country.

The Indian and His Problem

At the turn of the 20th century, Francis Leupp served as commissioner of Indian Affairs. He knew his predecessors in the position, and he knew the

Indian Problem he faced. Leupp also knew Indians relatively well, as he had worked with them for 25 years. In his book, *The Indian and His Problem*, published in 1910, Leupp described the white man's ignorance of the Indian, the resulting misconceptions, and the polarized views of the Indian and white man. In his preface, he wrote, "The Indian Problem has now reached a stage where its solution is almost wholly a matter of administration. . . . What is needed most from this time forth is the guidance of affairs by an independent mind, active sympathies free from mawkishness, an elastic patience and a steady hand." Four years later, Leupp wrote a second book, IN RED MAN'S LAND, to lobby for the Indian progress (Leupp 1914).

As Leupp addressed a better future for Native people, he recommended understanding the Indian's stamina as a strength to build on in the girls and boys, teaching them practical things about mainstream life and building on their individuality with the right ideals of civilization. "No one can understand the Indian problem without first understanding the Indian," said Leupp. But the Indian and the white man had to work together (Leupp [1910] 1971, vii).

Conclusion

During the late 19th and early 20th centuries, the Indian Problem remained one that could not be solved by reformers. However, multiple individuals, organizations, and parts of the federal government attempted a final solution. They failed. The one thing that they all agreed on was that Indians should be civilized for assimilation into the American mainstream. All of this proved to be timely to do something for Indians, but no one asked them. The paternalistic strong hand of certain individuals who were secretaries of war or commissioners of Indian Affairs told Indians what to do. This kind of paternalism has long been a part of U.S.-Indian relations and continued into the 20th century. By the end of the first decade, the Bureau of Indian Affairs employed an estimated 6,000 workers (Taylor 1959, 98). With the total Indian population dipping to its lowest ever of less than 238,000, one BIA employee was responsible for every 40 Indians.

Many people thought Indians were the vanishing race. The End of the Trail statue symbolized this concern among many people. Sculptor James Earle Fraser of South Dakota was asked to create the statue for the Panama-Pacific International Exposition in 1915, but due to the needs of World War I the planned bronze exhibit was made of plaster and began to dissolve. Ironically the presumed vanishing race did not dissolve while Fraser's statute had to be rescued with a bronze replica years later.

Indian reformers emerged from humanitarians, Christians, and some philanthropists. Outside of the federal government, they loosely became known as "Friends of the Indian." They considered themselves to be spokesmen on behalf of Indians who actually fell outside of the U.S. Constitution. This humanitarianism continued into the 20th century as long as Indians lived on reservations. By the end of the 19th century, an estimated 200 Indian reservations existed with many being formed by treaties following the Civil War.

References

"Abolition of Treaty Making Act." March 3, 1871. *U.S. Statutes at Large*, 16:566.

Andersson, Rani-Henrik. *The Lakota Ghost Dance of 1890*. Lincoln: University of Nebraska Press, 2008.

Board of Indian Commissioners Annual Report, 1890.

Commissioner of Indian Affairs Annual Report, 1891.

DeMontravel, Peter R. "General Nelson A. Miles and the Wounded Knee Controversy." *Arizona and the West* 28 (Spring 1986): 28–44.

Dobyns, Henry F. and Robert C. Euler. *The Ghost Dance of 1889*. Prescott, AZ: Prescott College Press, 1967.

Echo-Hawk, Walter R. IN THE COURTS OF THE CONQUEROR: THE 10 WORST INDIAN LAW CASES EVER DECIDED. Golden: Fulcrum Publishing, 2010.

Ewers, John C. *The Blackfeet: Raiders on the Northwestern Plains*. Norman: University of Oklahoma Press, 1958.

"Indian Commissioner Francis Walker on Indian Policy." *Annual Report of the Commissioner of Indian Affairs, 1872*. House Executive Document no. 1. 42nd Congress. 3d Sess. Serial 1560.

Jackson, Helen Hunt. *A Century of Dishonor*. Minneapolis, MN: Ross and Haines, 1964. Originally published 1881.

Kappler, Charles. comp. and ed. INDIAN TREATIES 1778–1883. New York: Interland Publishing Inc., 1972. Originally published 1904.

Leupp, Francis E. *The Indian and His Problem*. New York: Arno Press and The New York Times, 1971. Originally published 1910 by Charles Scribner's Sons.

Leupp, Francis E. IN RED MAN'S LAND. New York: Fleming H. Revell Company, 1914.

Lynch, Don, ed. and Michael Hittman, comp. *Wovoka and the Ghost Dance*. Lincoln: University of Nebraska Press, 1997.

Manypenny, George W. *Our Indian Wards*. Cincinnati, OH: Robert Clarke and Co., 1880.

Mardock, Robert Winston. *The Reformers and the American Indian*. Columbia: University of Missouri Press, 1971.

Miller, David Humphreys. *Ghost Dance*. New York: Duell, Sloan and Pearce, 1959.

Otis, Elwell S. *The Indian Question*. New York: Sheldon and Company, 1878.

Prucha, Francis Paul. AMERICAN INDIAN POLICY IN CRISIS: CHRISTIAN REFORMERS AND THE INDIAN, 1865–1900. Norman: University of Oklahoma Press, 1976.

Richardson, James D., comp. *A Compilation of the Messages and Papers of the Presidents*, Volumes 1 and 2. New York: Bureau of National Literature, 1897.

Savage, William. *Indian Life Transforming an American Myth*. Norman: University of Oklahoma Press, 1977.

Second Annual Address to the Public of the Lake Mohonk Conference. Philadelphia: Indian Rights Assn., 1884.

Tatum, Lawrie. *Our Red Brothers and the Peace Policy of President Ulysses S. Grant*. Lincoln: University of Nebraska Press, 1970.

Taylor, Theodore. "The Regional Organization of the Bureau of Indian Affairs." PhD diss., Harvard University, 1959.

United States *ex rel. Standing Bear v. Crook*, 25 Federal Cases, 695 (C.C.D. Neb. 1879) (No. 14,891).

Wissler, Clark. *Red Man Reservations*. New York: Collier Books, 1971.

FOUR

Federal Boarding Schools and Indian Education

The supervision of Indian education has been a responsibility of the federal government as a result of the trust relationship created by the 374 U.S.-Indian treaties. Seventy of the treaties contain provisions about introducing civilization to the tribal nations. Thirty-eight of the treaties have specific provisions about providing education. For example, on August 13, 1803, the Kaskaskia Indians made a treaty with U.S. officials that included a provision to introduce education. Article three of the agreement stated, "And whereas the greater part of the said tribe have been baptized and received into the Catholic church to which they are much attached, the United States will give annually for seven years one hundred dollars towards the support of a priest of that religion, who will engage to perform for the said tribe the duties of his office and also to instruct as many of their children as possible in the rudiments of literature" (Kappler 1975, 67–68).

In support of treaty obligations, Congress has established a long history of passing laws to promote the education of American Indians. Beginning with a missionary education, vocational training and academic learning later became a part of the Indian education experience.

Mission Schools in the Great Lakes and South

As various religious groups moved into Indian Country, they introduced the Bible and their Christian beliefs. The Baptists and Methodists actively sent their missionaries to the South where they lived among Native people, constructed churches, and built mission schools. Although the missionaries had not received authorization from the United States, they wanted federal protection when they needed it. The early treaties from 1778 to about 1817 pertained to military matters, land boundaries, returning prisoners, payments to tribes, and maintaining "peace and friendship" but nothing about missionaries. However, the missionaries used the opportunity of educating Indians as a means to introduce Christianity to them. As an example, the treaty of 1817 with the Wyandot, Potawatomi, Ottawa, and Ojibwa specifically stated the government's authorization and support of a Catholic education for the Native youth of these groups under article 16 of the treaty (Kappler 1975, 150).

In the South, Moravian, Presbyterian, Methodist, and Baptist missionaries worked among the tribes. Reverend John Gambold established an Indian school in Georgia in 1805 for the Creeks. In the same year, Reverend Gideon Blackburn, a Presbyterian, started a school at Hiwassee in the Cherokee Nation. In 1816 Cyrus Kingsbury, a Presbyterian, started a school near Missionary Ridge. A year later the Presbyterians established Brainerd School for the Cherokees near Chattanooga, Tennessee, and they maintained mission day schools at Pumpkin Vine and Etowah in Georgia.

As Native leaders and U.S. officials began to address education and civilization, the federal government became responsible for educating Native children. This obligation continued as more treaties were made but with the primary purpose of removing eastern Native people further westward. From the Jeffersonian idea to civilize Native people, education became a part of the civilization process, and missionaries volunteered to provide a Christian education. Yet more treaties followed, moving the same tribes again, and other agreements moved Indian groups of the Midwest and the South to west of the Mississippi known as Indian Country. This region would then become defined and known as Indian Territory, consisting of present-day Oklahoma, Kansas, and Nebraska. Eventually only the Oklahoma area would be the final site for eastern-removed tribes. Interestingly education and removal were both important in the treaty negotiations, although the latter became more significant due to settler expansion.

Indian Schools in Indian Territory

Missionaries continued to work among the tribes after their removal to Indian Territory during the 1820s and 1830s. As the eastern tribes began to rebuild their nations, they became well acquainted with Western ways, and many tribal members embraced the white man's education.

In Indian Territory the Choctaws started several public schools as well as Elliott Mission School, and they opened Spencer Academy and New Hope Academy in 1844. Armstrong Academy followed in 1845. Fort Coffee Academy opened in the 1850s, and it later became the Choctaw Female

Seminary. During the same decade, Bloomfield Academy opened for operation as well as Wapanucka Academy for girls.

Reverend Alfred Wright and his wife opened Wheelock Academy in 1833 and the Choctaws desired more education and Christianity. In 1850 Goodland Academy opened with the support of the Presbyterian Church. In 1897 Reverend William Henry Ketcham founded St. Agnes Mission School at Antlers in Choctaw country as a Catholic school. From 1892 to 1897, Father Ketcham started 13 missions throughout eastern Indian Territory.

The Seminoles followed the educational trend and opened Oak Ridge, a boarding school for manual training in 1848. The Presbyterians established the school, and Reverend John and Mary Anne Lilley ran it. Additional Seminole schools followed: Wewoka Mission in 1868, Sasakawa Female Academy in 1884, Mehasukey Male Academy in 1891, and Emahaka Female Academy in 1893.

Starting later than their Choctaw brethren, the Chickasaw opened Bloomfield Academy in 1852 as well as McKendree Academy about the same time and Manual Labor Academy in the same year. Chickasaw schools included Wapanucka Institute; Collins Institute, later called Colbert Academy; and Burney Institute, a Presbyterian-supported school (Gibson 1965, 159–166).

The five tribes realized the importance of education in order for their peoples to progress. The Cherokee male and female seminaries represented examples of tribal needs for education during the late 1800s. In Creek country, the Muscogees started Nuyaka Mission School. Reverend R. M. Louighbridge and Augusta R. Moore started a boarding school in Tullahassee, Oklahoma, near Muskogee for Creek boys and girls. After the Civil War, Reverend Theodore F. Brewer started Harrell Institute a Methodist school at Muskogee for the Creeks, and Alice Robertson started a Presbyterian school for Creek girls at Muskogee.

In 1880 missionary Almon C. Bacone started a school with three students in the Cherokee Baptist Mission at Tahlequah in Indian Territory. By the end of the first year, he had 56 students with 3 faculty, and the Creek Tribal Council gave Bacone a land grant of 160 acres where he moved his school outside of Muskogee. In 1885 the school was named Indian University and renamed Bacone Indian University in 1910 (Williams and Meredith 1980, 4–6). It is presently a four-year school and known as Bacone College.

In other parts of Indian Territory, government agency schools like Seneca Indian School, Chilocco and Fort Sill Indian School opened for operation in the late 1800s (Lomawaima, 1994; Williams and Meredith 1980, 250). The idea of educating Indian youth in the West turned into reality when 48 day schools existed near Indian reservations by the 1860s (Adams 1995, 28).

Much of the BIA's responsibility shifted to maintaining boarding and day schools on reservations. The late 19th century proved to be a critical stage in which the BIA sought to convert Indians to a different way of life and to educate them in Western ways, including manual as well as academic training. These busy years represented the high point of the Indian boarding school era. Throughout Indian Country, in 1900 the BIA operated 253 government schools (25 off-reservation, 81 reservation schools, and 147 day schools) (Adams 1995, 319).

Richard Pratt and Carlisle Indian School

The founding of Carlisle Indian School serves as the primary example of the Indian boarding school experience. Pratt had fought Indians in the Red River Wars in the 1870s and was concerned about the future of Indian children. The military transferred Pratt and placed him in charge of Kiowa, Comanche, and Cheyenne prisoners at Fort Marion in St. Augustine, Florida,

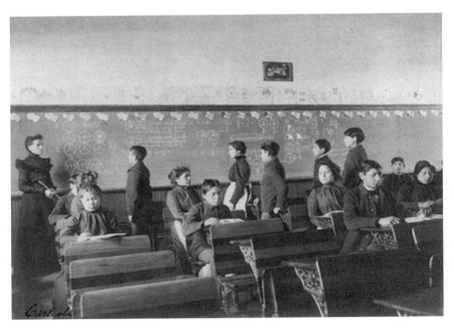

Native students participate in a mathematics class at the Carlisle Indian School in Carlisle, Pennsylvania, c. 1903. In 1900, the BIA reported 153 boarding schools and 154 day schools on reservations for a total of 307, enrolling 39,276 Native students. (Library of Congress)

from 1875–1878. At Fort Marion, Pratt authorized giving military uniforms to the Native prisoners. He ordered the Indians' hair to be cut. Pratt also ordered the Indians to be given lessons in English, Christianity, and other aspects of white civilization. Pratt believed that Indians could be changed with new surroundings.

In 1879 Richard Henry Pratt received permission to use abandoned army barracks in Carlisle, Pennsylvania to be converted into his Indian school. Pratt became an important supporter of the movement to educate American Indians in the late 19th century. He aggressively promoted his idea of combining industrial training with academic schooling while immersing Indian boys and girls in white society.

Carlisle was located far away from all reservations and close to the town of its name. This proximity allowed the students to be isolated from what Pratt saw as the demeaning influence of reservations. He believed the communities nearby would serve as role models for his students. After the students learned English and vocational skills, they entered the outing program. Pratt traveled widely, recruiting students and promoting Carlisle by stressing his system for off-reservation boarding schools. Pratt's military training and his stern attitude made him critical of federal policy. He disliked reservations, the continuation of tribal status, and reservation day schools. He stated:

It is a great mistake to think that the Indian is born an inevitable savage. He is born a blank, like the rest of us. Left in the surroundings of savagery, he grows to possess a savage language, superstition, and life. We, left in the surroundings of civilization, grow to possess a civilized language, life, and purpose. Transfer the infant white to the savage surroundings, he will grow to possess a savage language, superstition and habit. Transfer the savage-born infant to the surroundings of civilization, and he will grow to possess a civilized language and habit. (Adams 1995, 52)

Pratt believed his way represented the only proper method to teach Indians.

From 1879 to 1918, an estimated 1,200 Indian students attended Carlisle until the school closed due to military needs during World War I. While an impressive number of alumni attended Carlisle, less than 8 percent of the students actually graduated from the school. Lakota Luther Standing Bear, one of the first Indian students to attend Carlisle, described the way the experience changed his life: "At the age of eleven years, ancestral life for me and my people was most abruptly ended without regard for our wishes, comforts, or rights in the matter. At once I was thrust into an alien world, into an environment as different from the one into which I had been born as it is possible to imagine, to remake myself, if I could, into the likeness of the invader" (Standing Bear 1998, 191–193). The boarding school experience abruptly halted students' thinking in the traditional ways and forced them to learn a foreign culture.

Outing System

Pratt's "Outing System" after students completed training provided a practical education. The program involved placing the students with white rural families near the school, and the federal government paid the host family $50 a year for the student's medical care and clothing. The outing system placed students with rural families where they would gain firsthand knowledge of white society. The student was to live, eat, worship, and work with the family for three months over the summer or up to two years. For Pratt, the outing system had a dual purpose: it encouraged students to learn English and allowed them to earn money, while at the same time it broke down prejudice against them (Pratt 1964, 212–281).

The student was expected to learn the agricultural lifestyle from the farmer and his family. In this manner the Native student learned the civilized ways of Americans. Pratt did not get along with the Indian Bureau, and he also received criticism for his firm supervision of Carlisle in his military-like manner. Eventually Pratt's criticism of federal policy led to his dismissal from Carlisle in 1904 for insubordination.

Daily School Routine

Boarding school life proved to be demanding and unforgiving. At many schools the students wore cadet uniforms, marched to class in military fashion at the sound of a bell, and obeyed teachers' commands. A typical day's schedule was as follows:

5:30	Rising bell.
5:30–6:00	Dress and report for athletics.
6:00	Warning bell.
6:00–6:20	Setting-up exercise.
6:20–6:25	Roll call.
6:25	Breakfast bell; raise flag.

6:25–6:30	Line up; march to dining hall.
6:30–7:00	Breakfast
7:00–7:25	Care of rooms.
7:15	Sick call; bugle.
7:25	Work bell.
7:25–7:30	Line up; details report.
7:30–8:30	Industrial instruction.
7:30–8:15	Academic division.
8:15–8:25	Prepare for school.
8:25	School bell or bugle.
8:25–8:30	Line up. March to school building.
8:30	School application industrial division.
10:00–10:15	Recess; five minutes breathing exercise.
11:30	Recall bell; all departments.
11:30–11:45	Recreation; details return to quarters.
11:45	Warning bell.
11:45–11:55	Prepare for dinner.
11:55–12:00	Line up. Inspection. March to dining room.
12:00–12:30	Dinner.

A similarly rigorous schedule followed the rest of the afternoon. School officials accounted for every minute of the morning and the afternoons. They scheduled the evening meal at 5:30 and Taps at 8:30 to put the students to bed.

With the Indian tribes becoming less of a military threat, the federal government invested more into Indian schools. In 1877, a generous Congress appropriated $20,000; $75,000 in 1880; $992,800 in 1885; $1,364,568 in 1895; $2,060,695 in 1890; and $2,936,080 in 1900.

Indian student enrollment was 3,598 for 1877; 4,651 for 1880; 8,143 for 1885; 12,232 for 1890; 18,188 for 1895; and 21,568 for 1900 (Schmeckebier 1927, 209). Indian student enrollment began slow but increased noticeably in the late 1800s after the Ghost Dance and Wounded Knee Massacre in 1890.

Dr. Charles Eastman

Charles Alexander Eastman described the first day of entering a boarding school classroom at Flandreau, South Dakota. Eastman explained that he raced against another Indian youth on their ponies toward the school, and

By this time we had reached the second crossing of the river, on whose bank stood the little mission school. Thirty or forty Indian children stood about, curiously watching the newcomer [me] as we came up the steep bank. I realized for the first time that I was an object of curiosity, and it was not a pleasant feeling. On the other hand, I was considerably interested in the strange appearance of these school-children . . . The hair of all the boys was cut short, . . . When the teacher spoke to me, I had not the slightest idea what he meant, so I did not trouble myself to make any demonstration for fear of giving offense . . . He then gave some unintelligible directions, and, to my great surprise, the pupils in turn held their books open and talked the talk of a strange people . . . I had seen nothing thus far to prove to me the good of civilization. (Eastman [1916] 1936, 21–23)

Eastman's early days at Flandreau represented the stark entrance into the white man's boarding school system. This strict learning environment radically changed the life ways of Native youth and separated them from their families. Simultaneously, Native students stood at the threshold of a new beginning for themselves, even though many tears flowed miles away from their loved ones. In 1883, Sitting Bull, the wise and famed leader of the Hunkpapa Sioux, visited a boarding school and encouraged the Lakota students with the following words:

My dear grandchildren: All your folks are my relatives, because I am Sioux, and so are they. . . . When I was your age, things were entirely different. I had no teachers but my parents and relatives. . . . Now I often pick up papers and books, which have all kinds of pictures and marks on them, but I cannot understand them as a white person does. They have a way of communicating by the use of written symbols and figures; but before they could do that, they had to have an understanding among themselves. You are to learn that, and I was very much pleased to hear you reading. In [the] future business dealings with the whites are going to be very hard, and it behooves you to learn well what you are taught here. But that is not all. We older people need you. In our dealings with the white men, we are just the same as blind men, because we do not understand them. We need you to help us understand what the white man is up to. My Grandchildren, be good. Try to make a mark for yourselves. Learn all you can. (Diedrich, 1998, 168; Fiske 1933, 23–24)

Indian School Personnel

In 1891 an executive order placed Indian school personnel, including superintendents and agency physicians, under the classified civil service. The measure scrutinized those individuals in charge of reservation schools. This action dismantled the spoils system in which all that was required for employment on a reservation was a stated intent to work among Indians. Prior to 1890, Commissioner of Indian Affairs Thomas Morgan eliminated the position of Indian agent, which was replaced by school superintendents, but this difficult process lasted at least another 15 years.

By the late 19th century, an off-reservation boarding school movement had established a strong trend of emerging schools. By 1900 no less than 24 federal boarding schools had opened. Beginning with Carlisle in Pennsylvania in 1879, Chemawa, Oregon (Salem) opened in 1880 with others to follow. Four years later, four more schools opened at Chilocco, Oklahoma; Genoa, Nebraska; Albuquerque, New Mexico; and Haskell in Lawrence, Kansas.

Haskell experienced a series of important transitions. From a boarding school when 22 students started in 1884 under its official name—the United States Indian Industrial Training School—the school demonstrated an ability to adapt that allowed it to grow and even prosper while other Indian schools were forced to close. Boys learned trades involving tailoring, wagon making, blacksmithing, harness making, painting, shoe making, and farming. Female students learned cooking, sewing, and house cleaning or homemaking. By 1894 Haskell officials added academic training to the elementary grades. Later the government added a traditional school to Haskell in order to supply teachers to tribal communities. In 1927 the state of Kansas accredited the high school courses at Haskell as the Indian institution survived the Depression and World War II. In 1970 Haskell became a junior college, known as Haskell Indian Junior College; and in 1993 the school became Haskell Indian Nations University.

Schools continued to be established throughout Indian Country. A school opened in Grand Junction, Colorado, in 1886. In 1890 three schools opened in Santa Fe, Mexico; Fort Mojave, Arizona; and Carson, Nevada. Two schools opened their doors in Pierre, South Dakota; and Phoenix, Arizona, in 1891. Two more began operating the next year in Fort Lewis, Colorado; and Fort Shaw, Montana. Four schools opened in 1893 at Flandreau, South Dakota; Pipestone, Minnesota; Mount Pleasant, Michigan; and Tomah, Wisconsin. Two more started in 1895 at Wittenberg, Wisconsin; and Greenville, California; and Morris, Minnesota, began in 1897. In 1898 three schools opened at Chamberlain, South Dakota; Fort Bidwell, California; and Rapid City, South Dakota (Commissioner of Indian Affairs 1905, 41). The BIA had many responsibilities to carry out with the growing number of boarding schools, and each student had his or her own tale to tell about the schools. In Indian Country in 1925, the BIA operated 209 schools (18 off-reservation schools, 51 reservation schools, and 140 day schools) (Adams 1995, 319). The Great Depression and World War II would force the federal governemt to close many of the schools.

From a Native perspective, the schools scarred the Native children who attended them. Many sad stories lamented negative memories, but one that stands out is that of Maria Christjohn Hinton, an Oneida in Wisconsin. At the time Maria entered the school, she could not speak English. At the ages of four and five, she was too young for the first grade, so she played outside of the Oneida Government School throughout the day as the laundry woman kept an eye on her. When she did start school, the nuns punished her in different ways to stop her from writing with her left hand. They ignored the fact that Maria was left-handed (McLester and Hauptman 2010, 48–51).

Society of American Indians

By the late 1800s, the first generation of Indian boarding school students began to graduate or leave school. Many of the students abandoned the old ways of their tribal cultures and sought new lives in the American mainstream. These remarkable Native individuals became known to each other and discussed the plight of their people. In 1911 a group of educated Indians formed the Society of American Indians (SAI) in Columbus, Ohio, at the urging of Fayette McKenzie of Ohio State University. The founding six charter members included Carlos Montezuma (Yavapai-Apache), Charles Eastman (Dakota), Thomas L. Sloan (Omaha), Charles E. Dagenett (Peoria), Laura Cornelius (Oneida), and Henry Standing Bear (Oglala Lakota). Association members were called Red Progressives for their success in earning an education. Carlos Montezuma spoke out the loudest in criticizing the BIA for its mistreatment on the nearly 200 Indian reservations. As a united voice, the SAI called for the termination of the BIA.

Following the Roaring Twenties, which were not so prosperous for Native people, the Great Depression changed much of the country as the stock market crashed on Wall Street in New York City. By 1932 the country sank further into poverty as people panicked. Once elected president, Franklin Roosevelt introduced his so-called New Deal programs to solve the problems caused by the Great Depression. For Native people, the Indian Reorganization Act of 1934 laid the foundation for an Indian New Deal. The law began a new Indian policy of reorganizing Native communities as tribal governments patterned after the U.S. government. It also requested the tribes to write constitutions, and the government made loans available that the tribes had to apply for. A part of the bureau's solution, under the supervision of Indian Commissioner John Collier, was the passage of the Johnson-O'Malley Act in 1934. This act authorized the federal government to provide health, education, and social welfare services to Native Americans through state and territorial contracts. This important legislation has been amended to ensure that Indian and Alaska Native children have an equal opportunity for a public education. While the Society of American Indians dissolved in the early 1930s, Indian higher education became increasingly important.

Following World War II, the BIA began to offer scholarships to individual college students in need of financial support. Native students enrolled in a state- or federally- recognized tribe could apply for a BIA scholarship by contacting the BIA higher education program in their area. As a stipulation in the 1960s, scholarship recipients had to maintain a "C" grade point average in their college course work. The BIA scholarship program focused mainly on helping Native students to achieve their undergraduate degree, and it is presently helping to fund Indian college graduates via BIA-tribal contracts.

In 1968 American Indians opened the doors of operation for Navajo Community College and more tribal colleges to follow. Originally the college operated at the Rough Rock Community School until buildings for the community college could be completed in 1969 at Tsaile, Arizona. Dr. Ned Hatathli served as the first president of Navajo Community College when it moved to its new location in Tsaile. The Bureau of Indian Affairs funded the school from a modest amount to roughly $4 million in 1992 and increased the amount to $7.3 million in 2000. During the summer of 1997, the college changed its name to Diné College: Diné meaning the "People" in the Navajo language.

Kennedy Report

In 1969 the Kennedy Report for the Senate Special Subcommittee on Indian Education announced that formal education for American Indians had failed. Robert Kennedy initially chaired the committee until his assassination in 1968. Then, Senator Edward Kennedy became the chairperson that produced the report entitled "Indian Education: A National Tragedy, A National Challenge." The subcommittee set national goals, recommending,

> Maximum Indian participation in the development of exemplary educational programs for (a) Federal Indian Schools; (b) public schools with Indian populations; and (c) model schools to meet both social and educational goals; Excellent summer school programs for all Indian children; Full-year preschool programs for all Indian children between the ages of 3 and 5; Elimination of adult illiteracy in Indian communities; Adult high school equivalency programs for all Indian adults; Parity of dropout rates and achievement levels of Indian high school students with national norms; Parity of college entrance and graduation of Indian students with the national average; Readily accessible community colleges; Early childhood services embracing the spectrum of need; Bilingual, bicultural special educational assistance; Effective prevention and treatment procedures for alcoholism and narcotic addiction; Expanded work-study and cooperative education programs; Workable student financial assistance programs at all educational levels; and Vocational student financial assistance programs at all educational levels; and Vocational and technical training related accurately to employment opportunities. (Indian Education 1969, 1–220)

The report recommended that more Native involvement would help to advance the progress of Indian education. The report also included a recommendation for a National Indian Board of Education to develop a systematic plan for Indian education.

National Indian Education Association

As a part of this wake-up call for action, the National Indian Education Association (NIEA), composed of educated Native people, became incorporated in 1970. NIEA started with a 12-member board of directors with several committees to make certain that Indian educators and students were represented in various educational institutions and meetings throughout Indian Country and in Washington. At present, NIEA is the largest and oldest Indian education organization. Indian educators began to actively express Native views in various areas ranging from the need for more opportunities to the production of important academic works.

In the late 1960s and early 1970s, an Indian renaissance occurred with the publication of three important books, two of them written by Native scholars. In 1968 Vine Deloria Jr., Standing Rock Lakota Sioux, published his most well-known book, *Custer Died For Your Sins: An Indian Manifesto*. He challenged America to examine its past mistreatment of American Indians. At the same time, N. Scott Momaday published his novel, *House Made of Dawn*, which won the Pulitzer Prize for literature in 1969. A Kiowa - Cherokee Native from Oklahoma, Momaday's story of a returned Indian veteran from World War II rippled throughout Indian Country. In 1970 the most well-known publication appeared in print, Dee Brown's *Bury My Heart at Wounded Knee*. Published in 17 languages, the landmark book articulated the Native point of view to five million readers who have purchased this best seller. This book enabled readers to understand the perspective of American Indians from their side of the frontier as they watched invaders coming into their homelands.

In the early 1970s, Richard Nixon's administration in the White House brought about reform in both Indian education and in Indian self-determination more broadly. On July 8, 1970, President Nixon made a special message to Congress in which he explained that the government would help American Indians to achieve "Self-determination . . . without the threat of eventual termination." He stressed the importance of Indian empowerment and that "the Indian that he can assume control over his own life without being separated involuntarily from the tribal group." In the same message President Nixon remarked, "One of the saddest aspects of Indian life in the United States is the low quality of Indian education. Drop-out rates for Indians are twice the national average and the average educational level for all Indians under Federal supervision is less than six school years" (Nixon 1970). Nixon announced that for the fiscal year 1971, Johnson O'Malley (JOM) funding would be increased to $20 million (Public Law No. 638).

During the early 1970s the BIA operated schools for over 50,000 Indian students. Another 750 Indian students were enrolled in schools where the BIA contracted tribes to provide educational services. Another 141,000 Native students attended public schools. Of that number, 89,000 Indian students were eligible to receive JOM assistance.

Indian Education Assistance Act

In 1972 Congress passed the Indian Education Assistance Act, also known as Title IV of Public Law 92–318, Educational Amendments of 1972. This law offered new opportunities to Indian youth and adults. It provided federal assistance in education above the funds annually appropriated from the Office of Education; Department of Health, Education and Welfare; and the Bureau of Indian Affairs. Most important the law created the Office of Indian Education within the Office of Education with a deputy commissioner for Indian Education that reported to the commissioner of Indian Affairs. In addition the law established the National Advisory Council for Indian Education to consist of 15 Indians or Alaska Natives to be appointed by the president from a recommended list of Native people from tribes and organizations.

American Indian Higher Education Consortium

In the same year of the Indian Education Assistance Act, six tribal colleges gathered at a meeting to form the American Indian Higher Education Consortium (AIHEC). In 1973 the Ford Foundation, Carnegie Foundation, and Donner Foundation provided start-up funding to establish an AIHEC office in Denver, Colorado.

Since then, the tribal college members have met annually to deal with higher education issues as more tribal colleges are being established and joining the consortium. The members consist of tribal college presidents who provide updated progress reports of their schools, discuss issues of concern, and make recommendations to improve the overall progress of Indian higher education.

AIHEC succeeded in pressuring Congress to help tribal colleges. In December 1978, President Jimmy Carter signed into law the first Tribally Controlled Community College Assistance Act. Nonetheless, leaders quickly realized they needed additional assistance, and in 1988 the AIHEC established the American Indian College Fund to raise millions of dollars and other resources from nongovernment sources. In 1992 the fund received its largest donation to date from Theodore R. Johnson, a 90-year old retired executive of UPS of America, Inc., who gave $3.6 million with the statement, "I have always felt that Indians got a raw deal in this country" ("American Indian College Fund" 1992, 7; Szasz 1999, 237).

Coming together to work together, the tribal colleges have grown in number to help educate their tribal communities. As of 2010, 36 tribal colleges in the United States and Canada belong to the American Indian Higher Education Consortium.

American Indian Policy Review Commission Report

From 1973 to 1976, Morris Thompson served as commissioner of Indian Affairs. During his brief time in office, Thompson helped lead a reform movement that garnered federal support for Indian education at all levels. In a letter to Representative Lloyd Meeds of Washington, Thompson stated, "For the past five years the BIA, in cooperation with the U.S. Office of Education, has funded programs at the University of Minnesota, Pennsylvania State University, and Harvard University to train Indians and Alaska Natives to be school administrators. . . . The higher education assistance program operated by the Bureau provided assistance to 13,721 Indian college and university students in Fiscal Year 1974 and to more than 14,000 students in Fiscal Year 1975." The BIA planned for the future by helping universities to educate new administrators in directing schools at all levels. Thompson also informed Meeds that 169,482 Indian students had enrolled in BIA schools, contract schools, and Johnson O'Malley funded public schools. He added that 57,709 students had bilingual education needs.

In 1977 the American Indian Policy Review Commission released its final report with a section devoted to education. The commissioners in Task Force Five of the report reviewed 400 years of Indian education supervised by the federal government. The report called for a comprehensive education bill to achieve a higher quality of education services for American Indians. Commissioners recommended a set of policy guidelines to define clearly the commitment of Congress to meet the needs of Indians at the primary and secondary levels. The task force aimed this comprehensive effort at off-reservation schools, Indian community-controlled schools, and higher education (Report of Indian Education 1977).

Public Law 100–297 established a national Indian education conference, which called for developing recommendations to improve educational services. During the administration of President Bill Clinton, the White House Conference on Indian Education was held during January 22–24, 1992. A total of 234 delegates attended the conference, and they adopted 113 resolutions. The resolutions resulted from 30 states' tribal and regional reports gathered by state steering committees. The reports were condensed into 17 goal areas and were further consolidated under 11 topic areas. These topics included (1) "Governance of Indian Education/Independent Board of Education," (2) "Well Being of Indian Communities & Delivery of Services," (3) "Literacy, Student Academic Achievement and High School Graduation," (4) "Safe, Alcohol/Drug-Free Schools," (5) "Exceptional Education," (6) "Readiness for School," (7) "Native Languages & Culture," (8) "Structure for Schools," (9) "Higher Education," (10) "Native & Non-Native school Personnel," and (11) "Adult Education & Lifelong Learning/Parental, Community and Tribal Partnership" (Final Report of White House Conference on Indian Education 1992, 1).

On August 6, 1998, President Clinton signed Executive Order 13096 that committed the federal government to improving the academic performance of Indian students and reducing the dropout rate of American Indian and Alaska Native students attending public schools and Bureau of Indian Affairs schools. The order stated:

> The Federal Government has a special, historic responsibility for the education of American Indian and Alaska Native students. Improving educational achievement and academic progress for American Indian and Alaska Native students is vital to the national goal of preparing every student for responsible citizenship, continued learning, and productive employment. The Federal Government is committed to improving the academic performance and reducing the dropout rate of American Indians and Alaska Native students.

The order acknowledged the particular needs of American Indians and Alaska Natives pertaining to their various Native cultures and the government's historic responsibility to meet its commitment to Native people. Executive Order 13096 had six goals: (1) "Improving reading and mathematics," (2) "Increasing high school completion and postsecondary attendance rates," (3) "Reducing the influence of long-standing factors that impede educational performance, such as poverty and substance abuse," (4)"Creating strong, safe, and drug-free school environments," (5) "Improving science education," and (6) "Expanding the use of educational technology." Finally, "To accomplish these goals, Federal agencies are to develop a long-term comprehensive Federal Indian education policy that addresses the fragmentation of government services available to American Indian and Alaska Native students" (*Federal Register* 1999, 54622–54624).

Bureau of Indian Education

Previously known as the Office of Indian Education Programs (OIEP), the Bureau of Indian Education was renamed and expanded on August 29, 2006. The bureau provides services to an estimated 48,000 Indian students. The mission of the Bureau of Indian Education focuses on Indian education at various levels of education and works closely with tribal communities. The Bureau of Indian Education works with many tribes on a contract and service basis.

This division of the Bureau of Indian Affairs demonstrates the complexity of its rapidly increasing obligations and services in the 20th century. While it is an era of tremendous emphasis on education, it is also a means to the slow withdrawal of the government's participation in Indian affairs. Since the last two decades of the 20th century, this trend has become an established pattern.

Conclusion

By 2010 the Bureau of Indian Affairs indirectly operated 56 community-controlled schools via contracts made with tribal groups and Native communities. The BIA directly operated 103 elementary and secondary schools, which now have Indian school boards to assure Native input in the supervision.

Education has consistently been perceived by white Americans as the key to Native progress toward civilization and assimilation into the American mainstream. Following the 1960s, increasing numbers of Native people have come to accept this idea, as they have realized education is necessary to advance in the American mainstream and also to help their tribal communities. While this may seem ideal, a Westernized education for Native people also comes at the cost of losing traditional knowledge and decreasing its significance in Native communities. At the same time, the federal government recognizes its role in assisting Native people, tribal communities, and Indian organizations as more Native people are in leadership roles.

By the end of the 20th century and certainly at the end of the first decade of the 21st, Native leaders and tribal communities were very much prepared to direct their own educational progress for the coming generations of their people. This U.S.-Indian partnership achieved the full trust relationship in which both sides have confidence in each other to further Indian education.

References

Adams, David Wallace. *Education for Extinction: American Indians and the Boarding School Experience.* Lawrence: University Press of Kansas, 1995.

"American Indian and Alaska Native Education." Executive Order 13096. *Federal Register* 64, no. 194 (October 7, 1999).

"American Indian College Fund Receives $3.6 million from Theodore R. Johnson." *Tribal College* 3 (Winter 1992).

Commissioner of Indian Affairs Annual Report, 1905.

Diedrich, Mark. *Sitting Bull: The Collected Speeches.* Rochester, MN: Coyote Books, 1998.

Eastman, Charles A. *From the Deep Woods to Civilization: Chapter in the Auto-biography of an Indian.* Lincoln: University of Nebraska Press, 1936. Originally published 1916.

"The Final Report of the White House Conference on Indian Education," Volume One, May 1992, Washington, DC: U.S. Government Printing Office, 1992, 1.

Fiske, Frank B. *Life and Death of Sitting Bull.* Fort Yates, ND: Pioneer-Arrow Print, 1933.

Gibson, Arrell M. *Oklahoma: A History of Five Centuries.* Norman, OK: Harlow Publishing, 1965.

"Indian Education: A National Tragedy—A National Challenge." 1969 Report of the Committee on Labor and Public Welfare by Senate Special Subcommittee on Indian Education pursuant to S. Res. 80, 91st Cong., 1st. Sess., Senate Report No. 91–501. Washington, DC: U.S. Government Printing Office, 1969, 1–220.

Kappler, Charles, ed. *Indian Treaties 1778–1883.* New York: Interland Publishing, 1975.

Lloyd Meeds Collection. Accession No. 2900–9. Box 201. University of Washington Archives.

Lomawaima, K. Tsianina. *They Called It Prairie Light: The Story of Chilocco Indian School.* Lincoln: University of Nebraska Press, 1994.

McLester, L. Gordon, III and Laurence M. Hauptman, eds. *A Nation within a Nation: Voices of the Oneidas in Wisconsin.* Madison: Wisconsin Historical Society Press, 2010.

Nixon, Richard. "Special Message to Congress." July 8, 1970.

Pratt, Richard Henry. *Battlefield and Classroom: Four Decades with the American Indian, 1867–1904,* ed. Robert M. Utley. Lincoln: University of Nebraska Press, 1964.

Public Law No. 638. June 4, 1936 (49 Stat. 1458; 25 U.S.C. 452–455).

"Report of Indian Education—Task Force Five: Indian Education," *American Indian Policy Review Commission, Final Report, May 17, 1977.* Washington, DC: Government Printing Office, 1977.

Schmeckebier, Laurence F. *The Office of Indian Affairs.* Baltimore, MD: Johns Hopkins University Press, 1927.

Standing Bear, Luther. "Indian Education Should Not Destroy Indian Culture." In *Native Americans: Opposing Viewpoints,* ed. William Dudley. San Diego, CA: Greenhaven Press, 1998.

Szasz, Margaret Connell. *Education and the American Indian: The Road to Self-Determination Since 1928.* Albuquerque: University of New Mexico Press, 1999.

Williams, John and Howard L. Meredith. *Bacone Indian University: A History.* Oklahoma City: Western Heritage Press, 1980.

FIVE

Indian Land Allotment and U.S. Citizenship

The idea of Indians becoming U.S. citizens can be dated back to at least the presidency of Thomas Jefferson at the turn of the 19th century. Even earlier, in 1633 the General Court of Massachusetts ordered that Native people who came to the English plantations and lived in a civil and orderly manner should have allotments of their own land among the colonists. Land allotment became more popular in the early 1800s when missionaries believed that living conditions for the Indians could be vastly improved if they were allowed to become private landowners. In 1816 Secretary of War William Crawford recommended allotment for Indians. Three years later, President James Monroe concurred that allotment would be best for Indians. And three more years later, Secretary of War James C. Calhoun supported allotment, which has also been called allotment in severalty (as individuals).

Jeffersonians believed that Native people could become agrarian farmers and assimilate into the mainstream to participate in building a new country. The concept of assimilation has been a significant part of the supervision of Indian affairs. Secretary of the Interior Carl Schurz adopted it as a primary directive of his Indian policy in 1880. In his annual report, Schurz stated, "I look upon it [assimilation] as the most essential step in the solution of the Indian problem. It will inspire the Indians with a feeling of assurance as to the permanency of their ownership of the lands they occupy and cultivate; it will give them a clear and legal standing as landed proprietors in the courts of law; it will secure to them for the first time fixed homes under the protection of the same law under which white men own theirs; it will eventually open to settlement by white men the large tracts of land now belonging to the reservations, but not used by the Indians" (House 1880, 11–13). Schurz was both an assimilationist and expansionist who wanted Indians to have the same civilized life as whites. He viewed allotment as benefiting both Indians and whites, along with the West that needed to be civilized.

Bureaucrats involved in Indian affairs firmly believed that allotment preceded assimilation, and civilization would follow in preparing Native people for U.S. citizenship. The allotment idea of individual land ownership was to replace their communal living tradition.

Land Allotment by Treaties

In 1839 Congress authorized the allotment of land in "fee simple" (full ownership) to the Brotherton Indian group in the area east of Lake Winnebago in Wisconsin, an area the Menominees had ceded to the United States in a treaty. Arriving between 1831 and 1836, the Brotherton Indians were once a part of the Pequot and Mohican contingency in southern New England. Following conversion to Christianity, they joined their long-time allies, the Oneida and Stockbridge, who had accepted reservations in Wisconsin. As a part of the allotment arrangement, the Brothertons received full American citizenship. Four years later, an act called for similar provisions for the Stockbridge Indians in the same region. The majority of allotment provisions, however, occurred in treaties, although not all tribes signed such agreements with the U.S.

Occasionally during the 1830s and 1840s, the federal government distributed land to Native people, but allotment in severalty remained piecemeal until Indian Commissioner George Manypenny incorporated it into several treaties in 1854. Manypenny acted out of a popular belief that private land ownership would greatly increase the Indians' progress toward civilization. He also thought that allotment would help to resolve Indian-white competition for land. However, the BIA and Congress failed to realize the depth of Indian communal life. At the same time, local politicking in Kansas and Nebraska became persuasive for territorial development. In Congress the pressure for the Nebraska-Kansas Act of 1854 threatened to move Indians from the two areas that were a part of Indian Territory at the time. Kansas Territorial Governor Andrew Reeder called for statehood on behalf of his constituents. And settlers squatting on Indian reservations sensitized Manypenny to the wrongs the white man committed against Indians. The same westward expansion caused removal again. Treaties signed between Indians and the United States promised Native people new homelands in the Kansas-Nebraska area, which had been a part of Indian Territory.

Yet numerous interruptions created further problems. The gold rush of 1849 in California, other rushes, and the first transcontinental railroad in 1869 called for more accessible land liberated from tribes and the placement of tribes on smaller or newly established reservations. By the time Congress stopped making treaties in 1871, approximately 70 treaties had included specific provisions for allotment of lands to individuals. But allotment did not occur until 1879, when the Utes in Colorado received land after their outbreak of war and the ensuing treaty of 1868. This led to the end of the Ute War in 1882.

From 1879 onward, Congress entertained numerous allotment bills. Some of the bills drafted represented only the interests of white settlers. For example, a bill proposed to the House of Representatives in 1882 purported to provide "for the support and civilization of the various tribes of Sioux Indians" on the Great Dakota Reservation. But its content called for negotiations with the Sioux tribes and requested the cession of all their land north of the White River—the portion most suitable for agriculture. Such greed caused considerable debate in Congress over several drafts of the allotment bill, led primarily by Senator Richard Coke of Texas.

Henry L. Dawes

Instead of Coke, Henry L. Dawes of Massachusetts became most associated with the allotment of Indian land. Senator Dawes served as the chairman of the Committee on Indian Affairs. He initially opposed allotment until he realized that his congressional colleagues increasingly favored it. Unfortunately, more gold and silver strikes and the growing railroad industry made Native lands even more desirable as lobbyists pushed for the allotment of reservations that would create surplus land.

Senator Henry Dawes (R-Mass.), chair of the Senate Committee on Indian Affairs in the late 19th century, was the principal congressional sponsor of the General Allotment Act of 1887. Known unofficially as the Dawes Act, the legislation authorized the division of tribal land into allotments for individual Indians and surplus land was open to white settlement. (Library of Congress)

Dawes reminded Congress of the "Friends of the Indians" like the Women's National Indian Association, which had petitioned Congress to uphold its treaty obligations. This national group, with branch chapters throughout the country, became one of the staunch supporting organizations of Indians. Although the tribes possessed legal rights, according to the treaties, that the United States needed to respect, Dawes and the Women's National Indian Association realized that Congress was going to pass Indian allotment legislation. At this point, Dawes joined the allotment movement to make the allotment less damaging to the tribes by making sure that Native people received sufficient amounts of land to cultivate as farmers or livestock raisers.

Railroads

Railroad companies also became interested in the growing discussions of Indian allotment because of the large surplus lands to be gained. Railroad company officials did not directly lobby for the passage of the allotment act; they did not have to. Yet the government authorized railroad land grants through Indian lands on a wild scale that had never been seen before. From 1850 to 1870, the federal government made large cessions of land grants to states and railroads to promote railroad construction. The companies received rights-of-way that involved 20- or 50-mile strips of land, with alternating land sections for the public for the track laid. During these years, railroads received more than 175 million acres of public land.

In 1862 President Lincoln signed into law the Pacific Railroad Act "to aid in the construction of railroad and telegraphy line from the Missouri River to the Pacific ocean," which Congress amended four times. The legislation led to the creation of the first transcontinental railroad when the Union Pacific from Council Bluffs, Iowa, and the Central Pacific from Sacramento, California, connected at Promontory Summit, Utah, on May 10, 1869.

A corridor of wagon trails and a new railroad that excluded the Indian presence now connected the East and West. The railroads stood to gain the most as an estimated 23.8 million acres of Indian lands would be made available to railroads.

Bureaucratic Paternalism

Colonel William McMichael of the Board of Indian Commissioners had his own view on the progress of Native groups in Indian Territory. He believed that the tribes had schools, governments, and a governmental executive within a societal system "which, as I understand, there is no pauper there. And what is it they do not have? Why, they do not have the avarice and the selfishness, which are necessary to the acquisition of private property" (Priest 1972, 129).

McMichael also rejected Indian Agent H. J Armstrong's coercive benevolence: "We must protect the Indian," McMichael noted, "not against himself, but against ourselves" (Washburn 1975, 18). Because of Commissioner McMichael's positive paternal manner, the Indian interest had sincere support, like a father taking care of his children. Yet many, such as Armstrong, who worked among the Crows in Montana, believed that Indians should conform to the idea of allotment. Impatient when Indians resisted, Armstrong grew most frustrated with the traditionalists. Armstrong contended that the Indians should not be allowed to reject allotment in severalty. He said, "The truth is the Indians hate the white man's life in their hearts, and will not adopt it until driven by necessity" (Priest 1972, 129).

During the early 1880s, land allotment captured the attention of Congress. The interests of Indians, non-Indians who would benefit from surplus land available for homesteading, and railroad companies were addressed in the intensifying discussions. A revised bill in the House won support from the Committee on Indian Affairs, in spite of a strong minority report attempting to stop it from being discussed on the floor. In January and again in May, the Senate entertained new bills. Then, on May 19, 1880, Senator Richard Coke of Texas became the center of attention, sponsoring the bill that he and others debated vigorously over several days in January and February 1881. The Coke bill had the support of Secretary of the Interior Carl Schurz who insisted that the agricultural industry of Indians should be drastically improved. The Indian Rights Association also favored the bill, but the discussion continued in the congressional sessions that followed. During this lobbying in 1886, the association distributed 50,000 pamphlets on the subject of allotment of Indian lands. No one inquired about Indian input as pro-Indian organizations viewed it to be their societal responsibility to represent the tribes.

The severalty bill also had the support of the Lake Mohonk conferences and the Women's National Indian Association. But instead of the halls of Congress, reformers met in October 1885 at a resort hotel. Owned by the Smileys, a Quaker family at Lake Mohonk, the delegates ultimately decided that allotment would save the Indian population from extinction. At the instigation of Reverend D. Lyman Abbot and without any input from Indians, the reformers acted as a group in recommending a policy for allotting lands to individual tribal members. Dissatisfied with the general ill treatment of

Indians due to the government's restricted reservation program, the reform movement also viewed a dangerous non-Indian interest in illegally obtaining Indian lands against the wishes of Native people. When the allotment bill came before the Senate again on December 8, 1885, Senator Dawes, chairman of the Committee on Indian Affairs, introduced the bill himself. Interestingly, his name stuck to the final bill.

Continued opposition came from Representatives Russell Everett, Charles Hooker, and T. M. Gunter in a report to accompany a version of the allotment bill, H.R. 5038, in the 46th Congress. They reported:

> The real aim of this bill is to get at the Indian lands and open them to settlement. The provisions for the apparent benefit of the Indian are but the pretext to get his lands and occupy them. With that accomplished, we have securely paved the way for the extermination of the Indian race upon this part of the continent. If this were done in the name of Greed, it would be bad enough; but to do it in the name of Humanity, and under the cloak of an ardent desire to promote the Indian welfare by making him like ourselves, whether he will or not, is infinitely worse. (Washburn 1975, 39)

With congressional approval of allotment, Senator Henry Teller, a Republican from Colorado, foresaw doom for the Indians. Unfortunately, as a few congressmen had predicted, allotment failed to produce a change for the better as reformers and many government officials had envisioned. The cultural differences proved too great as Indians exhibited reluctance to change from their traditional economies to agrarianism. Even more, the lust for Indians lands proved greater as lobbyists pestered congressmen to pass the allotment bill.

Under the law, the adult head of the family normally received 160 acres; single adults over 18 years old and orphans less than 18 received 80 acres; and other single youths under 18 received 40 acres. The allottees could select their own land, but if they failed to do so in four years, the Department of the Interior would do it for them. This last stipulation resulted in absentee allottees. Furthermore, if the allotted land proved suitable for only grazing, the president could allot twice the amount of land.

Some tribes adamantly opposed the Dawes Act and the progress of many of their tribesmen convinced Congress to exclude them from allotment. These groups included the Creek, Cherokee, Chickasaw, Choctaw,

Seminole, Osage, Miami, Peoria, and Sac and Fox, all in Indian Territory. The escape for these tribes proved only temporary when Congress passed amendments to the Dawes Act calling for allotment of their lands.

Nelson Act and Great Lakes Allotment

Two years later, Congress passed the Nelson Act on January 14, 1889. Knute Nelson, a congressman in Minnesota, lobbied for the allotment of the Ojibwa lands in northern Minnesota. However, the law exempted the White Earth and Red Lake Reservations. The Nelson Act allowed the president to appoint a commission to allot Ojibwa tribal lands and it imposed a trust period on all Indian allotments, protecting them for a 25-year period. The United States became guardian and administrator of both individual and tribal lands. The measure also restricted Indians from selling their properties, thus this paternalistic effort could be interpreted either as inhibiting Indian independence or safeguarding them from business exploitation (Statutes at Large, 25:642).

Holding on to allotments proved to be problematic for Indian people. In the Great Lakes area, exploitative whites seized allotted lands from the Pillager Chippewas. The Mille Lac band of the Chippewas suffered most from land theft. After returning from a hunt or visiting relatives or friends, they found their homes taken by whites. Similarly, lumbermen seized Menominee timberland on which the Indians depended for their living. In addition, the lack of federal authorization restricted the tribe from cutting their timber.

In 1891 Congress approved a law that permitted aged and disabled Indians to lease their allotted land for 3 years to farmers and ranchers and for 10 years to miners (Statutes at Large 26:794–96). Secretary of the Interior John Noble strictly followed the law but became more lenient in allowing more allottees to lease their lands during his last months in office in 1893. In 1894 Congress made leasing restrictions more flexible and permitted any allottee "unable" to work to lease their land for 5 years to farmers and ranchers and for 10 years to miners and businessmen. Newly chosen Secretary of the Interior Hoke Smith authorized Indian agents to approve leases, resulting in 295 leases in 1894; 1,287 in 1897; and 2,590 in 1900.

Jerome Commission

The Bureau of Indian Affairs and Congress focused much of their attention on allotment in Indian Territory. By the 1880s, 67 different tribes had been removed to the territory to be safe from the pressures of white settlement. This effort to protect Indians did not last. During these years, the government created the Jerome Commission, also known as the Cherokee Commission, to supervise the allotment of the Cherokee and other tribes and negotiate with them for the sale of their surplus lands to the government. In July 1890, the commission began its work.

David H. Jerome led the commission that also allotted the Kiowa, Comanche, and Kiowa-Apache Reservation. Other members of the commission included Alfred M. Wilson (Democrat from Arkansas); Lucius Fairchild (Republican from Wisconsin); John Hartranft (Republican from Pennsylvania); and Horace Speed (Republican from Kentucky) who served as the secretary for the commission.

The selections of the Indians' allotments reflected the traditional community locations when the majority of Comanches selected allotments south of the Wichita Mountains in Indian Territory. The Kiowas and Kiowa-Apaches opted for lands to the north. When funding for the Jerome Commission ended in August 1893, the commissioners had negotiated with 11 tribes and purchased over 15.1 million acres made available to white settlement.

Boomers

Kansas "Boomers" led by David Payne also advocated the opening of Indian Territory for white settlement. On various occasions, Payne and his followers slipped onto Indian lands to start homesteads until army patrols escorted them back across the Kansas line. Further allotment of Indian lands fueled the Boomer Movement as cattlemen, miners, and railroad men pressured government officials to open the surplus lands to them. Other reservations experienced similar pressures for surplus lands, but the Boomer Movement precipitated actions for statehood for Indian Territory.

Starting at high noon on April 22, 1889, the military opened the Unassigned Lands in the heart of Indian Territory to white settlement when the first of six land runs began. Even prior to this famous day, eager settlers labeled as "Sooners" crossed into the Unassigned Lands to illegally claim the best lands. The Cherokee Outlet Run occurred two years later when settlers rushed to claim over 8.1 million acres that the Cherokee tribe had lost to the United States for fighting for the South in the Civil War. In addition, the Interior Department authorized land lotteries to settlers. Overnight, Oklahoma City began as a tent city on the prairie, and later it became the capitol site for the new state. Watching nervously, the Indians cautiously observed white men who coveted their lands. On May 2, 1890, the Territory of Oklahoma became official.

The allotment of reservation lands led to the demise of Indian landholdings throughout Indian Country. Frequently, white men married Indian women; such men became known as "squaw men," and they received allotments. In all, 17 such cases occurred on the Kiowa, Comanche, and Kiowa-Apache Reservations. Among the Five Civilized Tribes in 1906, the population consisted of 1,538 full-bloods and 4,146 mixed-bloods.

Finally, in 1897, the Choctaws and Chickasaws signed the Atoka Agreement with the Dawes Commission, enabling them to accept allotments of 320 acres each. A year later the Seminoles agreed to 120-acre allotments, the Creeks accepted 160 acres each in 1901, and the Cherokees received 110-acre allotments in 1902. The Dawes Commission had introduced allotment to all of Indian Territory.

Curtis Act

In the early months of 1898, U.S. Representative Charles Curtis of Kansas introduced H. R. 8581 as an "Act for the Protection of the People of Indian Territory." Curtis was part Kaw, also known as the Kansa tribe. Much of the original measure remained after five revisions. The Curtis Act established townsites, lease management of mineral rights, and disallowed the legal enforcement of any tribal laws created by the governments of the Five Civilized Tribes. In fact, section 28 stated, "That . . . all tribal courts of Indian Territory shall be abolished, and no officer of said courts shall thereafter have any authority whatever to do or perform any act theretofore authorized by any law in connection with said courts, or to receive any pay for same; and all civil and criminal cases then pending in any such court shall be transferred to the United States court in said Territory" (*Statutes at Large* 30, 497–498, 502, 504–505). In sum, the Curtis Act proved devastating, dashing the progress and hopes of the Five Civilized Tribes, the Osage, and other tribes in Indian Territory who wanted their own state.

Originally the General Allotment Act of 1887 excluded the Indians of Indian Territory on the basis of the bureaucratic view that the majority were civilized enough to run their own affairs. This proved not to be the case as many found themselves exploited by whites and mixed-bloods. Coal had been discovered in Choctaw country in the southeast part of Indian Territory, and oil had been experimented with in its early stages for industrial use. On March 3, 1901, Congress amended section six of the Dawes Act that granted U.S. citizenship to all Indians in Indian Territory (*Statutes at Large* 31, 1447). In this sweeping effort to make Indians a part of the growing society for assimilation, exploitation of Indian landowners occurred regularly, and many traditional Indians rejected both allotment and U.S. citizenship.

Crazy Snake Rebellion

As early as 1901, Chitto Harjo, a full-blood Creek, urged a resistance against allotment and the ways of the white man. This last patriotic fight for traditionalism became known as the Crazy Snake Rebellion. Also known as Wilson Jones, Harjo held the status as a town mekko (Creek king) and membership in the House of Kings in the Muscogee Creek National Council at Okmulgee. Born in 1846, Chitto Harjo grew up among the Upper Creeks, or Loyal Creeks, who sided with the Union during the Civil War when they fought to protect themselves against Confederate soldiers. In protest, Harjo led 94 "Snake" followers who took their name from one of the Creek clans. Attempting to establish a new Creek government based on ancient tribal laws, the Snakes gathered at Old Hickory Stomp ground, five miles east of Henryetta, Indian Territory. As the Snakes gathered, U.S. troops and federal marshals arrived, and the two sides fought two battles near Seminole and Wewoka. The action of the Snakes incited Choctaw traditionalists to oppose allotments, and federal officials had to use force to defeat them as well.

Immersed in turmoil, the House of Warriors of the Creek Government passed a series of 25 laws on December 7, 1903, to maintain the strength of the government. Harjo had been a member of the government, and his action divided the government, his community, and other communities.

Finally breaking the strength of the Snakes, federal officials arrested Harjo and some of his followers and filed legal charges against them. A federal court convicted Harjo and his rebels, although Harjo and the Snakes continued to voice opposition, claiming that allotment officials cheated their tribesmen during the assignments of land. Their protests fell on deaf ears as non-Indians and pro-allotment Indians campaigned for Oklahoma Territory to become the next state in the union.

Harjo's patriotic efforts to save his people's culture influenced the rise of the Four Mothers Society. The Cherokee, under the leadership of Red Bird Smith, gained the following of the Choctaw and Chickasaw as well as the Seminole. With the politics in Indian Territory working against the tribes and marshals in pursuit of Harjo and his Snakes, the Four Mothers Society met secretively and fought for their old ways of life by criticizing the white man's ways and continuing to practice traditions.

In 1906 Indian Territory joined with Oklahoma Territory as non-Indian officials happily anticipated statehood. The statehood movement convinced Harjo and several of his Snakes to make one last effort by sending a delegation to Washington. The delegates insisted that the Treaty of 1832 be upheld and believed that they had won a victory. Government officials opposed the Snakes' intentions, but Harjo responded that justice would ultimately prevail.

Lone Wolf v. Hitchcock

At the turn of the 20th century, Indian legal rights received a major blow in an important case known as *Lone Wolf v. Hitchcock*. In 1902 a Kiowa leader known as Lone Wolf filed a lawsuit against the Department of the Interior. According to article 12 of the Treaty of Medicine Lodge of 1867, no part of the Kiowa-Comanche Reservation could be ceded without the approval of three-fourths of the adult males. In fact, the Interior had disregarded the Medicine Lodge Treaty in seizing the land. However, the court ruled in favor of Interior Secretary Ethan A. Hitchcock. The final judgment acknowledged that the U.S. Congress had the ultimate authority in determining matters concerning Indians with its *plenary power* to abolish or change treaties that the Kiowa and other tribes had signed, a devastating blow to tribal sovereignty.

As Indian Territory remained a focal point of statehood politics, Congress became more involved, which diminished the position of the Bureau of Indian Affairs to a caretaker role. Settlers in Indian Territory began to move for territorial status for the western half of the region.

The creation of Oklahoma Territory on May 2, 1890 provoked the Indians of Indian Territory to desire a state of their own in the union when white settlers pushed for statehood starting in 1891. On August 21, 1905, the Sequoyah Constitutional Convention convened in Muskogee, Indian Territory. Delegates voted General Pleasant Porter, principal chief of the Creeks, to be president of the convention, and they proposed statehood. The five principal chiefs of the five tribes would serve as vice presidents. The efforts of the five tribes did not get far. When it seemed that the two territories would be combined into one state, convention delegates from the Okmulgee Convention had to accept their fate, and many joined the Oklahoma State Constitution Convention held in Guthrie in 1906. The House of Representatives passed the Enabling Act on June 14, 1906, to combine Oklahoma Territory and Indian Territory into one state, and President

Theodore Roosevelt signed the bill into law. This pursuit resulted in the new western state, Oklahoma, in 1907.

Burke Act

The Burke Act of 1906 altered the General Allotment Act in an important way. Congress amended the Dawes Allotment Act so that at the end of a 25-year probationary period, an Indian person who received an allotment would have fee patent (absolute) ownership of his or her land and properties. The secretary of the Interior had the authority to grant fee patent ownership to any Indian person that he deemed "competent" to run his or her own business affairs. Furthermore, at the end of the extended trust period of 25 years, every Native person who received an allotment would automatically become a U.S. citizen. The Burke Act affected the majority of allotted Indians throughout Indian Country, except "That the provisions of this Act shall not extend to any Indians in Indian Territory" (*Statutes at Large* 34, 182–83).

Both Congress and the courts undermined the legal rights of American Indians and denied tribal sovereignty. Courts of law determined whether a Native person was "competent" enough to run their own affairs or "incompetent" and could not, in which case, a guardian had to be appointed. As trustee to uphold the treaties, the role of the Bureau of Indian Affairs involved protecting the land and properties of those Native peoples deemed incompetent. Whether a Native person was competent or incompetent, opportunists lay waiting for chances to exploit or bilk Indians out of their lands and properties.

While the *Lone Wolf v. Hitchcock* court case clearly undermined tribal sovereignty and acknowledged the plenary power of Congress, a landmark court case involving water again ruled in favor of Indian treaty rights. In 1908 the U.S. Supreme Court ruled in *Winters v. United States* that the tribes on the Fort Belknap Indian Reservation had "reserve water rights" to the Milk River that crossed the reservation. Ranchers had constructed a dam upstream, but the Supreme Court ruled that the treaty that established the reservation included the resources to develop the land, allowing the Indians to have as much water as needed for agricultural and economic needs.

The second decade of the 20th century started with political rumblings in Europe. In the summer of 1914, the Great War broke out in Europe that came to be known as World War I because it involved so many countries in the world. In 1914 an estimated one-third of the Indian population were not

U.S. citizens, and many Native men fought in the war for the United States as noncitizens.

Green Corn Rebellion

In mid-summer of 1917, many Creek Indians gathered as usual at dance grounds to hold their Green Corn celebration ceremonies in Oklahoma. Instead of dancing, the Creeks and other Indians talked about mistreatment by the federal government and about the opportunists that were cheating them. They disagreed with the government drafting Native men into the army to fight the Germans in Europe. The Creeks had a long history of ill relations with the United States, dating back to when Andrew Jackson used Creeks against Creeks in the Creek War of 1813 and forced them to sign a removal treaty to the West. Then the federal government sharply reduced Creek tribal lands after the Civil War and punished the Creeks who actually fought the Confederates on their own without Union support. Next, the government reduced Creek tribal land again via land allotment and abolished their tribal government with the Curtis Act. The Creeks also cited the rejection of the state of Sequoyah that favored the white population and combined the twin territories to form Oklahoma Territory for statehood. The politics at the local, state, and federal levels were tilted against the Indians, and this corruption helped to fuel the Green Corn Rebellion.

World War I

While many Creek men served in World War I, others joined the Green Corn Rebellion against the drafting of Native men to serve in the trenches in Europe. In addition to other Indians joining the rebellion, African American men and some poor rural white farmers in three counties in Oklahoma also rejected the draft. They saw World War I as a rich man's war and a poor man's fight. On August 3, the rebels began cutting telegraph lines and burning bridges. Posses formed to suppress the rebellion, which resulted in the deaths of three men. Authorities arrested over 400 rebels, and courts convicted 150 of them and sent them to prison for terms up to 10 years.

An estimated 10,000 Native men served in World War I, many of whom were not citizens of the United States, although they fought against the Germans. Indian men served patriotically in the war and returned as heroes to their communities. Military officials designated a total of 14 Choctaw men in the army to put their indigenous language into a code. These men, known as code talkers, set an example that would be followed by the

Navajo, Comanche, Cherokee, and Choctaw in World War II. The Choctaw code talkers also helped in several battles in the Meuse-Argonne Campaign in France during the final German invasion.

For their patriotic service, Congress passed a law on November 6, 1919, for American Indian veterans of the war. The law stated, "Be it enacted . . ., That every American Indian who served in the Military or Naval Establishments of the United States during the war . . . and who has received or who shall hereafter receive an honorable discharge, if not now a citizen and if he so desires . . . be granted full citizenship with all the privileges" (*Statutes at Large* 41, 350). According to the law, honorably discharged Indians that served in World War I earned U.S. citizenship.

In 1921 Congress passed the Snyder Act, which authorized the secretary of the Interior to provide Indians with social, health, and educational services. This was a means to get Native people to begin to apply for state services as a part of the assimilation process (Statutes at Large, 42: pt. 1:208).

Roaring Twenties

Throughout the entire country, a portion of the population enjoyed prosperity that has been called the Roaring Twenties. Most American Indians did not enjoy such prosperity or progress, except for a small percentage that happened to have oil pools under their allotted lands, especially in Oklahoma. The small number of oil-rich Indians lived a different life than the impoverished Native communities in rural areas. Among the oil-stricken Creeks in Indian Territory, Woosey Deer owned highbred cattle that a court-appointed guardian had talked her into buying. Willie Berryhill had an allotment above the gushing Glenpool oil field south of Tulsa, and he died with an estate worth more than $40,000. Lucinda Pittman did not like the standard black automobiles, and she drove a custom painted purple Cadillac. Eastman Richards owned his own town in Eastern Oklahoma that he called Richardsville. During the Depression, Katie Fixico lived on a large farm outside of Okmulgee, Oklahoma. Katie fed crews of workers and their families who she hired to help on her farm, which consisted of several oil wells.

The richest American Indian proved to be Jackson Barnett, an oil-rich Creek full-blood who lived in the country near Henryetta, Oklahoma. A Kansas City prostitute read about Barnett in the local newspaper on her way to bilk Texas oilmen. Anne Lowe boasted about planning to marry Barnett and actually did marry him twice, once in Kansas and once in Missouri, against the protests of the guardian previously assigned to Barnett because he had been deemed "incompetent" to handle his own affairs by a court of law, a circumstance commonly faced by American Indians at this time. Then she had Barnett's monthly allowance increased to $2,000 and moved him, lock, stock, and barrel to Los Angeles to enjoy his wealth (Fixico 1998, 3–260).

In addition to certain allotments under Creek and Seminole lands, pools of oil made some Native people rich from its royalties. Windfalls of oil royalties created unwanted opportunities for Indians who were being exploited even if their allotments did not contain oil pools beneath their lands. To fill out the rest of the picture, in Oklahoma 54 out of 77 counties produced oil to meet 20 percent of the world's need during the early 1920s.

Osage Reign of Terror

People outside of the Osage tribe married Osages, and these opportunists exploited the rich Indians. With each tribal member holding a "headright," meaning an equal share of the mineral rights, each Osage person had a guaranteed monthly income until the oil ran dry under the Osage Reservation. The first oil well, drilled on the Osage Reservation in 1897, failed to create any indication of large oil pools resting below ground. In the first decade of the 20th century, oil and gas wells brought a windfall of royalty monies. In 1925, Osage families enjoyed royalty money of more than $65,000 per year, compared to less than $200 per year for average Indian families and over $1,000 for the average white mainstream family.

What became known as the Reign of Terror arose when individuals carried out the murder of as many as two dozen Osages, beginning in spring 1921 and lasting until 1926. The killings centered around the Lizzie Q. Kyle family in which each family member had a "headright." On the western part of the reservation, a Texas cowhand watched the Osages getting rich. William K. Hale began to mastermind a plot to murder relatives of Lizzie Kyle. In the end, the sole heir would be married to Hale's slow nephew, Ernest Burkhart. Hale hired ex-convicts and others who wanted Osage money to kill Kyle's relatives. One by one, Hale's hired murderers got the Osages drunk, shot them, planned accidents, and also killed non-Indians who got in his way.

Calling himself the "King of the Osages," Hale brought too much attention to himself. For three years, the Bureau of Investigation planted spies and collected evidence to arrest Hale and his culprits. In the end, the Bureau of Investigation arrested Hale and his nephew for the murders, and they served time in prison (Fixico 1998, 27–54). (In 1934, the bureau became known as the Federal Bureau of Investigation.)

Committee of One Hundred

Clearly American Indians, many of whom were not U.S. citizens, needed help. John Collier and the American Indian Defense Association led a charge to protect Indian rights, particularly their religious ceremonies. The American Indian Defense Association widely distributed a pamphlet in July 1924 called "The Indian and Religious Freedom," and the Eastern Association on Indian Affairs put out a special bulletin under the title of "Concerning Indian Dances," referring to the missionaries' and assimilationists' attempts to degrade Pueblo ceremonies as pagan (Prucha 1984, 276–277).

Newly appointed Secretary of the Interior Hubert Work created the Advisory Council on Indian Affairs to help the BIA commissioner, and it became known as the Committee of One Hundred. During spring 1923, Work appointed roughly 100 men and women to meet from December 12–13. The committee included John Collier, some of his friends in the defense association, members of the Indian Rights Association, Board of Indian commissioners, missionaries, journalists, anthropologists, and Indians. The committee reviewed past federal policies and made recommendations about better supervision of Indians affairs. The committee recommended studying peyote use in the ceremonies of the Native American Church, as they were concerned with the morals of peyote usage because it acted as a hallucinogen.

Overall, the committee focused on the improvement of Indian health and mainly recommended that updated information was needed about conditions in Indian Country. Secretary Work listened to the group and in 1926 requested an independent organization, the Institute for Government Research, to visit reservations and compile a study of conditions in Indian Country.

U.S. Citizenship Act

Representative Homer Snyder introduced a bill for general citizenship for all American Indians. On June 2, 1924, President Calvin Coolidge signed the Indian Citizenship Act, which affected all Indians born within the United States who had not yet been made citizens. The act read:

> To authorize the Secretary of the Interior to issue certificates of citizenship to Indians. . . . That the granting of such citizenship shall not in any manner impair or otherwise affect the right of any Indian to tribal or other property. (*Statutes at Large* 43, 253)

Some tribes like the Iroquois and Hopi declined American citizenship on the basis that it usurped their tribal sovereignty—the right to govern their communities. At the same time, New Mexico and Arizona denied Native people the right to vote until 1948.

Meriam Report

At the request of Interior Secretary Hubert Work to the Institute for Government Research on June 2, 1926, an appointed commission of experts began to assemble during October of that year. In a comprehensive field report, the team examined the general policy for Indian affairs, health, education, general economic conditions, and family and community life as well as the activities of women, migrated Indians, legal aspects of the Indian Problem, and missionary activities among Native communities.

Headed by Lewis Meriam, the commission included Ray A. Brown, assistant professor of law, University of Wisconsin; Henry Roe Cloud, president of the American Indian Institute in Wichita, Kansas; Edward Everett Dale, head of the History Department, University of Oklahoma; Emma Duke, specialist in health in Washington, DC; Herbert R. Edwards, medical field secretary of the National Tuberculosis Association; Fayette Avery McKenzie, professor of sociology and dean of men, Juniata College; Mary Louise Mark, professor of sociology, Ohio State University; W. Carson Ryan Jr., professor of education, Swarthmore College; and William J. Spillman, agricultural economist, Bureau of Agricultural Economics, U.S. Department of Agriculture. The commission made its final report two years later on February 21, 1928, as "The Problem of Indian Administration" published by Johns Hopkins Press.

The report began by stating: "An overwhelming majority of the Indians are poor, even extremely poor, and they are not adjusted to the economic and social system of the dominant white civilization. The poverty of the Indians and their lack of adjustment to the dominant economic and social systems produce the vicious circle ordinarily found among any people under such circumstances. Because of interrelationships, causes cannot be differentiated that are part of this vicious circle of poverty and maladjustment" (Meriam et al. 1928, 3).

The commission's most important finding was that the allotment program introduced by the Dawes Act in 1887 had failed. Furthermore, the commission suggested a new federal policy needed to be developed.

The final report also included findings on the health status of Native peoples. Among the Indian communities, the commission found that from

1921 to 1925, the Indian death rate had reached 62 percent and that another 22 percent or more of the Native population had trachoma, an eye disease. In Arizona, which had a heavy Native population, tuberculosis killed at a rate of 17 times the national average. The government made funding available for health treatment, yet the commission discovered that of $756,000 spent, only $200,000 actually addressed treatment in the Native communities. This meant that on average, the government spent about 50¢ annually on each Native person. In other words, misappropriation cost the lives of many American Indians.

Preston-Engle Report

In 1928, Congress called for its own study of Indian conditions but focused on agriculture. A federal government study produced the Preston-Engle Report. Porter Preston of the Bureau of Reclamation and C. A. Engle of the BIA studied irrigation and agriculture among western tribes.

The report disclosed that thieves stole Indian cattle, and squatters built homes and farmed on tribal lands. Whites used roughly 68 percent of the irrigated farmland. The fact that many Indians did not become U.S. citizens until 1924 worked against them, and the laws favored non-Indians. Furthermore, Indians raised wild hay instead of profitable crops (Boldt 1987, 104).

The report recommended further that the government halt support of several Indian irrigation projects due to cost and the little value they had for Native communities. The remaining irrigation projects were assigned to the supervision of the Bureau of Reclamation.

Tribal Membership

It had been common practice for tribal governments to establish the membership of their communities. During the late 1800s, some tribes had constitutions that established the criteria for tribal membership. Native communities determined membership by kinship and residence in the community. Cultural kinship norms governed membership according to the tradition of maternal or paternal preference.

In Indian Territory, the Creek, Seminole, Cherokee, Choctaw, and Chickasaw developed tribal constitutions that defined membership criteria. Unfortunately, the Cherokee or Jerome Commission (1890–1893) and Dawes Commission (1893–1914) reestablished tribal memberships as the commissions developed tribal rolls that determined who was and who was not a member for land allotment purposes.

Tribal constitutions became more common after the Indian Reorganization Act of 1934, as tribes patterned their governments after the United States. With U.S. citizenship, American Indians possessed dual citizenship, as they were also members of their tribes by assignment on a tribal roll. Presently those people who have enough Indian blood to be recognized by the Bureau of Indian Affairs can apply for a certificate of degree of Indian blood (CDIB).

Conclusion

The allotment of tribal lands and U.S. citizenship were a part of the large plan to help reform Indian conditions and to solve the so-called Indian Problem. At the same time, the General Allotment Act proved to be devastating to Native people. The traditional Native emphasis on the community rather than the individual contradicted the federal government's plan to make Native people into individual landowners. The allotment individualization process drastically altered Native cultures. While allotment and citizenship seemed achievable from a bureaucratic standpoint, the reality was plagued by problems. For these two ideas to succeed meant that Native people would have to undergo a transformation of embracing mainstream cultural ways and foregoing their traditional cultures.

Furthermore, tribal land allotment reduced the reservations, making large areas open to settlers, railroad companies, timber companies, ranchers, and miners. By the end of the allotment era that would last until 1934, American Indians retained less than 2 percent of all of the land in the United States. At the same time, the impoverished living conditions became characteristic of many individual allotments. As a result, the Indian population declined sharply, sinking to its lowest level at less than 238,000 people by 1890 from an original total of more than 5 million people. To many people, American Indians did not seem capable of taking up and succeeding in a new culture. More importantly, the question needed to be asked, in times of Jim Crow laws and the Chinese Exclusion Act of 1882, would the mainstream accept Indians into white society? Furthermore, the supervision of Indian affairs decreased in bureau personnel to 5,000 by 1890 (Taylor 1959, 98). The clear message from bureaucrats designated that assimilation meant that less of the BIA was needed.

Finally, the Dawes Act brought considerable change to Indian cultures, and some Native people could not survive the ordeal. This created the Indian Problem, as discussed earlier, with the Bureau of Indian Affairs being held totally responsible for providing solutions to saving the indigenous American as he entered a new age of modernity in the 20th century.

References

"An Act Amending Section Six of the General Allotment Act." Also known as "Burke Act." May 8, 1906. *U.S. Statutes at Large*, 34.

"Act for the President of the People of Indian Territory." Also known as "Curtis Act." June 28, 1898. *U.S. Statutes at Large*, 30.

Annual Report of the Secretary of the Interior. November 1, 1880. *House Executive Document* no. 1. 46th Congress. 3rd Sess. Serial 1959.

Boldt, Christine. *American Indian Policy and American Reform: Case Studies Campaign*. New York: Routledge, 1987.

"Citizenship for World War I Veterans." November 6, 1919. *U.S. Statutes at Large*, 41.

Fixico, Donald L. THE INVASION OF INDIAN COUNTRY IN THE TWENTIETH CENTURY: AMERICAN CAPITALISM AND TRIBAL NATURAL RESOURCES (Niwot, CO: University Press of Colorado, 1998).

"Indian Citizenship Act." June 2, 1924. *U.S. Statutes at Large*, 43.

"Land Allotment (Leasing) Act," February 28, 1891, U.S. Statutes at Larage, 26:851–54.

Meriam, Lewis et al. *The Problem of Indian Administration*. Baltimore: The Johns Hopkins University Press, 1928.

"Minnesota Chippewa Allotment Act," January 4, 1889, U.S. Statutes at Large, 25:642.

Priest, Loring. "The Congressional Decision to Use Force." In Richard Ellis, ed., *The Western American Indians, Case Studies in Tribal History*. Lincoln: University of Nebraska Press, 1972.

Prucha, Francis Paul. *The Great Father: The United States Government and the American Indians*. Lincoln: University of Nebraska Press, 1984.

"Synder Act," November 2, 1921, U.S. Statutes at Large, 42 pt. 1:208.

Taylor, Theodore. "The Regional Organization of the Bureau of Indian Affairs." PhD diss., Harvard University, 1959.

"U.S. Citizenship for Indians in Indian Territory." March 3, 1901. *U.S. Statutes at Large*, 31.

Washburn, Wilcomb. *The Assault on Indian Tribalism: The General Allotment Law (Dawes Act) of 1887*. Philadelphia, PA: J. B. Lippincott, 1975.

SIX

John Collier and the Indian New Deal of Tribal Reorganization

Following World War I, Americans celebrated the aftermath during what became called the Roaring Twenties. Progress and prosperity typified this age in which America broke with conservative traditions of the Victorian 19th century. The United States bounced back from the immediate recession after the war as returning soldiers entered the workforce and factories converted to peacetime production of consumer goods. An improving economy allowed society to experiment with social and cultural changes. Americans went well beyond Warren G. Harding's "return to normalcy" as jazz music helped to forge a new national identity composed of consumerism, new technology, and a modern lifestyle. New automobiles, moving pictures, and radio became a part of family life as the mid-20s earned the name of the Golden Twenties. On November 6, 1920, the first radio station went on air broadcasting from KDKA in Pittsburgh, and by 1922, 3 million American families listened to programs. By 1926, a Model T Ford had decreased in price to $290 so that a new automobile leaving the assembly line became available for one of every five Americans.

For American Indians, these times proved less prosperous. Indians, African Americans and most farmers, as well as new immigrants, earned less than $2,000 per year. Yet mainstream America became urbanized and electrified, and telephone lines connected people who enjoyed indoor plumbing. For most American Indians, the postwar years and the 1920s represented a continuing plight of poverty. Fighting in the war enabled many American Indians to leave reservation areas for the first time as they became exposed to the rest of the country and even parts of Europe. Importantly, the worst seemed behind them, as Native people saw their population stabilize and then begin to increase in spite of poverty and poor health conditions. The myth of Indians disappearing as relics of the past proved wrong as the resilience of Native people responded.

Assimilating into Western society became a goal more difficult for Native people. Now citizens of the United States, American Indians struggled to change their cultures in order to become a part of the mainstream. Instead they adopted parts of the mainstream culture that made their lives easier. They found it difficult to separate from their communities.

In 1928 the Brookings Institute reached the end of a task force assignment when members of the group, led by Lewis Meriam, delivered its report. The Meriam Report made its final conclusion that the allotment program of individualizing tribal lands had failed. The report halted the allotment experiment that had persisted for 40 years. The experiment had initially been intended to civilize Native people as individual farmers for assimilation into the American mainstream.

Great Depression

The late 1920s also shocked the entire country and the rest of the world. On October 29, 1929, what became known as Black Tuesday, the stock market on Wall Street in New York crashed, and stock market prices continued falling for a month. Black Tuesday followed Black Friday in Europe's sharp stock market decline. The crash on Wall Street sent the United States into economic turmoil for the next decade.

The Great Depression gripped the nation as everyone suffered and panic began to spread. The worst came next. The following year brought no relief as dust storms hit the American West and Canada. A long-term drought struck the region and overplowing prevented the topsoil from being anchored as winds affected some 100 million acres, mainly in the Texas panhandle, western Oklahoma, and parts of New Mexico, Colorado, and Kansas. Local farmers learned a tough lesson. These years became known as the Dirty Thirties, with the heaviest dust storm occurring during Black Sunday on April 14, 1935. This black storm rendered the name "Dust Bowl," convincing numerous people that the world was coming to an end.

Many Oklahomans left the state to find farm work in the San Joaquin Valley of California, and John Steinbeck depicted these "Okies" in his classic novel, *The Grapes of Wrath*, which won the Pulitzer Prize for literature in 1940 and the Nobel Prize for literature in 1962. Other migrants from Texas, New Mexico, Kansas, and Colorado, added up to as many as 7,000 migrants who snaked along Route 66 in Model Ts or Hudson trucks entering California each month. Some of the Okies included American Indians, mostly mixed-bloods, who found a second chance in Southern California with other migrants. The majority of Native people, however, had no choice but to endure nature's wrath with no solutions in sight.

The laissez-faire approach in business permitted unstable growth during the 1920s. President Herbert Hoover's belief in "rugged individualism" fell out of sync with the corporate growth in the country as fewer people farmed and more people worked for companies. As the nation became industrialized, cities grew from urbanization. Businessmen ran the country with little restrictions, as people generally wanted the government to stay out of the business of Americans.

The Bureau of Indian Affairs faced difficult times. Charles H. Burke served as commissioner of Indian Affairs from 1921 to 1929. From near Batavia, New York, Burke had political ambitions as a young man, moved to South Dakota, and was elected to the House of Representatives as a Republican in 1895 and 1897. In 1906 Burke served as a member of the House Committee on Indian Affairs and introduced the amendment to the Dawes Act, resulting in the Burke Act. President Warren G. Harding chose Burke as his second choice for the Indian commissionership, and after the first person refused, Burke took office on May 7, 1921. In his first couple of years as head of the BIA, Burke endured the heavy hand of Interior Secretary Albert Fall who made the commissioner powerless. But Fall tried and failed to secure passage of the Bursum bill that would have surrendered Pueblo irrigated lands to white squatters. Nevertheless, Fall succeeding in getting the General Leasing Act of 1920 passed, which allowed all reservations created by executive order to enter negotiations with oil companies. The law enabled two-thirds of all oil royalties to not be paid to Indian allottees who actually deserved them.

Burke's own agenda for the BIA focused on Indian education and health. In 1921 when Burke took office, no high schools existed on any reservations. Curriculum in most day and small reservation boarding schools went to the third grade level. Roughly 65,000 Native children attended schools of different kinds. The government estimated that another 25,000 youth between 5 and 18 years old did not attend any schools. Regarding health, an Indian service physician earned $2,100 a year, and nurses earned $1,500. Both doctors and nurses had a high turnover rate as diseases like trachoma plagued reservation populations.

Trouble with Oil

In 1922, Secretary Fall ruled that the General Leasing Act could be applied to oil development on reservations created by executive orders. Commissioner Burke found himself solving problems without the support of the

Interior Department, due to Fall's personal ventures. The commissioner struggled to overcome the secretary's illegal actions. He had to operate the BIA without oversight from the Interior while Fall was under investigation.

One of Burke's reform actions included ending the policy of former Commissioner Cato Sells who awarded all adult Indians of less than one-half Indian blood fee patents to their lands and properties on the assumption that they could run their own affairs. Burke wanted to protect Indian allottees by keeping their properties in trusteeship with the government to stop opportunists from gaining control over such properties. Oil on Indian lands proved to be the biggest challenge for Burke and the BIA during the 1920s. Drilling for oil on treaty-created reservations called for the BIA to protect these tribal lands like the Osage Reservations and those of the Five Civilized Tribes in Oklahoma. However, oil discovered on the Navajo Reservation in 1922 caused problems because no law provided for drilling for oil on reservations established by presidential executive order. Officials like Fall believed that Indian natural resources only extended to the surface level, thereby making executive order tribal lands vulnerable to oil companies. Fortunately for Burke and Indians, Fall's tenure as interior secretary ended in 1923. Ill deeds forced Secretary Fall to leave office due to the Teapot Dome oil scandal in Wyoming and the Elk Hills affair. Without requesting competitive bids as required by the government, Fall had leased the Teapot Dome fields to Harry F. Sinclair of Sinclair Oil and the Elk Hills field in California to Edward L. Doheny.

FDR

The nation's financial problems enabled the Democrats to win the presidency in 1932. The American people elected Franklin Delano Roosevelt (FDR) to the White House to get the country out of the Depression. In his first "Hundred Days" in office, Roosevelt introduced a series of unprecedented reform programs. Unlike the Republican approach favoring small government, Roosevelt believed that the federal government needed to get involved in people's lives to help them. He launched his "New Deal" platform, determined to get people back to work. With his inspirational optimism during fireside chats on the radio, FDR and his administration forged a fairly united country of organized communal spirit for labor, big city political systems, poor white southerners, and African Americans.

In the following months, President Roosevelt named Harold Ickes as the secretary of the interior. Ickes served for 13 years from 1933 to 1946. Born in Pennsylvania, Ickes became a Republican in Chicago politics, and he supported civil rights. Roosevelt selected officials from both political parties and recruited Ickes for his cabinet; and Ickes did much for FDR's New Deal administration. Ickes also served as director of the Public Works Administration and carried out many of the New Deal programs, including approving those for American Indians.

New Deal and Indian New Deal

FDR's New Deal represented a call to arms to combat the Depression. In his early days in office, Roosevelt called an emergency session of Congress to launch his program of federal involvement to get the country back on its feet, both morally and economically. U.S. citizens voted in favor of forming a bipartisan Congress, which allowed Roosevelt's bills to pass easily. Congress passed the Emergency Banking Act, Glass-Steagall Act, Agricultural Adjustment Administration Act, and National Industrial Recovery Act in FDR's first administration. The Emergency Conservation Act proved to be the most popular among the people by putting 250,000 young men back to work immediately.

After Roosevelt appointed Ickes as secretary of the interior, the next step was to decide who would serve as the commissioner of Indian Affairs. Among several candidates for the job, John Collier quickly stood out. Based on knowledge and experience in Indian affairs, Collier was the most qualified. In naming the next Indian commissioner, Roosevelt called Ickes into the oval office and inquired who he wished to recommend. Collier had expressed ideals that depicted him as a reformer, but he knew Indians and their ways. With Ickes's recommendation, Roosevelt named Collier as BIA commissioner. The Ickes-Collier team ushered in a new era of federal-Indian relations. The secretary of the interior, the commissioner of Indian Affairs, and President Roosevelt produced tremendous change that transitioned tribal communities from dependence on old cultural ways to a combination of new and old.

Collier devised an Indian New Deal from FDR's overall plan, as the Roosevelt administration introduced a second New Deal for the country in 1935. His second New Deal continued the momentum with more legislation, including the Works Progress Administration, Social Security, and National Labor Relations Act.

John Collier

To say the least, Collier's personality struck people as odd. Born in Atlanta, Georgia, Collier came from a troubled, prominent Southern family that sent him to Columbia University for his higher education. He first got involved in Indian affairs in support of Native rights during the early 1920s. He then joined the American Indian Defense Association. As a member, he actively helped to defeat the Bursum bill that threatened to take away irrigated land from the Pueblo communities in New Mexico.

A driven individual soul, Collier knew only one way to get things done—his way. His determination to establish a workable Indian policy raised criticism from those who disagreed with him—such as missionaries who viewed his hands-on approach as interfering in converting Indians to Christianity. Collier admired the Native ways and made it known that he believed Indians should keep their traditional religions.

Historian Kenneth Philp described Collier as "a small stooped-shouldered man who wore glasses and kept his hair untidy." A "long-legged, somewhat humorless" man who blazed "with zeal for the Red Man," he had the reputation of being a dreamer, which soon aroused the suspicions of Congress (Philp 1977, 117). Philp wrote, "At the office, Collier often sat in his swivel chair coiling his legs into a kind of nest, and he frequently smoked a corncob pipe, which he kept in an empty water glass on his desk. Instead of wearing a suit, Collier usually came to work in a baggy old long-sleeved green sweater. Gossips in Washington rumored that the commissioner sometimes kept a pet frog in his pocket" (Philp 1977, 117).

Many people underestimated the weak-looking Indian commissioner who wore glasses. In fact, Collier proved to be intimidating when he carried his own drafts of legislation to put into the hands of congressmen; they

John Collier was the founder of the American Indian Defense Association and, later, commissioner of Indian Affairs (1933–1945). He supervised the Indian New Deal. (Library of Congress)

learned to try to avoid him. A man of tremendous energy, Collier became the most effective Indian commissioner of the 20th century. He said,

> If we can relieve the Indian of the unrealistic and fatal allotment system, if we can provide him with land and the means to work the land; if, through group organization and tribal incorporation, we can give him a real share in the management of his own affairs, he can develop normally in his own natural environment. The Indian Problem as its exists today, including the heaviest and most unproductive administration costs of public services, has largely grown out of the allotment system which has destroyed the economic integrity of the Indian estate and deprived the Indians of normal economic and human activity. (Annual Report of CIA 1933)

All of what he said did not make Collier popular, especially on religious issues. Throughout his years as commissioner, Collier provoked missionary organizations and their leaders like G.E.E. Lindquist who despised the commissioner. The missionaries' long support from the government, especially Congress, since the formation of the Board of Indian Commissioners in 1869 allowed them to easily carry out their missionary work among Indians. Collier flatly disagreed. He wanted tribal communities to build their own governments without necessarily assimilating. Indians would assimilate when they wanted to, he believed. To achieve his goal, Collier viewed the missionaries, largely Republican Protestants dominating the board, as the problem, and he succeeded in pressuring Congress to terminate the Board of Indian Commissioners on May 25, 1933.

Indian Reorganization Act 1934

In Congress, Representatives William Zimmerman and Nathan Margold introduced the Wheeler-Howard bill with Felix Cohen, one of the earliest authorities on federal-Indian law. The collaborative effort produced the original draft of four sections covering 48 pages. Somewhat staggering for its time, Congress had entertained few such bills (although it amended the bill several times and later, when it became a law). The act changed the course of federal-Indian policy from allotment to reorganizing tribal communities and their governments.

Representative Edgar Howard introduced the bill in the House, and it passed 258 to 88. Senator Burton Wheeler introduced the bill in the Senate. The bill passed as the Indian Reorganization Act (IRA), and President Roosevelt signed it on June 18, 1934. According to the bill's wording, the IRA was:

An Act to conserve and develop Indian lands and resources; to extend to Indians the right to form business and other organizations; to establish a credit system for Indians; to grant certain rights of home rule to Indians; to provide for vocational education for Indians; and for other purposes. (Statutes at Large 48 pt. 1:984–88)

Many Indian communities, like the Oneida in Wisconsin, favored the Indian Reorganization Act. During these years the majority of the Wisconsin tribe spoke Oneida, and individuals like Oscar Archiquette explained the provisions of the IRA to his people. Following the first meeting in a small log private home, the Oneida called a second meeting that took place at the Methodist Church Hall. Following the voting to accept the IRA, the Oneida changed their tribal enrollment to accept members who were one-quarter Oneida by blood, and they amended their constitution to have nine members on the tribal council. The tribe purchased 2,400 acres under the IRA.

Other Indian groups debated the bill as well. On June 10, 1934, Collier flew to Arizona to make a last appeal in an unofficial meeting with the Navajo tribal council at Fort Wingate. One week after Collier's visit, the Navajos voted on the IRA. Collier's effort fell short by 518 votes with 7,679 Navajos voting for the IRA and 8,197 voting against it (Parman 1976, 76). The Crow and Seneca also rejected the IRA.

The IRA offered comprehensive reform by encouraging tribes to keep their traditional communities and to form charters to protect them. Collier and his BIA personnel also encouraged tribes to adopt constitutions and form new government structures patterned after the two-house model of the United States. The IRA proved to be the most important law regarding Indians in the first half of the 20th century.

In all, Native communities held 258 elections to accept or reject the IRA. In the end, 181 tribes voted to accept the IRA, affecting 129,750 Indians. Seventy-seven tribes rejected the IRA, totaling 86,365 Indians, which included the Navajo population of 45,000. To accept the IRA, the law required the tribes to have only one-fourth of their adult members approve it. The

BIA sent individuals from Washington to reservations to explain the benefits of the IRA programs and to convince them to vote to accept the law. By 1946 a total of 161 tribal constitutions and 131 corporate charters had been adopted favoring the IRA.

Indian New Deal

Based on the Indian Reorganization Act of 1934, Commissioner Collier ushered in what became called the Indian New Deal. Collier had considerable support from Secretary Ickes, and the two often talked about Indian affairs before their workday began (Parman 1976, 29). The Indian New Deal meant considerable change for tribal communities where living conditions had not improved much since the late 19th century. Native American tribal governments were given the authority to create their own constitutions, establish criteria for tribal membership, pass tribal laws, and were encouraged to form business corporations.

On the practical side, Collier had his own daily policy for Indian progress. He envisioned Native families living in their tribal communities, working out tribal governments with their leaders, and being home for their children at the end of each school day. Collier also respected Native ceremonies, which got him into trouble with religious organizations, but he became accustomed to criticism. Being a target of complaints did not improve the reputation of the Bureau of Indian Affairs, but Collier defined and shaped the Indian New Deal as he saw fit, earning the approval of an interested Ickes and an observing FDR.

One of the serious problems that the commissioner encountered involved conservation of soil on the Navajo Reservation, so that the land could provide a livelihood to its people. The BIA's conservation effort called for the reduction of at least 200,000 sheep and 200,000 goats. Collier met with the Navajos on the reservation and broached the subject carefully. He guessed that the government could pay the Navajos $2 or $3 per sheep or goat. Collier did not force the reduction, but his persuasive pressure gave the Navajos little time to consider the move, and they agreed to the livestock reduction. In the November 16 meeting, the tribal council met at Tuba City to learn that the Interior Department and Federal Emergency Relief Administration would make a grant of $200,000 for the BIA to purchase 100,000 sheep from the Navajos.

One Navajo woman described what it felt like to lose her sheep and her husband who died from the experience of reducing the family herd. She said,

When I had a husband and a lot of sheep I was happy. Then when it came my sheeps' turn to be acted upon, they were all driven away from me. They were driven into a corral and I was told to select the ones that were the best. That hurt me and I just bowed my head. I just sent my children over and they selected some. . . . My husband became sick from worry, and these officials went about in their cars even at night. (Nabokov 1991, 330–331)

Indian Service workers collected the sheep and shipped them via railroad to packing plants. The Southern Navajo district sold 32,000 sheep; the Northern Navajo district 20,000; Eastern Navajo 15,000; Western Navajo 15,000; the Hopi 10,000; and the Leupp district 8,000. A second stock reduction of 50,000 sheep and 148,300 goats soon followed (Parman 1976, 48, 63).

Johnson-O'Malley Act

As a part of the Indian New Deal, Senator Hiram W. Johnson of California introduced Senate Bill 2571 on February 2, 1934, and Thomas P. O'Malley introduced House Joint Resolution 257 in the House of Representatives. The collaboration of the two congressmen on this measure focused on making sure that Indian children received the same educational opportunities in attending public schools, although Native people lived on tax-exempt reservation lands.

Congress passed the Johnson-O'Malley Act (JOM) at the strong urging of Collier on April 16, 1934. With this legislative measure, the federal government authorized health, education, and social welfare services to Native people through state and territorial contracts. JOM permitted Indians to use state-operated schools, hospitals, and other social services. However, the fifth section of the act excluded Oklahoma from the law, which Congress later amended. In an effort to improve Indian education, JOM redirected Native students to public schools rather than boarding schools or day schools on reservations (Statutes at Large 48, 596).

In the beginning, JOM had little effect because the BIA had no control over the provisions of the law. Federal and state officials failed to agree about the programming. In addition, conservative public schools refused to establish any special programs for Indian students. JOM remained less than successful until after World War II and the 1960s. Thereafter, and still today, JOM programs in public schools became a central part of the progress of many Native students obtaining education.

Civilian Conservation Corps Indian Division

One of the relief programs began with the passage of the Emergency Conservation Act in 1933. FDR called an emergency session of Congress in early March to present his plan to put 250,000 unemployed men to work to preserve the natural resources of the country. The bill was quickly approved, and he signed it into law on March 31.

The program that would become known as the CCC called for the reforestation of federal, state, and private lands with related projects planned for public lands. Reforestation involved controlling soil erosion, reseeding rangeland, constructing recreation facilities, and related projects. By 1936 nearly a half million men worked for the program, often jokingly called Roosevelt's Tree Army, which attempted to rescue dust bowl-ridden states. From 1933 to 1941, more than 3 million young men served in the CCC. They worked 40 hours per week; often on Saturdays, due to bad weather during the week; and they received $30 per month with another $22 to $25 designated to a family dependent, which also included food, clothing, and medical care.

Secretary Ickes pressured CCC Director Robert Fechner to create an Indian Division of the program and one for African Americans. In April the CCC set aside nearly $5.9 million for 72 camps on 33 reservations. Fechner scheduled 43 camps for Arizona and New Mexico. To apply to the CCC, young men had to be between 17 and 35 years old. The army ran the CCC projects. The required physical examinations and immunization shots were provided by the Indian Service and mission doctors (Parman 1976, 32). For many of the 14,000 Indians that joined, this became their first off-reservation experience as they left with other tribal members and worked on bridges, roads, and public facilities in other states. Following their service, they traveled and returned with stories to tell their families and relatives about what they saw and experienced. These rewarding experiences continued until the outbreak of World War II.

Indian Arts and Crafts Board Act

Long before he became commissioner, John Collier encouraged Native people to continue the production of their arts and crafts. He envisioned Indians selling their goods off reservation to supplement their limited incomes while simultaneously carrying on their cultural traditions. His view won the support of anthropologist Oliver La Farge, who shared the same cultural idealism of preserving Native traditions and rebuilding their communities.

During these years some non-Indians began to produce goods to be passed off to the public as being made by Indian craftsmen. These imitations became a lucrative business for opportunity-minded individuals. Their actions took away a part of the economy of Native artists and crafts-men who depended on selling their products to tourists and collectors.

In 1935 Congress passed the Indian Arts and Crafts Board Act, which Collier heavily advocated. This protective law created a board to authenticate arts and crafts made by American Indians. With this certification, the board protected the Native arts and crafts industry and made it a crime for non-Indians to produce similar goods for sale under the assumption that they were Indian made (Statutes at Large 49, 891–93).

Commissioner Collier appointed Rene d'Harnoncourt as the manager of the Indian Arts and Crafts Board to encourage the production of Indian arts and crafts by Native people and to attract public interest in these Native-made goods (Meyn 2001, 57–58). The law remained in effect during the following decades. In 1990 Congress amended the act for more secure protection.

Oklahoma Indian Welfare Act

Like the Dawes Act of 1887, Congress left Oklahoma Indians out of the Indian Reorganization Act of 1934. Many Indians had done well in Oklahoma in becoming assimilated, but the majority of them had only part Indian blood. As tribal communities made progress, more work needed to be done, at least according to John Collier's Indian policy of community restoration. Tribal communities there had promising potential, but they needed financial assistance most of all.

Collier found an ally in Senator Elmer Thomas of Oklahoma. Thomas sponsored legislation in the Senate to amend the Indian Reorganization Act. The resulting legislation produced the Oklahoma Indian Welfare Act (OIWA) of 1936. Also known as the Thomas-Rogers Act, the law extended the authorization of the secretary of the interior to obtain quality lands, including Indian ones, to be held in trust for Native people (Statutes at Large 49:1967–68).

The OIWA provided for the restructuring of tribal governments, funding for economic development, loans for land purchases, and the options of tribes to decide whether they wished to participate in the Indian New Deal program. The act also permitted tribal towns and communities to form cooperative associations. Originally, approximately 40 Oklahoma tribes with a population of 140,000 had been excluded from the IRA because of their progress in emulating the mainstream lifestyle. The Oklahoma Indians, especially many members of the Five Civilized Tribes, had made substantial progress as farmers and had little need of reservations. Some IRA services had been available to the Oklahoma Indians, but federal officials believed that Oklahoma tribes, like the Muscogee Creek, had little need of services in comparison with reservation tribes in the West. Farmers by nature, the eastern tribes of the state in particular made progress as the nation tried to pull itself out of the Depression.

Between the years of 1937 and 1942, 18 tribal groups accepted the provisions of the law. In all, the BIA processed a total of 51 tribal communities and credit associations under the Oklahoma version of the IRA (Strickland 1980, 73).

Alaska Native Reorganization Act

Like the Oklahoma Indians, Alaska Natives were left out of the Indian Reorganization Act, and Congress passed the Alaska Native Reorganization Act in 1936 (Statutes at Large 49, 1250–51). Originally, the Wheeler-Howard bill included Alaska Natives, but the former territorial delegate to Alaska, Anthony J. Dimond, convinced congressmen to exclude them. Furthermore, the Alaska Native Brotherhood (ANB) preferred their own villages instead of the creation of reservations. The ANB had formed at Sitka in 1912 as a group of Christianized educated Natives who believed in white ways while retaining their Native identity (Philp 1981, 309–313).

In 1936 Congress enacted the Alaska Native Reorganization Act, this time with Dimond's support. Dimond believed that the Natives needed financial assistance and titles to their homesteads. The new law permitted Alaska Natives to establish self-government in their villages as well as borrow money from a credit fund to overcome Depression conditions. BIA personnel convinced Alaska Natives to draw up constitutions and begin charters of incorporation to reorganize their villages.

Basically the act offered the same opportunity to the Alaska Natives to accept provisions. Alaska Native communities voted to accept the act or to reject it. Many of the Alaska Native communities accepted the act and became eligible for receiving assistance from the IRA programs that the bureau offered. Interior Secretary Harold Ickes and John Collier used the reorganization act to establish five reservations, and the Interior Department held hearings to determine Haida and Tlingit claims to fishing rights and land in southeastern Alaska (Philp 1981, 309–313).

National Congress of American Indians

In the early 1940s BIA Commissioner Collier encouraged Indians who worked for the bureau to share information about federal progress in Native communities. They met in restaurants and elsewhere. Collier and his assistant commissioner, William Zimmerman, especially urged the Indian employees of the BIA in the Chicago office to meet. Sometimes they met at the local YMCA on South LaSalle Street. The idea of a national Indian organization had been on the minds of individuals like D'Arcy McNickle (Flathead), Archie Phinney (Nez Perce), Charles E. J. Heacock (Lakota Sioux), Ben Dwight (Choctaw), and others. McNickle, Phinney, and Heacock, in particular, pushed for forming the National Council of American Indians that later changed its name to the National Congress of American Indians (NCAI).

As the fighting in World War II winded down, Native leaders became concerned. The IRA remained controversial among Native communities, and some did not trust Collier and the BIA workers. Living conditions on most reservations had improved, but more needed to be done. John Collier did much to help Native communities, but his heavy-handed paternalism proved to be too much for Native leaders who criticized the BIA and the federal government for being too restrictive.

In 1944 Native tribal leaders gathered at the Cosmopolitan Hotel in downtown Denver, Colorado, to establish a national organization that became the National Congress of American Indians. In the planning meetings for the convention, the founders made efforts for as equal representation as possible among the tribes. In his keynote address at the first national meeting in November, Ben Dwight stated, "Now I know that you can't put the same blanket over everybody because when you do that you are going to pull it off of somebody else. The same blanket won't go over everybody at the same time, but if you use some judgment you can spread the blanket out so that the one that is a little bit colder can get warmth from it" (Cowger 1999, 30). NCAI used this wisdom in the following decades to speak against the wrongs of federal-Indian policies that it deemed inappropriate, especially the termination of federal trust relations with tribes and Native individuals.

Governed by an executive council, the convention delegates elected Cherokee Judge Napoleon B. Johnson from Oklahoma as the first president of the National Congress of American Indians. This national meeting of Indians identified common concerns, thus creating a pan-Indian effort to protect Indian lands, rights, and culture and to improve reservation life.

NCAI members found themselves continually questioning federal-Indian policy and challenging the BIA when they felt threatened.

Indians in World War II

When the Japanese attacked Pearl Harbor in the early morning of December 7, 1941, the United States joined World War II. From that point on, Indian affairs changed in Native communities and for the Bureau of Indian Affairs. In preparation for war, Congress terminated the entire CCC program on July 2, 1942, to appropriate support for the armed forces. In the summer, the decision was made to move the BIA to Chicago, on South Dearborn Street, due to more space being needed in Washington for the war effort. This temporary move disrupted Collier's supervision of Indian matters, and budget cuts to all nonwar agencies made him feel exiled from Washington. Continued disruptions and budget decreases over the next three years demoralized Collier, and he resigned on January 22, 1945 (Prucha 1984, 337).

As many as 25,000 Indian men and several hundred Indian women served in the U.S. armed forces. Roughly 22,000 Native men served in the Army, 2,000 in the Navy, 120 in the Coast Guard, and 730 men joined the Marines. A BIA report toward the war's end in 1944 announced that most of the able-bodied Indian men in the service were from 18 to 50 years of age. This presence represented 7 percent of the total American Indian population. Several hundred Native women served as well, although they have not received nearly as much attention as Native men have. Mainly, Native women served in the Women's Auxiliary Army Corps, which was a branch of the U.S. Army that became the Women's Army Corps, Women Accepted for Volunteer Emergency Service (WAVES, a navy division), and Army Nurses Corps.

On the home front, Native women and the elders worked in factories to produce war goods needed overseas. Roughly 50,000 Native women and elders worked in the war industries by sewing uniforms and making jeeps, planes, and tanks for the armed forces. On the 250 reservations, elders and women worked the farms and timberlands where available to feed their families.

The U.S. Marines followed the example of using the Choctaw language in World War I and looked for another tribal language to use. The Navajo code talkers became well known for the coded messages they sent on the battlefield. Other tribal code talkers in World War II included the Comanche of Oklahoma and Mesquakie of Iowa.

In the invasion of Normandy, 14 Comanche code talkers in the Fourth Infantry Division created a vocabulary of over 100 code terms. The Comanche used their tribal language in code on battlefields at Utah beach on June 6, 1944. The French government awarded the Comanche code talkers the Chevalier of the National Order of Merit in 1989, and on November 30, 1999, the U.S. Department of Defense awarded the Knowlton Award to Charles Chibitty, the last living Comanche code talker of World War II. In North Africa 24 Mesquakie soldiers used their language in the same coded manner.

American Indians serving in the war won six Medals of Honor as well as many other awards. Those who earned America's highest military award were Thomas Van Barfoot, Choctaw of Mississippi; Pappy Boyington, Coeur D'Alene of Idaho; Ernest Childers, Muscogee Creek of Oklahoma; Ernest Edwin Evans, Muscogee Creek and Cherokee of Oklahoma; Roy W. Harmon, Cherokee of Oklahoma; and Jack Montgomery, Cherokee of Oklahoma. In the end American Indian service men earned a total of 71 air medals, 51 silver stars, and 47 bronze stars in addition to the 6 Medals of Honor.

The most celebrated American Indian in World War II was Ira Hayes, a Pima from Arizona. Hayes served in the U.S. Marines at Iwo Jim in the Pacific. He became famous following the battle at Mount Surabachi when the Marines took the site following hand-to-hand combat with Japanese soldiers. Hayes was one of the six servicemen to help raise the American flag following the hard-fought battle, and the picture of the flag raising made him a celebrity to help sell more war bonds to finance the war in the United States. World War II changed Hayes's life and the lives of many American Indians who left their reservations for the first time.

The end of the war also meant changes in the organization of the Bureau of Indian Affairs. From 1946 to 1949, the BIA reorganized itself into 12 area offices to supervise 90 offices on reservations. The main BIA office returned to Washington, and much of the authority of the commissioner of Indian Affairs was transferred to the 12 area offices.

Conclusion

The Indian Reorganization Act changed federal-Indian relations and placed the Bureau of Indian Affairs in a more positive light. Critics claimed that federal paternalism was apparent. Yet the efforts of a single-minded John Collier had helped to alter Indian Country and the Bureau of Indian Affairs. The Indian New Deal made the bureau more responsible and directly involved in helping to reorder the infrastructures of tribal communities.

Collier set the tone for the rest of the 20th century by enlarging the bureau, providing a zeal for leadership in the federal government and bringing Indian affairs to the forefront. As head of the BIA, Collier had no easy task during the Great Depression and the international events that led to World War II. Undoubtedly Collier left a huge legacy in the Indian commissioner position; and the Bureau of Indian Affairs developed a reputation for being out in Indian Country and talking to Indians about their concerns.

Although Collier proved to be stubborn, he was a successful Indian commissioner and raised the Bureau of Indian Affairs to a new level of modern complexity in serving the Indian population. The commissioner listened to Native people, but he persisted in doing what he believed was best, including pressuring congressmen to go along with his version of the Indian New Deal. And it appeared that it was Collier's Indian New Deal.

At the same time, Collier met stubborn Indian resilience. The Navajo in particular refused the IRA, even after Collier flew to Arizona to lobby tribal members to vote for it. Other tribes like the Crow and Seneca rose to meet Collier and became a part of the movement that was critical of both Collier and the BIA. While Collier helped to lay the foundation for modern tribal governments, his actions also mounted complaints from both Indians and non-Indians. Indeed, Collier's work would not be equaled by other Indian commissioners for the rest of the 20th century.

As a result of the war, a large number of Indians became exposed to the off-reservation experience, and this influenced their desire to begin to assimilate. At the same time, the economies of the reservations struggled to get back on their feet like the rest of the country did in changing back to peacetime. The Indian New Deal provided a solid foundation for tribal governments that would be challenged by the oscillating pendulum of federal-Indian policy as defined by Congress and carried out by new BIA leadership coming into office.

References

"Alaska Native Reorganization Act," May 1, 1936, U.S. Statutes at Large, 49 pt. 1:1250–51.

Collier, John. *Annual Report of the Commissioner of Indian Affairs*, 1933. Microfilm. Marquette University Library, Milwaukee, WI. Reel 5, p. 11.

Cowger, Thomas W. *The National Congress of American Indians: The Founding Years*. Lincoln: University of Nebraska Press, 1999.

"Indian Arts and Crafts Board Act," August 27, 1935, U.S. Statutes at Large, 49:891–93.

"Indian Reorganization Act," June 18, 1934, U.S. Statutes at Large, 48 pt. 1:984–88.

"Johnson-O'Malley Act," April 16, 1934, U.S. Statutes at Large, 48:596.

Meyn, Susan Labry. "Fighting for Indian Artisans: John Collier, Rene d'Harnoncourt, and the Indian Arts and Crafts Board." In *Politics and Progress: American Society and the State Since 1865*. Westport, CT: Greenwood Press, 2001.

Nabokov, Peter, ed. *Native American Testimony: A Chronicle of Indian-White Relations from Prophecy to Present, 1492 to 1992*. New York: Penguin, 1991.

"Oklahoma Indian Welfare Act," June 26, 1936, U.S. Statutes at Large, 49:1967–68.

Parman, Donald. *The Navajos and the New Deal*. New Haven, CT: Yale University Press, 1976.

Philp, Kenneth. *The Crusade for Indian Reform, 1920–1954*. Tucson: University of Arizona Press, 1977.

Philp, Kenneth. "The New Deal and Alaska Natives, 1936–1945." *Pacific Historical Review* 50, no. 3 (August 1981): 309–327.

Prucha, Francis Paul. *The Great Father: The United States Government and the American Indian*. Lincoln: University of Nebraska Press, 1984.

Strickland, Rennard. *The Indians of Oklahoma*. Norman: University of Oklahoma Press, 1980.

SEVEN

Dillon S. Myer, Termination and Relocation

World War II changed the world, and it altered the attitudes of many people, including American Indians. As the United States led the rest of the world into the atomic age and the Cold War, people changed their political views and held steadfast to values that had been recently protected. The rise of communism in the Soviet Union compelled defenders of democracy in America to cling to their freedom and the American way of life. However, American optimism began to retreat to defensive and conservative thinking. This postwar retrenchment climaxed with the sudden rise of McCarthyism and the Red Scare of the early 1950s. Rhetorically anything that seemed un-American was perceived as a threat to the United States. In this light, Indian cultures and the previous Indian Reorganization policy went against this new strand of protective Americanism. In Indian Country, many Native people had experienced the outside world due to the war. They retained their tribal identities, but many—particularly those who had attended boarding schools—began to become a part of the mainstream, at least on a daily basis of working off-reservation jobs.

The Indians' new mobility influenced those in Washington as they worked to develop a new Indian policy. Two instrumental programs dominated the eight years of the Dwight Eisenhower administration from 1952 to 1960, and they found their roots even before then. These programs became known as termination and relocation, and they threatened Native identity. Relocation involved moving Indians again, this time to cities; and termination intended to assimilate Native peoples by dissolving their sovereignty.

Indian Claims Commission

In 1945, BIA Commissioner William Brophy proposed House Resolution 237 to create a congressional committee to study the claims of Indian tribes against the United States. Brophy's idea derived from suggestive reforms during the Indian New Deal. Some congressmen, however, were not sure that this would bring about any final solutions and thus were wary of spending millions of dollars on the endeavor. In October, Representative Henry Jackson of Washington introduced House Resolution 4497 that articulated the need for an Indian Claims Commission and a process to handle the claims. President Harry Truman signed the bill on August 13, 1946, and the Indian Claims Commission (ICC) Act became P.L. 79–726 (Fixico 1986, 28).

In the postwar years, Congress passed this first important law pertaining to Indian affairs. Truman referred to the law as a "Fair Deal" that opened a new era of federal-Indian relations, and he emphasized the loyalty of many Native men serving in the armed forces. The law called for establishing a claims commission for 10 years in which the members would assist tribes for the first 5 in preparing claims and would make decisions on them over the next 5. The original commission had three members: Chief Commissioner Edgar Witt, Louis J. O'Marr, and William L. Holt. In the first five years of operation, the commission heard 852 cases. In 1961 and 1966, the act had to be amended to include an extension because of the large number of claims. In 1967, with advice and consent from the Senate, the commission increased to 5 members (Lurie 1978, 100–101). The ICC continued until 1978 (Statutes at Large 60, 1049–56).

With John Collier's resignation in 1945, the bureau's leadership faced a daunting decision. Should they continue the Indian New Deal, or should they try to rid federal Indian relations of stiff government paternalism? In the following months, Commissioner William Brophy criticized Collier's bureaucratic structure of numerous offices within the BIA. Trained as a lawyer with legal experience with the Pueblo communities, Brophy believed too much bureaucracy existed. He planned to dissolve 40 district offices, thereby saving money and reducing personnel. Brophy streamlined the bureau in setting up five geographic area offices in Minneapolis, Minnesota; Billings, Montana; Portland, Oregon; Phoenix, Arizona; and Oklahoma City, Oklahoma. With these changes, Brophy seemed well on his way to putting his own stamp on federal-Indian affairs.

Zimmerman Plan

During a tour of Native communities throughout Alaska in early 1947, Commissioner Brophy fell ill with pneumonia. His illness developed into tuberculosis, and the mantel of the bureau fell on the shoulders of Assistant Commissioner William Zimmerman. By this point, Congress had begun entertaining ways of getting out of the Indian business that Collier's Indian New Deal had heavily invested in. On February 8, 1947, Zimmerman testified before the Senate Committee on the Post Office and Civil Service on the subject of cutting back on personnel and expenses in the BIA. Zimmerman presented his three-part plan listing tribes to be terminated of their trust status. He divided all the tribes into 3 groups, based on their readiness to handle their own business affairs. This became known as the Zimmermann Plan, and it named the first group of tribes for immediate trust withdrawal and asserted that the second group would be ready at the end of 10 years. The last group had an indefinite time limit for termination of trust status (Kvasnicka and Viola 1977, 286).

The winter of 1947–1948 produced a blizzard that gripped the Southwest. Hopi and Navajo communities became endangered due to the freezing cold, compelling the federal government to act. Airlift drops of food, supplies, and hay for livestock provided temporary relief to the communities. Ultimately the federal government made the decision to temporarily relocate Navajo families to Salt Lake City, Denver, and Los Angeles, providing them with housing and jobs. This became an early precursor to the Relocation Program of the 1950s (Fixico 2000, 8–25).

Hoover Task Force Commission

In 1949 the Department of the Interior authorized the formation of the Hoover Task Force Commission to conduct a national study of the conditions and status of American Indians. The commission included 14 individuals: Ferdinand Eberstadt served as chairman, Dr. Raymond B. Allen, Thomas Archer, Hanson W. Baldwin, Chester I. Barnard, Dr. Charles W. Cole, John Cowles, James Knowlson, John J. McCloy, Dr. Frederick A. Middlebush, Robert P. Patterson, Lewis L. Strauss, J. Carlton Ward Jr., and General Robert E. Wood.

The commission recommended that the federal government decrease its involvement in Indian affairs in order for American Indians to assume more responsibility for their own business. The commission explicitly recommended that the government stop funding Indian programs once the trust status was removed from Native tribes. Furthermore, the Department of the Interior began to entertain the idea of moving the BIA to a new department. The Hoover Report suggested establishing a Department of Natural Resources. Some of the tribal affairs involved resources on reservations with national conservation and the development of forests, water, and other natural resources.

Fiscal conservatism became a part of the federal retrenchment while President Eisenhower held office. In a speech to the 81st Congress, Senator Hugh Butler of Nebraska asked, "Does the Indian desire to be considered Uncle Sam's stepchild forever?" He then answered, "No: Wardship with all its paternalistic trappings is increasingly distasteful to him" (Fixico 1986, 55). Butler's point of view dovetailed with the growing sentiment that enough of the Indian business was enough.

McCarthyism

The postwar years witnessed the rise of McCarthyism when Senator Joseph McCarthy of Wisconsin began rumors about individuals being communist or sympathizers of the Communist Party. Suspicion proved to be McCarthyism's greatest tool in convincing the public that some workers in the federal government believed in communism, while other believers worked in the entertainment business. McCarthy and his followers singled out teachers for teaching about communism, and union activists were rumored to be a part of the political infiltration to convince people to rebel against the United States. Naturally Indians' community-oriented traditions placed them in the un-American category. Meanwhile Congress thought Native people should be liberated from their beliefs to be redirected toward American values of individuality.

To compound this situation, also known as the Second Red Scare, the Korean War broke out on June 25, 1950. In the following six months, 2,500 American Indian men enlisted in the armed services to once again prove their loyalty as they did in World Wars I and II. By the end of the Korean conflict on July 27, 1953, roughly 10,000 Native men had served in the war, and Charles George, Raymond Harvey, and Mitchell Red Cloud earned the Medal of Honor.

Relocation Program

In 1951 the Bureau of Indian Affairs under Commissioner John Nichols entertained the idea of extending the Navajo relocation experiment to all American Indians. Nichols's time in office extended for only14 months as Truman soon named Dillon Myer to be the BIA commissioner. From Ohio, the conservative Republican believed in American idealism and proved to be a staunch supporter of Eisenhower. In fact, Myer's previous appointment was the director of the War Relocation Authority that ironically relocated some Japanese Americans to the Gila Indian Reservation in Arizona.

Myer moved other Japanese American citizens to nine internment camps in six other states throughout the West. His action represented the paranoid fear that the estimated 120,000 locked-up Americans might fight for Japan. Ironically 7,000 Japanese American men and women fought in the armed services for the United States.

In 1952 the Bureau of Indian Affairs supervised the Relocation Program to arrange for Indians from rural areas and reservations to move themselves to major cities in the West. By the end of relocation in 1973, thousands of Indians found themselves living in crowded and dilapidated ghetto apartments. Furthermore, these Indians worked jobs, often seasonal, for less than standard pay, and many were laid off from the jobs that had been arranged for them. To Native people, relocation proved to be a great disappointment as it became a disliked word throughout Indian Country. The bureau used the preferred name of Employment Assistance to replace the ill-named Relocation Program.

The Indian Bureau searched for stable leadership, naming Glenn Emmons as commissioner. Emmons, a former banker from New Mexico, knew Indians, and he served during Eisenhower's eight years in office.

Termination Policy

In 1953 the 83rd Congress began to take action, entertaining numerous bills to streamline the Bureau of Indian Affairs and to liberate tribes from federal restrictions. During the 83rd congressional session, congressmen introduced a record number of bills. Congress entertained 288 public bills and resolutions involving Indian affairs; 46 bills became laws. As a part of its legislative studies on Indians, the Bureau of Indian Affairs submitted 162 reports to the Senate and House of Representatives. In early June, Congress sealed the fate of Indian people when it approved a general resolution that established the termination policy affecting all tribal groups. Senator Henry Jackson of Washington introduced House Concurrent Resolution 108 in the Senate, and Representative William Harrison of Wyoming sponsored the legislation in the House of Representatives. The essence of this landmark resolution reads as follows:

Whereas it is the policy of Congress, as rapidly as possible, to make the Indians within the territorial limits of the United States subject to the same laws and entitled to the same privileges and responsibilities as are applicable to other citizens of the United States, to end their status as wards of the United States and to grant them all of the rights and prerogatives, pertaining to American citizenship; and

Whereas the Indians within the territorial limits of the United States should assume their full responsibilities as American Citizens. (HCR 108 1953)

HCR 108 laid the foundation for the most dangerous Indian policy that the United States government ever devised. Once and for all, Congress intended to abrogate all obligations to American Indians as promised in 374 treaties signed with the United States.

Public Law 280

As another action of federal withdrawal, Congress passed Public Law 280. P.L. 280 authorized five states to have criminal and civil jurisdiction over tribal lands within their state boundaries. These states included Nebraska, California, Minnesota (except for the Red Lake Reservation), Oregon (except for the Warm Springs Reservation), and Wisconsin (except for the Menominee Reservation). Later when Alaska became a state on January 3, 1959, Congress amended P.L. 280 to include Alaska.

Passed by the 83rd Congress, P.L. 280 represented the belief of the predominately Republican Congress that it was time to get out of the Indian business. As a form of termination, the law placed the jurisdiction of most Indians in these states under state authority, thereby decreasing the traditional federal-Indian relationship that the founders of the United States once wanted so badly (Statutes at Large 67, 588–90).

Menominee Termination

In 1954 Congress terminated the first tribe to undergo withdrawal of trust status. Listed in the first group of the Zimmerman Plan, Congress passed P.L. 399 to terminate the Menominee of Wisconsin (Statutes at Large 86, 250–52). This law set the final date for 1958, but extensions delayed termination until 1961. The former Menominee Reservation of 357,960 square miles became the last and poorest county in Wisconsin. Terminationist leader Senator Arthur Watkins of Utah and BIA Commissioner Emmons had mistakenly presumed that the Menominee could develop its timberland industry based on an estimated $10 million in tribal assets. Unfortunately, opportunists preyed upon them, and factionalism divided the Native community. In the same session, Congress terminated the timber-rich Klamath of Oregon, and their termination deadline followed the Menominee with similar results (Statutes at Large 68, 718–28). In this period Congress terminated 61 tribes, communities, bands, and groups of Indians from 1954 to 1961.

In March 1957 a private organization established the Commission on the Rights, Liberties, and Responsibilities of the American Indians to make a comprehensive evaluation of Indian conditions and status. The commission, led by former Commissioner Brophy and O. Meredith Wilson, made a final report in 1966, *The Indian: America's Unfinished Business*. The commission made recommendations against termination, stating, "Indians should be allowed full hearings before the appropriate Congressional committees. The government's responsibility should be relinquished only when the Indians are no longer in the lower segment of our culture in education, health, and economic status" (Brophy and Aberle 1966, 211).

Chicago Conference

The termination policy spread caution and fear throughout Indian Country. In response the National Congress of American Indians (NCAI) held annual meetings and more activities to give tribes updated information on new congressional bills. Professor Sol Tax of the University of Chicago, Professor Nancy Lurie of the University of Michigan, and others worked with NCAI to plan the national meeting. In 1961 a major pan-Indian conference occurred at Midway on the University of Chicago campus. Some 500 Indians representing 90 tribes and bands met at the American Indian Chicago Conference for several days, focusing on education for children, job training, reservation housing, health care, tribal economies, and job employment. In the end, the conference produced its own Indian policy, "Declaration of Indian Purpose," to present to President John Kennedy the following year (Cobb 2008, 31–42).

Indian youth attended the Chicago conference, and they wanted more to happen politically. Many of the angry Indian young men and women had attended boarding schools, some experienced relocation, and a few had attended college. The young people called their elders "Uncle Tomahawks" and spread the word that they wanted to meet among themselves. In the following months, the National Indian Youth Council (NIYC) formed in Gallup, New Mexico, from August 10–13, 1961, as an advocate group to deal with problems. They continued to meet annually as their numbers grew, and individuals like Clyde Warrior, a charismatic Ponca from Oklahoma, articulated a new era for Indian concerns.

The Chicago conference drew the attention of the White House even during the tenuous times of the Cuban missile and the Bay of Pigs affairs. Matters became worse with the assassination of President Kennedy in November 1963. Sworn into office as the new president on Air Force One returning to Washington, Vice President Lyndon Baines Johnson (LBJ) of Texas inherited national problems involving Vietnam and civil rights protests. Johnson responded to them with his Great Society program. As a part of his efforts to make America better, LBJ's administration created the Office of Economic Opportunity (OEC) to reduce poverty, including the poverty experienced by so many American Indians. OEC did not allow the BIA to administer the funds or be the principal organization for controlling the funds. OEC's allocated funds went directly to the tribal governments, becoming a primary example of LBJ and his politically plagued administration's support of a self-determination policy.

As Congress terminated tribes in the 1960s, NCAI continued to meet to devise ways to fight the federal policy of withdrawing trust status. In 1965 NCAI Executive Director Vine Deloria Jr. and tribal representatives presented a united front protesting congressional action to pass Senate Bill 1442 to terminate the dozen Confederated Colville Tribes in Washington. The effort succeeded as the Colville Indians avoided termination.

Indian Fish-Ins

National headlines shifted to the Pacific Northwest when Indians in the region protested that they possessed legal rights to fish in several rivers in the state of Washington. State laws and court rulings denied Native people the right to use traditional net fishing and traps. The Native fishermen tried to assert their treaty fights as laid out in the Treaty of Medicine Creek in 1854, which allowed them to fish in ceded waters, but they clashed with local officials on this point.

In February 1966, local authorities arrested Nisqually tribe members who held the fish-ins. Hank Adams of Fort Peck Reservation in Montana emerged as the leader of the local tribal fishermen as racial confrontations occurred between local Indians and whites. The challenge of Indian fishing rights led to the establishment of the Survival of American Indian Association (SAIA) in 1968 under Adams. Confrontations continued, compelling SAIA membership to grow to about 200 members. And local authorities arrested SAIA members and Adams on a regular basis. On one occasion, an unknown assailant shot Adams in the stomach, yet Adams survived.

In May 1968, in *Puyallup Tribe v. Department of Game*, the Supreme Court ruled that the state of Washington could ban net fishing by Native people in the name of conservation. This court ruling usurped tribal sovereignty and threw Indian fishing rights into abeyance, as it became a contested issue added to a long list of concerns. The heated fishing rights issue sent the case to higher courts and eventually to the U.S. Supreme Court. (The final ruling in 1974, which would be called the *Boldt* Decision, confirmed the treaty rights and declared that the Native people of Washington had the right to fish in the state rivers. The landmark *Boldt* Decision became a reference for other Indian fishing cases.)

Robert Bennett

LBJ believed that Indian people could help themselves and that they knew their conditions better than anyone else. Along this line, LBJ appointed Robert LaFollette Bennett as commissioner of Indian Affairs in April 1966. Bennett, an Oneida from Wisconsin, became the second Indian person to hold the position of commissioner of Indian Affairs. Educated at Haskell Indian Boarding School in Kansas, Bennett graduated from Southeastern University Law School in Washington, DC and began his ascension up the Indian Bureau ladder of appointments. Bennett represented the prime example of Indian assimilation, and he served in the U.S. Marines during World War II. Bennett maintained positive BIA relations with Interior Secretary Stewart Udall and LBJ's administration.

In the spring of 1966, the Navajo established the Rough Rock Demonstration School by contracting with the BIA. Allen D. Yazzie, chairman of the Navajo Tribal Education Committee, and others presented a proposal to the newly created Office of Economic Opportunity. With support from Commissioner Bennett and the BIA, as well as $214,300 from OEO, Rough Rock succeeded in meeting its students' needs with a curriculum that fit well with the community. Rough Rock represented the first school in modern history to be completely controlled by a tribe.

During the following months, old friends in Alaska needed Bennett's attention. In October 1966, members of the Alaska Federation of Natives gathered in Anchorage, Alaska, to discuss plans to conserve their land. An estimated 400 Alaska Natives representing 17 Native organizations met for three days. The group focused on stopping state land claims and bringing to attention "aboriginal title," especially concerning Alaska Natives who did not sign treaties with the federal government. From 1966 to 1971, the Alaska Federation of Natives worked with the BIA to recognize Alaska

Native claims. Bureau Commissioner Bennett became heavily involved, drawing from previous experience as director of the Juneau Area Office.

Bennett continued his effort to improve Indian education by working with Congress. In 1965 Congress passed the Elementary and Secondary Education Act. As a part of the law, the BIA improved educational services to Native students by creating a kindergarten program and starting local school boards for bureau schools. In January 1967 the BIA created the National Indian Education Advisory Committee as an effort to increase Native participation to improve the educational level of all Indians.

In March 1967, Congress passed a bill allowing the Indian Claims Commission to function until 1972. Several weeks later, in June, the U.S. Claims Court upheld a previous decision made by the Indian Claims Commission that stated that the Seminole of Florida, according to an 1823 treaty, had claims to 32 million acres. In August, eight Lakota Sioux groups received $12.2 million in compensation from the Indian Claims Commission for lands totaling 29 million acres taken from them by treaties in the 19th century.

Forgotten American

On March 6, 1968, President Lyndon Johnson delivered his noted "Forgotten American" speech to Congress. In the speech, President Johnson stated, "The American Indian, once proud and free, is torn between white and tribal values; between the politics and language of the white man and his own historic culture. His problems, sharpened by years of defeat and exploitation, neglect and inadequate effort, will take years to overcome. But recent landmark laws—the Economic Opportunity Act, the Elementary and Secondary Education Act, the Manpower Development and Training Act—have given us an opportunity to deal with the persistent problems of the American Indian. The time has come to focus our efforts on the plight of the American Indian through these and the other laws passed in the last four years . . . I propose a new goal for our Indian programs: A goal that ends the old debate about 'termination' of Indian programs and stresses self-determination; a goal that erases old attitudes of paternalism and promotes partnership of self-help" (Johnson 1968).

During his speech, Johnson requested a 10 percent increase in funding for Indian programs. He also reviewed three goals: (1) an equal standard of living, (2) freedom to live where they please, and (3) equal economic opportunity and social justice. On March 6, 1968, Johnson signed Executive Order 11399. As a part of the order, the National Council on Indian Opportunity came into existence. This council, consisting of the vice president and selected Indian leaders, had the task of presenting the problems of American Indians to the highest levels of the federal government.

Members of Congress took Johnson's plea in his speech to heart. In April 1968, Congress passed the American Indian Civil Rights Act. This act gave American Indians living on reservations under tribal governments many of the same civil rights that all persons under state and federal governments already possessed, according to the U.S. Constitution. The law established guidelines for tribal courts and required updated versions of *Indian Affairs: Laws and Treaties*, compiled by Charles Kappler; and *Handbook of Federal Indian Law*, edited by Felix Cohen, to be published by the secretary of the Interior (*Statutes at Large* 82, 77–81).

American Indian Movement

In July 1968, Dennis Banks, Clyde Bellecourt, and George Mitchell—all Ojibwas from Minnesota—organized other Indians living in the Twin Cities to protest against police brutality against Indian people. During that summer the three cofounders established an urban Indian organization that called itself the American Indian Movement (AIM). The principal goal of AIM focused on stopping police from harassing Indians and improving social services to city neighborhoods.

The first meeting of AIM occurred at 8:00 P.M. on July 28, 1968, in the basement of a rundown church in south Minneapolis. Clyde Bellecourt arranged for attorney Gus Hall to attend to answer any legal questions that might arise. Several noted individuals such as Dennis Banks, Clyde Bellecourt, Eddie Benton Benai, Mary Jane Wilson, and George Mitchell—all Ojibwa—persisted in pushing for organizing the American Indian Movement (Banks 2004, 61).

The year 1968 marked a turning point with the rise of AIM; the end of Bennett's term as BIA commissioner; and the election of a new president, Richard Nixon. In October, Congress authorized a $5 million settlement to the Yavapai of Arizona and established the Central Arizona Project. The settlement was in response to the illegal taking of nine million acres of Yavapai land by the federal government in 1874.

In March 1969, President Richard Nixon signed a law to establish the Office of Minority Business Enterprise. The goal of this venture was to ensure that government contracts and purchases could also form agreements with minority owned businesses, including American Indians. The act also called for the government to aid tribes in the development of their reservation economies.

The BIA and the Nixon administration found themselves involved in Indian issues in all areas. In March, seven Mohawks protested against the Canadian government. These individuals demonstrated against the Canadian custom duties on Mohawk goods. They stated that the Jay Treaty of 1794 allowed border tribes to freely pass the borders and exempted them from paying import and export taxes on their goods. While this protest has been one of several, the Canadian government refused to recognize a Mohawk exemption from export taxes based on the Jay Treaty.

In May 1969, the Indian Claims Commission awarded the Klamath tribe of Oregon $4.1 million. This settlement resulted from bad surveys that government workers conducted on their reservation in 1871 and 1888. The claims settlement eventually led to the actual termination of the Klamath Tribe in 1973.

Nixon's Special Message to Congress

In August 1969, President Nixon appointed Louis Bruce, a Mohawk-Oglala Sioux, as commissioner of Indian Affairs. Bruce was one of the founding members of the National Congress of American Indians in 1944. Commissioner Bruce remarked, "The will for self-determination has become a vital component of the thinking of Indian leadership and the grassroots Indian on every reservation and in every city. It is an irreversible trend, a tide in the destiny of American Indians that will eventually compel all of America once and for all to recognize the dignity and human rights of Indian people" (Bruce 1976, 242).

In the following weeks, angry Indians fulfilled plans to take over Alcatraz Island in the San Francisco Bay. Once the location of an infamous federal penitentiary, urban Indians seized the island and occupied it for 18 months as a symbolic gesture of suppressed Indian legal rights and American colonization of indigenous people. AIM members joined the occupation as headlines escalated.

Nixon listened to AIM protests and began to help Native people. On July 8, 1970, Nixon gave a special message to Congress in regard to American Indians, calling for a new direction of Indian self-determination. President Nixon began the speech stating:

The first Americans—the Indians—are the most deprived and most isolated minority group in our nation. On virtually every scale of measurement—employment, income, education, health,—the condition of the Indian people ranks at the bottom. . . . It is long past time that the Indian policies of the Federal government began to recognize and build upon the capacities and insights of the Indian people. Both as a matter of justice and as a matter of enlightened social policy, we must begin to act on the basis of what the Indians themselves have been long telling us. (Nixon 1970, 565–576)

Nixon strongly advocated self-determination without termination as the basis for the next era of Indian policy. Nixon ended his speech by calling for Indian input. He stated, "It is a new and balanced relationship between the United States government and the first Americans that is at the heart of our approach to Indian problems" (Nixon 1970, 565–576).

Indian Preference

As early as the Indian Reorganization Act of 1934, "Indian Preference" became a part of BIA policy to employ American Indians to run Indian affairs. This policy enabled many Indians to work for the BIA at entry-level positions and to work in area offices. After World War II, Indians began to work for the BIA in increasing numbers. They worked mainly in area offices and at reservation agencies, and they were being promoted to higher posts.

The tendency to place American Indians in lower-level BIA positions changed during the Nixon years. Following his commissioner appointment, Louis Bruce and Interior Secretary Rogers C.B. Morton began to implement Indian preference when filling all BIA positions. By the next decade, BIA personnel included 75 American Indians (Taylor 1984, 41). This policy continued, including the top position of commissioner of Indian Affairs and afterwards with the newly created position of assistant secretary of the Interior.

Native American Rights Fund

During the turbulence of AIM activism and civil rights protests, Indian legal rights remained a critical issue in Indian Country. California Indian legal services received funding from the Ford Foundation in 1970 to provide legal representation to Indians in California. A year later, Native American Rights Fund (NARF) separated from California Indian Legal Services and opened its own office in Boulder, Colorado.

This pilot program quickly developed into a national effort when it received its name as the Native American Rights Fund (NARF). David Getches served as the initial director of NARF, which worked to help Native people and Indian organizations. During these years, the Office of Economic Opportunity funded a legal support program to assist in providing legal services to the disadvantaged and poor sectors of society. Lawyers and organizations realized that the complexity and long history of federal-Indian law was not generally taught in law schools, until the University of New Mexico offered federal-Indian law as a part of its curriculum, and other law schools followed.

By 1975 NARF grew from a 3-lawyer operation into an organization of 40 full-time staff employees with 15 attorneys. In the following decades, NARF established itself as the most effective legal assistance program to support, advise, and represent Indian people.

Americans for Indian Opportunity

After founding Oklahomans for Indian Opportunity (OIO), LaDonna Harris followed a similar model in establishing Americans for Indian Opportunity (AIO) in 1970. Harris, a Comanche activist, had been married to Fred Harris for 21 years. They lived in Oklahoma where Fred Harris graduated from the University of Oklahoma Law School and entered politics. During this time, LaDonna Harris organized individuals who felt compelled to advance the economic conditions of Native people living in the state. Oklahomans for Indian Opportunity began as an information organization in her living room during the 1960s.

As Fred Harris's success in Oklahoma politics continued, he announced his candidacy for the U.S. Senate, and he won by a narrow victory over Republican Bud Wilkinson, a famed college football coach. As Fred and LaDonna established themselves in Washington, LaDonna continued to be active in working for American Indians. Operating at a national scale, she opted to organize a national organization, Americans for Indian Opportunity.

LaDonna became a nationally recognized figure in her own way as she worked to bring about Indian reform. President Johnson appointed her to serve on the National Council for Indian Opportunity. However, AIO remained LaDonna's main focus: emphasizing economic opportunity to help tribal communities to become economically self-sustaining. Since its founding, AIO continues to advance American Indians and Indian organizations by helping them to obtain grants and supplying expertise to those who request it.

National Tribal Chairmen's Association

For two days in February 1971, tribal leaders met in Billings, Montana, to discuss specific concerns on their reservations. The meeting involved representatives from 50 reservations in 12 states. They met and established the National Tribal Chairmen's Association (NTCA). NTCA members believed that the federal government under Nixon shaped federal Indian policy too much to appease the protests of young Indian activists. NTCA wanted federal assistance to help improve conditions on reservations in tribal communities.

The American Indian Movement voiced concerns of urban Indians, and this swung the attention of federal officials, including President Nixon, to respond to the rapidly growing urban Indian population. Although Nixon asked the Bureau of Indian Affairs and other federal agencies to help in carrying out self-determination, NTCA continued to hold annual meetings to monitor each presidential administration and Congress.

The tribal chairmen found a useful ally in Commissioner of Indian Affairs Louis Bruce, and they worked together well following the founding of NTCA. In the following decades, the National Tribal Chairmen's Association and the National Congress of American Indians became the two most effective organizations to represent the general interests of Native people to the Bureau of Indian affairs and other federal agencies.

Alaska Native Settlement Act

In 1971 Congress passed the largest claims case in the history of Indian-white relations. The Alaska Native Claims Settlement Act gave the Alaska Natives $962 million for relinquishing the remainder of their claims in Alaska. Congress set an unheard-of precedent of returning an enormous area of land back to Native people. In this unusual occurrence, the United States returned 44 million acres to the Alaska Natives (Statutes at Large 85, 688–92, 702–03).

Although the act passed easily in the House and by a voice vote in the Senate, Alaska Natives had concerns about the impact of the law. Some Native people claimed that the act would alter the traditional culture by focusing on the village. Reorganizing into regional corporations under state law in order to manage funds and lands went against traditional ways.

Finally the Alaska Native Federation held a convention to hear and vote on the act. In the end, the delegates at the convention voted 511 to 56 to accept the law. After the Alaska Natives accepted the act, President Nixon signed into law the largest Indian and Native land claims settlement to date on December 18, 1971. (In 1978 Narragansett Indians received a $3.5 million settlement followed by the Massachusetts Wampanoag's $4.5 million in 1987; Washington Puyallup's $162 million in 1989; New York Seneca's $60 million in 1990; Montana Crow's $35 million; New Mexico Santo Domingo Pueblo's $23 million and California Cahilla's $14.2 million in 2000; Oklahoma Cherokee's, Choctaw's and Chickasaw's $40 million together) (Rosier 2003, 61–81)

In 1972 the Nixon administration listened to AIM protests and supported the protestors' views on self-determination. Native activists and the Nixon administration both saw education as an important key to help Native groups and their people. In 1972 Congress passed the American Indian Education Act. Learning much from the Kennedy Indian Education Report released in 1969, Congress passed this legislation to help Native people become more educated. This important law increased spending and called for more personnel to raise the education level of American Indians.

Occupation of the BIA Building

On October 26, 1972, two caravans from Seattle, Los Angeles, and San Francisco moved out for a cross-country expedition to end in Washington, DC. Another group of Indians left Oklahoma on October 23 to retrace the "Trail of Tears" of the 1830s. AIM leaders planned for all three to join as one caravan along the way. The large caravan arrived in Washington about 6:00 A.M. on November 3, and members went to rest at a church. The church's accommodations angered the AIM members, and they criticized bureaucrats for having fine office surroundings in the Indian Bureau. The AIM members left for the BIA. Arriving at the Bureau of Indian Affairs building located at Constitution Avenue and 19th Street, the Indians soon became involved in a heated argument with the building guards and lower bureau officials. At that critical point, the Indians seized the BIA building. Once inside the activists renamed the building the Native American Embassy.

The Indians requested an audience with President Nixon to present a list of "Twenty Points." These points outlined a new framework for federal-Indian relations. They included a proposed repeal of the act of 1871 that forbade additional treaty making. AIM leaders also demanded that a treaty commission be created within the next year, and they wanted a government review of past and present treaty violations.

Federal Judge John H. Pratt issued a court order setting a midnight deadline for the Indians to leave the building, but negotiations lasted past 4:00 the next morning. Hours later U.S. Marshall Wayne Colburn arrived with a court order for eviction, accompanied by armed federal officers.

Threats to remove the Indians by force compelled them to barricade themselves in the building with desks, office furniture, and other items. During the chaos the activists destroyed office files and furniture. On November 9, newly appointed Indian Commissioner Forest Gerard finally negotiated a release of the building after he said the federal government would listen to the Indians' grievances and follow up on them. Federal officials agreed to look into the administration of Oglala Sioux leader Richard Wilson at Pine Ridge who AIM accused of corruption. Officials also agreed to a federal review of the past treaty violations and the release of the Indians in the building without criminal charges. AIM and its supporters had occupied the Bureau of Indian Affairs building for seven days, mounting $2.28 million in damages (Banks 2004, 126–144).

Wounded Knee Occupation

In response to tribal leader Richard Wilson's manner of governing the Pine Ridge Sioux Reservation and his abuse of tribal members, the American Indian Movement met in South Dakota. AIM members examined the situation and discussed the past mistreatment by the United States, and this led to the takeover of Wounded Knee in South Dakota. In response, the Department of Justice sent 50 marshals to subdue the AIM protestors, and support arrived from the U.S. Army as well.

Dennis Banks acted as the primary negotiator for the Wounded Knee occupants. The federal government had as many as 500 personnel with ranchers and vigilantes joining who wanted to defeat the Indian militants. The government supplied the federal agents with an extraordinary amount of hardware. This effort included 100,000 rounds of M-16, 1,100 parachute illumination flares, 20 sniper rifles with night-vision scopes, powerful searchlights, submachine guns, bulletproof vests, gas masks, C-rations, ponchos, blankets, and helmets. In addition, army planes flew low over the village as reconnaissance missions.

Finally, on May 8, the two sides laid down their weapons after the Oglala chiefs and federal government signed an agreement. The agreement called for an investigation to be held into charges against Wilson. It also called for treaty meetings with the Oglala Sioux in order to review the 1868 Fort Laramie Treaty. The occupation of Wounded Knee ended on Friday, May 8, 1973. On that day, 146 Native men and women surrendered. The federal officials lowered the AIM flag and raised the Stars and Stripes while a helicopter hovered overhead.

For 71 days, members of the American Indian Movement held the small town, building barricades against the U.S. Army, FBI, and U.S. marshals. This action stood as the last major Indian occupation of the 20th century, much like the Wounded Knee Massacre that ended the last major Indian stand in the previous century (Banks 2004, 157–180).

Restoration Policy

During the upheaval of federal-Indian relations, the Nixon administration continued to listen to Indian concerns that became now more than mere actions of protest, but militancy. The Indians protested that past and present wrongs needed to be addressed like the termination of the Menominee as a federally recognized tribe. The termination of the Menominee in 1954 via P.L. 399 caused many problems for the tribal members. In becoming the last county in Wisconsin, the former Menominee Reservation also became the poorest. Sales of the timber from the reservation caused more problems when opportunists exploited tribal members by underpaying them. The mismanagement of the Legend Lake real estate development caused additional hardship.

Ada Deer, a Menominee activist; her sister Connie; tribal member James White; and others launched a grassroots movement to overturn the Menominee termination with new legislation. Their organization, Determination of Rights for Menominee Shareholders (DRUMS), began with people on the former reservation and all the legal help they could get. The legacy of termination still continued, and to turn it on its head seemed impossible. But other people in Washington listened in addition to the president. BIA Commissioner Louis Bruce, who was in office at this time, and other Indians in high positions wanted to help.

"I began knocking on doors and making friends with everybody. . . . It was exhausting work," said Ada Deer. "I would just pick up the phone and called people and I took direction from them: LaDonna Harris and Fred Harris, Senator [Ted] Kennedy's staff, Senator [Gaylord] Nelson's staff, Senator [William] Proxmire's staff. People got on board because this was the early '70s, when Nixon's presidential message on Indian affairs provided background for self-determination without termination" (Deer 2010, 106).

The restoration bill moved through congressional procedure and reached the desk of the president. Richard Nixon signed the Menominee Restoration Act on December 22, 1973, thereby repealing the termination act of 1954. A new policy began under the umbrella of Indian self-determination called "restoration" as other terminated tribes began to be restored. With this new momentum of 60 plus restoration cases, more than 100 nonfederally recognized Indian communities attempted to obtain federal recognition as an Indian tribe under the law, forcing the government to consider developing a federal branch of acknowledgment (Ulrich 2010, 247).

Conclusion

Of all of the federal-Indian policies, termination may very well have been the worst that threatened American Indians. With the goal to once and for all assimilate Indians into the mainstream by not allowing any return to the old ways or even to their tribal communities, termination represented a one-way avenue toward Americanizing Native people. Circumstances and a strong congressional movement forced tribes to accept termination that led to 109 total cases of tribes, bands, communities, and individuals being terminated of their trust status.

In addition, relocation proved to be more harmful than helpful in its early years of moving Native people to cities. BIA relocation officers offered promises of a better life in urban areas and convinced many individuals and families to move to cities. The jobs waiting there proved to be seasonal or short term as Native workers were the first to be fired due to lack of training or inexperience, and they faced discrimination from an urban society that was troubled by civil rights activism.

At the same time Indian protests called for a new era of federal-Indians relations. President Nixon understood this perspective, and his administration took action to help Native people. At the same time, qualified Native people began to be appointed to positions in the Bureau of Indian Affairs, which made Indians responsible for federal-Indian affairs. At the beginning of the 1970s, an estimated 477,000 individuals worked for the BIA. By the end of 1980, an increase of 54 percent in personnel to 734,895 indicated the enormous demands on the bureau to meet the service needs of American Indians and their tribal governments (Taylor 1984, 32).

Commissioner Louis Bruce resigned on January 20, 1973, leaving the commissioner position vacant. During this time the Interior Department reassigned the BIA from reporting to the assistant secretary for Public Land Management and created a special assistant on Indian affairs, naming Marvin Franklin, former Iowa chief and officer of Philips Petroleum Corporation. The number of BIA workers in the main office was reduced from 1,318 to 715 as many of the positions became vacant due to people being fired or transferred. In addition, the titles of key staff positions were changed from assistant commissioner to office director, causing some confusion. Morris Thompson entered as the new BIA commissioner in 1973, and he reported directly to the secretary of the Interior (Taylor 1984, 40). The Bureau of Indian Affairs had some responsibilities dispersed to other federal agencies, and many of the daily services carried out by area offices and reservation agency offices.

References

"Alaska Native Claims Settlement Act," P.L. 92-203, December 18, 1971, U.S. Statutes at Large, 85:688–92, 702–03.

Banks, Dennis with Richard Erodes, OJIBWA WARRIOR: DENNIS BANKS AND THE REST OF THE AMERICAN INDIAN MOVEMENT. Norman: University of Oklahoma Press, 2004.

Brophy, William A. and Sophie D. Aberle, comps. *The Indian: America's Unfinished Business*. Norman: University of Oklahoma Press, 1966.

Bruce, Louis. "The Bureau of Indian Affairs, 1972." In *Indian-White Relations: A Persistent Paradox*, ed. Jane F. Smith and Robert M. Kvasnicka. Washington, DC: Howard University Press, 1976.

"Criminal and Civil Jurisdiction Act," August 4, 1953, U.S. Statutes at Large, 67:588–90.

Daniel M. Cobb, NATIVE ACTIVISM IN COLD WAR AMERICIA: THE STRUGGLE FOR SOVEREIGNTY. Lawrence: University Press of Kansas, 2008.

Deer, Ada E. "Termination and the Menominee Restoration Act." In Brian Hosmer, ed. *Native Americans and the Legacy of Harry S. Truman*. Kirksville, MO. Truman State University Press. 2010.

Fixico, Donald L. *Termination and Relocation: Federal Indian Policy, 1945–1960*. Albuquerque: University of New Mexico Press, 1986.

Fixico, Donald L. THE URBAN INDIAN EXPERIENCE IN AMERICA. Albuquerque: University of New Mexico Press, 2000.

"House Concurrent Resolution 108." August 1, 1953. Box 120, Klamath Agency Files, no accession number, Reord Group 75, Federal Archives and Records Center, Seattle, WA.

"Indian Civil Rights Act." April 11, 1968. *U.S. Statutes at Large*, 82, 77–81.

"Indian Claims Commission Act," August 13, 1946, U.S. Statutes at Large, 60:1049:56.

Johnson, Lyndon B. Special Message to Congress on the Problems of the American Indian: "The Forgotten American." March 6, 1968. *Public Papers of the Presidents of the United States; Lyndon B. Johnson, 1968–69*. Washington, DC: National Records and Archives Administration. 1, 336–344.

"Klamath Termination Act," P.L. 587, August 13, 1954, U.S. Statutes at Large, 68 pt. 1:718–28.

Kvasnicka, Robert M. and Herman J. Viola, eds. *The Commissioners of Indian Affairs, 1824–1977*. Lincoln: University of Nebraska Press, 1979.

Lurie, Nancy Oestreich. "The Indian Claims Commission." *The Annals of Political and Social Science* 436 (March 1978): 97–110.

"Menominee Termination Act," P.L. 399, June 17, 1954, U.S. Statutes at Large, 68:250–52.

Nixon, Richard. "Special Message to Congress." July 8, 1970. *Public Papers of the Presidents, 1970*. Washington, DC: National Records and Archives Administration, 565–576.

Rosier, Paul C. NATIVE AMERICAN ISSUES. Westport, CN: Greenwood Press, 2003.

Taylor, Theodore W. *The Bureau of Indian Affairs*. Boulder, CO: Westview Press, 1984.

Ulrich, Roberta. AMERICAN INDIAN NATIONS FROM TERMINATION TO RESTORATION, 1953–2006. Lincoln: University of Nebraska Press, 2010.

EIGHT

Indian Self-Determination and Government to Government

In the midst of Vietnam, Watergate, and Richard Nixon's foreign diplomacy to open the doors of trade with China, Indian land returns occurred for the first time ever under any president of the United States. Nixon and his aides listened to American Indian protesters, and they understood their concerns. Furthermore, the Nixon administration laid the foundation for the prevailing policy of self-determination with significant improvement in Indian education. Indian input replaced federal paternalism, marking the Nixon era as the most pivotal in modern BIA history.

On July 8, 1970, President Nixon delivered a special message to Congress that the government would help American Indians to achieve "Self-determination . . . without the threat of eventual termination." He said that "the Indian [could] assume control over his own life without being separated involuntarily from the tribal group." In this same message, Nixon remarked, "One of the saddest aspects of Indian life in the United States is the low quality of Indian education. Drop-out rates for Indians are twice the national average and the average educational level for all Indians under Federal supervision is less than six years" (Nixon 1970). During the early 1970s, the BIA operated schools for over 50,000 Indian students. Another 750 Indian students continued to be enrolled in schools where the BIA contracted for educational services to be provided. Another 141,000 Native students attended public schools. Of that number, 89,000 Indian students were eligible to receive JOM assistance. Nixon announced that for the fiscal year 1971, Johnson O'Malley funding would be increased to $20 million (Statutes at Large 88, 2203–2217).

BIA Commissioner Louis Bruce found federal-Indian affairs to be a swirling vortex of energy, politics, ideas, and not enough funding. Yet he remained very optimistic though his job as head of the bureau proved daunting. He stated, "I have only to read my daily mail to know that no matter how hard we try or how sincere our efforts are, it is never fast enough and there is never money enough. We are fortunate if we accomplish just a little and please a few. We will keep trying as best we can for more. This is our assigned task, our solemn responsibility. Indian self-determination is going to be a complete reality not too far ahead of today, and when it is, one of the incomplete chapters of American history will then have been completed" (Bruce 1976, 250).

Land Returns and Natural Resources

The return of Taos Blue Lake to the Taos Pueblo people set an extraordinary precedent in 1970 when President Nixon signed this bill into law. Originally seized by President Theodore Roosevelt, the 48,000 acres containing the lake became a part of the Carson National Forest. Since then, the Taos Pueblo people lobbied and fought for the return of their sacred lake. During these same years, Congress passed legislation to return another sacred site, Mount Adams, to the Yakama Indians in Washington, and Nixon signed the bill into law.

Tribal lands became a growing concern as energy companies began to look at Indian reservations for their vast quantities of coal, oil, uranium, gas, and water. In the 1970s, more than half of the nation's coal rested under lands in the West. As much as one-third of the western coal existed on reservations. The Northern Cheyenne in Montana, Crow in Wyoming, Hopi in Arizona, and Navajo in the Four Corners area held large coal veins. In New Mexico the Jicarilla Apache Reservation had 154 million barrels of oil and 2 trillion cubic feet of natural gas.

In the Black Hills as many as 25 mining companies operated during these years. In the Four Corners area, strip mining for coal on the Navajo Reservation became the largest operation in the world. Peabody Coal Company, Shell, and General Electric led the list of numerous companies harvesting natural resources on tribal lands (Fixico 1998, 123–158). The pressure for natural resources put the politics of energy usage in disarray. In 1992 Congress passed the Energy Policy Act to promote energy efficiency, conservation, and management of natural gas, alternative fuels, radioactive waste, coal, and renewable energy. The rest of the 20th century witnessed the growing pressure that energy companies placed on tribal leaders for reservation resources.

As the 21st century began, American usage of fossil fuels continued at an increasing rate. President George W. Bush signed into law the Energy Policy Act in August 2005. In this lengthy act, Title V is known as the Indian

Tribal Energy and Self-Determination Act, which amended the original law passed in 1975 (*Statutes at Large* 119, 594). At the same time, the United States imported 54 percent of the crude oil that it used in the first decade of the 21st century. American Indian tribes have a little over 2 percent of the entire land in the United States, while an estimated 30 percent of the fossil fuels used in the country come from this small percentage of Indian lands.

Council of Energy Resource Tribes

In 1975, representatives from 25 tribes gathered in Washington, DC to discuss their common concerns of protecting their natural resources. Chairman Peter MacDonald of the Navajo Nation recalled the first meeting in which the representatives from the tribes met for hours and hours. MacDonald described the early effort to recognize their potential resources. Later in the meeting, the representatives elected MacDonald as the first chairman of the newly formed Council of Energy Resource Tribes (CERT). MacDonald described, "I decided to organize several tribes into a coalition I liked to call the Native American OPEC [Oil Petroleum Exporting Countries]. The coalition came about during a trip to Washington, DC, where we attempted to seek support for our efforts to evaluate our energy resources. Following our first meeting with the president's special assistant in the Department of Energy, we were told to organize ourselves in order to gain White House backing. This we did in a room assigned to us in the D.O.E" (MacDonald 1993, 228).

CERT opened its new office in 1977, and the Bureau of Indian Affairs aided in opening a mineral technical assistance center in Denver, Colorado. Initial federal support permitted 5 of the 12 needed positions to be filled (Boeth et al. 1978, 40). Soon, CERT began confronting energy companies. Since the 1920s, energy companies had obtained leases for natural resources from tribes, with the government as the tribes' trustee. In addition to dealing with energy companies and tribes, the government found itself in a pressured situation with oil-exporting countries. A foreign oil embargo caused the federal government to ration gasoline in 1979, creating long lines of cars at gasoline stations. A second gasoline shortage occurred within the next five years. The Council of Energy Resource Tribes had started with a chairman and executive board of eight tribal leaders. Within four years, CERT employed 65 people. Twenty-three CERT employees worked in the Washington office, and 42 worked in the Denver office.

In 1976 the United States celebrated its bicentennial and elected a former Navy officer and governor from Georgia to the presidency—Jimmy

Carter. As a Democrat outside of Washington's Watergate politics, Carter had a fresh start to settle into the presidency. An optimist, idealist, and believer in justice, President Carter continued the reform that Nixon had started to help Native people. The Nixon and Carter years increased the federal-Indian relations that extended beyond the Bureau of Indian Affairs as more federal agencies in the Interior Department, health service, and courts dealt with Indian issues. As American Indian families struggled during the political ridden years of the 1960s and 1970s, many Native youth became separated from their parents. In many cases, the loss of employment after relocation made it impossible for Native parents to provide for their families. Many Indian youth were removed from the custody of their parents and placed in boarding schools.

American Indian Policy Review Commission Report

In 1973, U.S. Senator James Abourezk of South Dakota proposed Senate and House Joint Resolution 133. Following several revisions, the resolution became a public law on January 3, 1975, and established a federal-Indian policy. The Indian Self-Determination and Education Act increased funding in various areas of health, business, and education and also helped tribal communities form governments in order to become self-sustaining. As a part of the act, the American Indian Policy Review Commission made a comprehensive study of conditions throughout Indian Country, which ended in 1977.

The commission consisted of congressional members and Indian representatives divided into 11 task forces addressing the status of reservations, Indian urban areas, community services, economic development, education, federal-Indian relationship, federal legislation, governance, natural resources, public policy, self-determination, socioeconomic status, taxes, treaties, tribal sovereignty, and trust responsibility. In a hurry to complete their assignments, the task forces submitted their separate reports that staff compiled into a final report of various parts. With the objective to further the development of self-determination, the commission recommended access to federal funds from other government agencies in addition to those from the BIA and Public Health Service. Recommendations also included putting the tribes in charge by allowing them to negotiate contracts with the BIA and Public Health Service to provide services to their communities.

Like previous comprehensive studies, the law charged the commission to complete field surveys for producing a report on the conditions on Indian reservations. The report strongly recommended a federal recognition procedure for new tribes. It also advocated implementing reform measures in other important areas of health, economics, and education. This congressional study laid the direction for Indian policy based on sovereignty and the federal-Indian trust relationship for the rest of the 20th century. Divided into several reports as a set of documents, this information updated the bureau, Congress, and other federal agencies with information and recommendations.

Assistant Secretary of the Interior

Another major effort in the Carter administration involved dissolving the office of commissioner of Indian Affairs and replacing it with a new position called assistant secretary of the Interior. This promotion negated the long history of the position of Indian commissioner that 47 individuals had held since 1824.

The takeover of the BIA following the Trail of Broken Treaties march to Washington had a backlash effect for the bureau. The resignation of Commissioner Louis Bruce after the takeover left the position unoccupied until the Senate confirmed the presidential appointment of 34-year old Athapascan Morris Thompson. Thompson supported Indian self-determination policies that shifted much of the BIA's power to the tribes, which entailed seeking the recommendations of the National Tribal Chairmen's Association and the National Congress of American Indians. Nixon had listened to Indians, and now the BIA supported the new policy. At the same time, Native leaders viewed the commissioner's position as second-class treatment in the power structure in Washington. Thompson resigned in November and at this time Ben Riefel, who had been appointed by President Gerald Ford, served as the last BIA commissioner. Many people expected Riefel to remain in the position during this turbulence in federal Indian affairs, but newly elected President Jimmy Carter asked for and received the commissioner's resignation on January 28, 1977.

On July 12 1977, President Carter nominated Forrest J. Gerard as assistant secretary for Indian Affairs to replace the position of commissioner of Indian Affairs. Although Gerard had the support of the National Tribal Chairmen's Association, Senator James Abourezk was not so pleased and delayed the confirmation hearings for Gerard until mid-September. The new assistant secretary received approval (Department of the Interior 1977).

This political promotion gave more power to the head of the Bureau of Indian Affairs, especially as federal-Indian relations have become more complicated since the late 1970s. The move also enabled the assistant

An American Indian rights activist noted for her fight in overturning the Menominee Termination Act of 1954, Ada Deer became the first Native woman appointed assistant secretary of Indian Affairs in the Interior Department, in 1993. (Bureau of Indian Affairs)

secretary to communicate on a more even level with other officials in the many agencies of the federal government on the behalf of the government's trust responsibilities to Native people. This position became one of five assistant secretaries of the Interior.

From 1978 to 2010, 14 persons have held the new position of assistant secretary, and all have been American Indian, with Ada Deer (Menominee) appointed July 1993 being the only Native woman ever to hold this position. With the new responsibilities for carrying out Indian policy in the hands of area offices and agencies on reservations, a United States Government Manual for 1981 and 1982 defined six main functions of the BIA in Washington:

1. Develop bureau-wide policies, programs, budgets, and justifications;
2. Develop bureau-wide legislative programs and reports;
3. Provide a liaison with other federal agencies and national Indian organizations regarding Indian programs and bureau activities;
4. Monitor and evaluate the performance of the field establishment;
5. Participate in periodic and specific management and program reviews of field operations; and
6. Advise the commissioner and director of the Office of Indian Education Programs on bureau programs, policy matters, regulations, and related matters. (Taylor 1984, 50)

The complexity of Indian activities caused the bureau to work with other federal agencies where Native affairs related to other projects and programs. Since 1980 the BIA works with eight other bureaus and offices in the Interior: Fish and Wildlife Service, Geological Survey, Bureau of Land Management, Bureau of Mines, Office of Surface Mining, National Park Service, Bureau of Reclamation, and Office of the Solicitor (Taylor 1984, 71).

American Indian Child Welfare Act

From 1958 to 1967, the Indian Adoption Project adopted 395 American Indian children and placed them in white families in Illinois, Indiana, New York, Massachusetts, Missouri, and other states in the East and Midwest. Funded by a federal contract from the Bureau of Indian Affairs and the U.S. Children's Bureau, the Child Welfare League of America administered the project.

When the Indian Adoption Project ended, the Adoption Resource Exchange of North America was founded in 1966. This organization continued the work of the Indian Adoption Project in adopting more Indian children to non-Indian families. Indian activists became concerned about the Indian youth not having a right to know their Native culture. The activists and support groups challenged the work of the two organizations and pushed to obtain legislation to stop the adoptions of American Indian children by non-Indians.

In 1978 Congress passed the American Indian Child Welfare Act. Known also as Public Law 95-608, the measure aimed for Indian children to retain their identity and culture. The law established that the child's relatives had first priority to adopt the youth. Second, other members of the same tribe had priority. An Indian family of any tribe had third priority before a non-Indian family could adopt an Indian child.

In June 2001, Shay Bilchik, Child Welfare League executive director, formally apologized for the Indian Adoption Project and put his organization on record as supporting the Indian Child Welfare Act. As quoted on a Web page entitled "The History Adoption Project," Bilchik stated: "No matter how well intentioned and how squarely in the mainstream this was at the time, it was wrong; it was hurtful; and it reflected a kind of bias that surfaces feelings of shame" (Child Welfare League 2001).

American Indian Religious Freedom Act

In the same year Congress passed the American Indian Religious Freedom Act (AIRFA) as a law and joint resolution. This law came out of the recommendations of the American Indian Policy Review Commission. Passed on August 11, 1978, the law is also known as P.L. 95-314 or AIRFA (*Statutes at Large* 92, 469).

Government officials had violated American Indian religions and denied Indians protection under the First Amendment of the U. S. Constitution. AIRFA legislation intended to protect and preserve the traditional religious rights of American Indians, Eskimos, Aleuts, and Native Hawaiians. The scope of this protection included access to sacred sites and freedom to worship in ceremonies with the usage of sacred objects.

In signing AIRFA, President Carter stated, "In the past, Government agencies and departments have on occasion denied Native Americans access to particular sites and interfered with religious practices and customs where such use conflicted with Federal regulations. In many instances, the Federal officials responsible for the enforcement of these regulations were unaware of the nature of traditional Native religious practices and, consequently, of the degree to which their agencies interfered with such practices. This legislation seeks to remedy this situation" (*Statutes at Large* 92, 469). Although the law seemed clear, it has been challenged in discussions and in communities where sacred sites are located.

Federal Acknowledgement Branch

On September 5, 1978, the Bureau of Indian Affairs published federal regulations for the federal recognition of Indian communities. This action came out of the recommendations of the American Indian Policy Review Commission Report of 1977. The action demonstrated another major Indian reform of the Carter administration, which established the Federal Acknowledgement Program.

The Office of Federal Acknowledgement (OFA) was set up in the office of the assistant secretary of the Interior. The OFA staff included anthropologists, genealogists, and historians using their professional training to review petitions by Indian groups for consideration for federal recognition as a "tribe."

Following the establishment of OFA, 82 groups submitted petitions for federal recognition. The Interior Department resolved 47, and Congress resolved 19 that also were decided in court. Another 250 groups submitted at least letters of intent to file petitions.

Oliphant v. Suquamish Indian Tribe

On March 6, 1978, in a six to two decision, the U.S. Supreme Court ruled in favor of Oliphant in the *Oliphant v. Suquamish Indian Tribe* case. The decision reversed the decision of the lower courts. This noted ruling stated that tribal courts and their officials had no authority over non-Indians arrested on their reservations. But in addition, tribal courts had no authority over non-enrolled Indians living on their reservations.

The details of the case derived from August 1973. Mark Oliphant, a non-Indian, lived as a resident with the Suquamish Tribe on the Port Madison Indian Reservation in northwest Washington. Tribal police arrested Oliphant for assaulting a tribal officer and resisting arrest. In response Oliphant filed a suit that the Suquamish Tribe had no jurisdiction over him.

With the established federal-Indian policy of Indian self-determination in 1975, the *Oliphant* case usurped tribal sovereignty to protect Mark Oliphant's legal rights. This was not the first time, although the legal gymnastics of federal courts continued to produce unpredictable results. Tribal sovereignty and self-determination would be tested again.

Santa Clara Pueblo v. Martinez

On May 15, 1978, the U.S. Supreme Court ruled in *Santa Clara Pueblo v. Martinez* that the tribe had the right to determine its tribal membership and had not violated the rights of Julia Martinez. Mrs. Martinez and her daughter Audrey Martinez had filed a suit in a federal court against the tribe, claiming that her rights as a tribal member had been violated.

The Santa Clara Pueblo tribal court had ruled that the tribe could legally deny membership to Julia Martinez and her daughter since Mrs. Martinez married a non-tribal member Sergio Martinez outside of the community. Julia Martinez had in fact married a Navajo man; thus the tribal court ruled that her membership went with her when she left Santa Clara Pueblo.

In this landmark case, the Supreme Court ruled that Santa Clara Pueblo had the right to establish its own governance over tribal members, thus upholding tribal sovereignty.

Tribal Courts

In the early 1970s the number of tribal courts began to rapidly increase, and jurisdiction over non-tribal Indians and non-Indians on reservations became a common issue of concern. Based on guidelines laid out in the Indian Reorganization Act of 1934, many tribal courts modeled their legal systems after that of the United States.

P.L. 280, passed in 1954, caused a jurisdictional shift in allowing five and then six states to have crimination and civil jurisdiction over lands within their state boundaries. At times P.L. 280 conflicted with tribal courts over jurisdiction and the prevailing federal Indian policy of self-determination as illustrated by the *Santa Clara* court case.

As a part of the Indian Self-Determination Act introduced in 1975, by the end of the decade, 16 traditional courts existed with 32 BIA-operated courts operating that addressed Indian offenses. In addition, 71 tribal courts and 15 hunting and fishing courts operated on reservation lands (Taylor 1984, 90). Tribal courts consisted of judges and court staff appointed by the tribes, and BIA-operated courts had judges and staff assigned by the government.

Indian Bingo and Casinos

Economically, tribal communities continued to struggle, and tribal leaders began to explore new ways to help their people. By the end of the 1970s, the average income for families in the nation, according to the 1980 U.S. Census, was $19,917. Native people averaged a family income of $13,724. The unemployment rate for Native people was 13.2 percent compared to 6.5 percent for the rest of society. As some Indians enjoyed privileges of the mainstream middle class, a significant portion of Indians lived in poverty (Fixico 1985, 75–87). In the 1970s, only 55 percent of Indians who were 25 years and older graduated from high school. This amount compared to 66.5 percent of all Americans. In 1980, the Census reported that 23.7 percent of Indian families lived below the poverty line (Nagel, Ward, and Knapp 1988, 40).

In mid-1979 the Seminoles of Florida began considering opening a bingo establishment. Chief James E. Billie and the Seminole Tribe negotiated an agreement with Eugene "Butch" Weisman and George Simon to locate financial backers for opening a bingo hall on the Hollywood Reservation, located north of Miami. The agreement called for a split of 45 percent to the financial backers and 55 percent to the Seminole Tribe. Plans called for a bingo hall to accommodate 1,500 players, complete with valet parking, security guards, closed-circuit television, and a large announcement board, as well as climate control. Billie and other tribal officials planned for all of this to happen on 480 acres at Stirling Road and U. S. 441 on the Hollywood Reservation. The business was scheduled to open its doors in December 1979. The price of admission was $15, but a person could also purchase chances to win from $10,000 to $110,000. Soon, bingo players came by the busloads from as far north as Jacksonville and as far west as St. Petersburg to play (Covington 1993, 254–255).

Within the first six months, the Florida Seminoles operated a successful and profitable bingo operation. An estimated 1,200 people crowded into the bingo hall, and the Seminoles learned to pamper the players with valet parking, drink service, and armed escorts to players' cars after collecting their winnings. The super jackpot ran as high as $19,000 per night. The Seminoles chartered buses to pick up players as far away as Tampa, who spent an average of $35 per night. In early July, Chief Billie speculated that the tribe would earn $1.5 million after paying 45 percent of the earnings to their financial backers, who held a partnership with the Seminole Tribe. Chief Billie commented that "Indians have historically been able to adapt to their environment," and "Generating money is now the name of the game" ("Bingo" 1980, 18). After windfall success, the Seminole Tribe opened a second bingo hall on the Brighton Reservation in November 1980.

During the first several months of the Seminoles' bingo operation, Robert Butterworth, sheriff of Broward County, encountered increased auto traffic at late hours. Butterworth filed suit against the Seminoles, arguing that the tribal bingo hall's hours of operation violated state regulations restricting bingo operations and jackpots (Covington 1980, 255).

The court case *Seminole Tribe of Florida v. Butterworth* (658 F. 2d 310 [1981]) became increasingly significant as a legal precedent for other Indian gaming rights. The court ruled that the state of Florida had no jurisdiction over the Seminoles and could not regulate Indian gaming. Other Indian nations followed soon, thereby opening bingo operations, with many people approving. Others criticized gambling as "dirty money," viewing it as unethically earned.

Cabazon Band of Missions Indians et al. v. California

On March 3, 1983, in Riverside Country in Southern California, the Cabazon Tribe of 25 enrolled members opened Cabazon Bingo Palace. For three years the Cabazon Band operated a bingo room, according to a management agreement with an outside firm. The Morongo Band of about 730 enrolled members had a similar agreement, the Morongo Band of Mission Indians Tribal Bingo Enterprise Management Agreement, in running its bingo operation.

In California the local and county governments regulated card games since they were legal. On May 6, 1983, the Riverside County Sheriff Ben Clark closed down the Cabazon gambling establishment, and Judge Laughlin E. Waters issued a preliminary injunction against the county. The Cabazon tribe received bad publicity when Wayne Reeder, Peter Zokosky, John Patrick McGuire, and Jimmy Hughes attempted a takeover of the tribe. Unfortunately, the Geraldo Rivera *20/20* show broadcasted the story. The state of California argued that it was one of the original five states under P.L. 280 that had the right of criminal and civil jurisdiction over Indian reservations within its boundaries.

In 1987 unregulated "high-stakes" bingo faced a serious test, *Cabazon Band of Mission Indians et al. v. California* (480 U.S. 202). In this case, two Indian groups, the Cabazon and Morongo Bands of Mission Indians, had opened successful bingo operations in Riverside County, California. The state of California contested the bingo operations when the Cabazon Band opened a card club, offering draw poker and other card games to the public that was predominately non-Indians.

On February 25, 1987, the U.S. Supreme Court ruled that high-stakes bingo and other gaming on Indian reservations could not be regulated by state and local governments, even if state law allowed such forms of gaming by anyone (Lane 1995, 126–127). Justice Byron White stated the ruling of the court with Chief Justice William Rehnquist and with Justices William J. Brennan, Thurgood Marshall, Harry Blackmun, and Lewis F. Powell Jr. in agreement.

Pequot and Foxwoods

One day after the Fourth of July in 1986, the Pequots opened their doors for bingo. Congressman Sam Gejdenson cut the red ribbon to officially open the bingo parlor with closed-circuit television, electronic scoreboards, and fried chicken dinners for players. Thousands of New Englanders passed through the doors to play bingo. The crowds did not stop coming to Ledyard, Connecticut, to gamble. By the end of 1987, the Pequot bingo parlor grossed $20 million a year with 25 percent accounting for pure profit. The tribal population stood at about 100 members, figuring out to be an estimated $60,000 for every man, woman, and child on the reservation (Eisler 2001, 107–110).

The man behind the growing Pequot empire was Richard "Skip" Hayward. Born the day after Thanksgiving in 1947, Skip was one of nine children of Theresa Plouffe Hayward. Theresa Plouffe had married Richard Hayward, a Navy man. While Richard Hayward served in the Navy, the family lived at Quonset Point, Rhode Island. Theresa brought her young large family to visit their grandmother on the reservation. Skip recalled the difficult conditions: cold floors, thin walls, no hot running water, and no electricity. His grandmother's house had been built in 1856. Skip's father intended for his son to attend the U.S. Naval Academy, but at the final hour, Skip believed that being in the Navy would send him to Vietnam. Upon graduation from high school in North Kingston, Rhode Island, Skip went to work for $229 a week as a pipe fitter and welder at Electric Boat, a submarine manufacturer, in Groton. During these years, Skip spent more time with his grandmother, who died on the reservation on June 6, 1973. Skip received his Indian blood from his mother's side, making him about one-sixteenth Indian (Eisler 2001, 55–56).

In the early 1990s, gaming tribes earned $1.5 to $2.5 billion annually, and by 1999 the intake had risen to over $7 billion a year. By the year 2000, a total of 212 tribes of 562 federally recognized tribes operated businesses involving Indian gaming in 24 states. At the end of the first decade of the 21st century, over 350 Indian gaming operations existed throughout Indian Country, and the Pequot operated the largest gaming facility in the world.

Indian Gaming Regulatory Act

As the holder of trust responsibilities to tribal governments, the federal government is legally obligated to protect the Indian interest. The Indian Gaming Regulatory Act of 1988 established the National Indian Gaming Commission located in Washington, DC. By law, tribes negotiate state compacts with state governments to introduce new gaming operations. These operations fall into three categories of gaming. Class I involves traditional games. Class II pertains to bingo and card games. Class III involves Las Vegas style gaming (Statutes at Large 102, 2467–88).

In 1987 President George Bush appointed Eddie Brown as assistant secretary of the department of the Interior, and he served from 1988 to 1993. An enrolled Pascua Yaqui tribal member, Brown earned a doctorate in social work from the University of Utah in 1975. Brown had also served as associate dean and director of the Center for American Studies at the George Warren Brown School of Social Work at Washington University in St. Louis. In addition, he served as executive director of the Department of Human Services for the Tohono O'odham Nation as well as the director of Arizona Department of Economic Security and chief of the Division of Social Services for the Bureau of Indian Affairs in Washington, DC.

In the capacity of assistant secretary, Eddie Brown was the first assistant secretary to respond to the 1988 Tribal Self-Governance amendment of the Indian Self-Determination and Education Assistance and the Indian Gaming Regulatory Act of 1988. Brown establish the Self-Governance Office in his office. Established a nationwide communication network, which laid the foundation for federal partnership with tribal governments. He also implemented the Tribal Governance Demonstration legislation, restructured the Office of Indian Education Programs, and his administration supervised the first state-tribal gaming compact. Brown also served

Assistant Secretary of the Interior Eddie Brown
(Pascua Yaqui, Tohono O'odham) also served
briefly as acting secretary of the interior. (Courtesy of Dr. Eddie Brown)

for several days as acting secretary of the Interior prior to Bruce Babbitt
coming to the office, making him the only Native person to serve in this
capacity at this date.

Native American Grave Protection and Repatriation Act

On November 16, 1990, Congress passed the Native American Grave Protection and Repatriation Act (NAGPRA), also known as Public Law 101-601
(Statutes at Large 104, 3048–58). The primary reasons for the passage of
this law involved the lack of enforcement in the American Indian Religious
Freedom Act of 1978. Litigators said it had no teeth to actually protect
American Indian religious rights. At the same time, Native people complained long enough to finally be heard as museums, including the Smithsonian, collected tribal artifacts and skeleton remains. Private collectors
and grave robbers stole artifacts and remains from Indian graves to make
matters worse. In addition, rock climbers and others desecrated American
Indian religious sacred sites such as Devils Tower via recreational rock
climbing that has disregarded the sacred nature of such sites for Native
people. In the early 1970s Maria Pearson began to lobby for legislation
to protect Native skeletal remains. Her engineer husband informed her
that the skeletal remains of white individuals and a Native woman and her
child were treated differently when a road construction crew uncovered
the bones in Glenwood, Iowa. The crew immediately took the white remains to be buried properly in a cemetery. Conversely, the crew took the

Indian bones away for study at a laboratory. Pearson demanded a meeting with Iowa Governor Robert D. Ray and sat outside of his office until he agreed to meet with her. When he asked what he could do for her, she replied, "You can give me back my people's bones and you can quit digging them up" (Bataille, Gradwohl and Silet 2000, 131–141). The efforts of Pearson and like-minded activists produced the Iowa Burials Protection Act of 1976. Next she pushed with others for national legislation that resulted in the Native American Graves Protection and Repatriation Act.

Since the passage of NAGPRA in 1990, the human remains of approximately 32,000 Native individuals have been returned to tribal communities. In addition, 670,000 funerary objects have been returned as well as 120,000 non-funerary objects, including 3,500 sacred objects.

The presidential election in 1992 put William J. Clinton, a Democrat, in the White House. Five hundred years after the arrival of Columbus in the Americas, Americans celebrated this event, but Indians did not. However, President Clinton's administration introduced several pieces of legislation to help Native people. In 1992 Congress passed Public Law 102-573 that amended the Indian Health Care Improvement Act, and in 1996 Congress amended Public Law 104-313 for further appropriations to fund health services.

BIA Apology to Indians and 175th Anniversary

Under President Clinton, Kevin Gover served as assistant secretary of the Interior from 1997 to 2000. A graduate of Princeton University, Gover is

Assistant Secretary of the Interior Kevin Gover (Pawnee), officially apologized to American Indians for their mistreatment on behalf of the BIA at the 175th anniversary of the BIA in the Sidney Yates Auditorium of the Interior Building. He is currently the director of the National Museum of the American Indian. (AP/Wide World Photos)

an enrolled tribal member of the Pawnee in Oklahoma. In 2003 he joined the law school faculty at Arizona State University (ASU) and served as co-founding director of the American Indian Policy Center at ASU. In 2009 he began his tenure as the second director of the National Museum of the American Indian.

On September 8, 2000 in the Sidney Yates Auditorium of the Interior Building, then-assistant secretary of the Interior Kevin Gover made a national apology to American Indians at the 175th anniversary of the founding of the Bureau of Indian Affairs. The long overdue apology was ironically made by an Indian person to Indian people and from the BIA and not from the rest of the federal government. Gover stated:

I do not speak for the United States. That is the province of the nation's elected leaders, and I would not presume to speak on their behalf. I am empowered, however, to speak on behalf of this agency, the Bureau of Indian Affairs, and I am quite certain that the words that follow reflect the hearts of its 10,000 employees. Let us begin by expressing our profound sorrow for what this agency has done in the past. Just like you, when we think of these misdeeds and their tragic consequences, our hearts break and our grief is as pure and complete as yours. We desperately wish that we could change this history, but of course we cannot. On behalf of the Bureau of Indian Affairs, I extend this formal apology to Indian people for the historical conduct of this agency. And while the BIA employees of today did not commit these wrongs, we acknowledge that the institution we serve did. We accept this inheritance, this legacy of racism and inhumanity. And by accepting this legacy, we accept also the moral responsibility of putting things right. (Gover 2000)

Following Assistant Secretary Gover's BIA apology, the bureau began to navigate more carefully as Congress passed more favorable legislation for American Indians. In 2000 Congress passed legislation that returned the Sand Creek Massacre site to the Cheyenne and Arapahoe tribes of Oklahoma. At dawn on November 29, 1864, John Chivington, a former Methodist minister, led the First and Third Colorado Cavalry, foot soldiers, and transporting cannon against Peace Chief Black Kettle's camp of Cheyenne and Arapahoe who had agreed to live on a reservation and were located there that morning. Ignoring a white flag of peace and an American flag held by the Indians, Chivington and his men massacred the Indians. Publicly,

Chivington proudly claimed a victory. Like the BIA's national apology, Congress's 2000 legislation was a way of acknowledging past federal wrongs.

On November 7, 2000, President Clinton signed the bill into law. The actual site of the massacre had to be located, and this was accomplished in August 2005. The historic site was located eight miles north of the ghost town Chivington, a few miles east of present-day Eades, Colorado.

National Museum of the American Indian Act

On November 28, 1989, Congress passed the National Museum of the American Indian Act, P.L. 101–408 (*Statutes at Large* 103, 1336). Introduced by Hawaii Senator Daniel Inouye, the bill called for the construction of the National Museum of the American Indian on the Smithsonian Mall in Washington, DC.

In the process, the law called for an inventory of the massive holdings of the Heye Foundation's collection. George Gustav Heye was a private collector in the late 1800s who collected indigenous artifacts from all over the Western Hemisphere, and he created the Museum of the American Indian in 1916 in New York City. The inventory results recorded that the Smithsonian had an estimated 4,000 American Indian remains that the Surgeon General of the United States Army had requested army medical officers to collect and send to the Army Medical Museum. The Smithsonian had also acquired about 14,000 additional Indian remains. The donation of the Heye Foundation added 800,000 artifacts to the Smithsonian American Indian collections that included items from all over the Western Hemisphere.

In 2004 the Smithsonian's National Museum of the American Indian held its grand opening full of activities for an entire week. With its architecture of a mesa design from the Southwest, the National Museum of the American Indian has no right angles in its outer shape. The museum began with its first director, Richard West Jr., and has been directed since 2009 by Kevin Gover, former assistant secretary of the Interior.

Congressional National Apology to American Indians

Following Assistant Secretary Gover's BIA apology to Indians, Kansas Senator Sam Brownback began to plan a national apology to the Native people of the United States. He asked the advice of other congressmen, Native groups, Director Donald Fixico of the Center of Indigenous Nations Studies at the University of Kansas, and others about his idea regarding a national apology. After discussing and forming the apology with Senators Ben Nighthorse Campbell of Colorado and Daniel Inouye of Hawaii, Brownback introduced Senate Joint Resolution 37 on May 6, 2004, the national day of prayer, in Washington.

On December 19, 2009, President Barack Obama signed Brownback's apology resolution into law as section 8113 of the 2010 Defense Appropriation Act also known as Public Law 111-118. The apology states:

> Section 8113—States that the United States, acting through Congress: (1) recognizes that there have been years of official depredations, ill-conceived policies, and the breaking of covenants by the federal government regarding Indian tribes; (2) apologizes on behalf of the people of the United States to all Native Peoples for the many instances of violence, maltreatment, and neglect inflicted upon them by U.S. citizens; (3) urges the President to acknowledge such wrongs; and (4) commends state governments that have begun reconciliation efforts and encourages all state governments to work toward reconciling their relationships with Indian tribes within their boundaries. ("Native American Apology Resolution," 2010)

Cobell v. Salazar Case

The greatest blunder in American Indian history to this date was exposed in the *Cobell* court case, known as *Cobell v. Salazar*. Elouise Cobell, a Blackfeet banker for her tribe in Montana began to realize that the government had problems accounting for the funds it held in trust for American Indians. She filed suit on June 10, 1996, with Mildred Cleghorn, Thomas Maulson, and James Louis Larose. The case has been known at various times as *Cobell v. Babbitt*, *Cobell v. Norton*, *Cobell v. Kempthorne*, and also *Cobell v. Salazar*.

In 2009 a federal court reached a final settlement in the *Cobell* case. The suit claimed that the U.S. government mismanaged individual Indians' trust accounts and could not tell the individuals what had happened to their monies. According to the Cobell Settlement web page, the settlement called for the federal government to create a $1.4 billion accounting/trust administration fund and a $2 billion trust land consolidation fund. President Obama signed the settlement legislation into law. In addition the settlement created an Indian Education Scholarship fund of up to $60 million to improve access to higher education for American Indians.

The final repercussions of *Cobell* are yet to be seen, but it has made the federal government and the Bureau of Indian Affairs much more accountable for monies involved in the overall trust relationship with American Indians and American Indian tribes.

Conclusion

By the end of 2010, 95 percent of the Bureau of Indian Affairs' 12,000 employees were American Indian or Alaska Native. The BIA has 12 regional offices with 83 agencies throughout Indian Country. These offices and agencies serve 564 tribes on 326 federal reserved land areas (reservations, *rancherias*, pueblos, villages, and communities) covering about 87,000 square miles (or about 2.3% of the United States) in 33 states.

The history of the Bureau of Indian Affairs from its beginning in 1824 to this date of 2011 involved 47 commissioners and 14 assistant secretaries of the Interior. With each new Indian policy, the job of the BIA became more daunting, resting on the shoulders of the commissioners and now the assistant secretaries. Although many incompetent individuals were repaid political favors and received appointments as BIA commissioner, since the Grant administration the office has had heads of the BIA that have taken their job very seriously. These years included when the United States fought against Indian tribes. They also included the military wanting the BIA back in the War Department in the late 1800s, missionary involvement from the mid-1800s to the early decades of the 20th century, and activist

Larry Echo Hawk (Pawnee), head of the Bureau of Indian Affairs, appointed by President Obama in 2009 as Assistant Secretary of the Interior. He is an attorney, legal scholar and former Attorney General of Idaho. (U.S. Department of the Interior)

Indians in the 1960s and 1970s recommending their own Indian policy for the bureau.

At the individual level in the self-determination era, the bureau succeeded in providing education for numerous Indian students from K–12 to higher education. According to the Department of the Interior Indian Affairs website, as of July 31, 2007, the Indian and Alaska Native population, including those of more than one race, was 4.5 million with over 1.9 million enrolled tribal members. The bureau worked with the emerging tribal colleges and continues to do this in a partner-to-partner relationship that is positive. More progress needs to be made, but tribes are more in control of educating their own communities and are able to provide scholarships with BIA assistance to individuals attending public and private universities or colleges. In the United States the average family income had risen by the end of the twentieth century. In 2008 the average income for the American Indian family was $33,627 compared to the American family income average of $46,326, according to the U.S. Office of Minority Health website.

In many ways, the Indian Problem of poverty on reservations reached resolution, and new challenges faced the bureau toward the end of the 20th century. Indian affairs had entered a new era of self-determination as a federal policy, but tribes endeavored to sustain their tribal sovereignty and viewed it as an important issue to them. Many tribes had prospered from Indian gaming and stood on their own, well above the rest of the tribes. In the 21st century, government-to-government relations exist between the federal government and tribes with the Bureau of Indian Affairs remaining as a liaison with much hard work ahead to achieve progress and prosperity for American Indians.

References

"American Indian Religious Freedom Act." August 11, 1978. P.L. 95-341. *U.S. Statutes at Large*, 92.

"Bingo Is the Best Revenge." *Time*, July 7, 1980.

Boeth, Richard et al. "A Paleface Uprising." *Newsweek*, April 10, 1978.

Bruce, Louis. "The Bureau of Indian Affairs, 1972." In *Indian-White Relations: A Persistent Paradox*, ed. Jane F. Smith and Robert M. Kvasnicka. Washington, DC: Howard University Press, 1976.

Child Welfare League website. Statement by Shay Bilchik, June 2001. http://www.cwla.org/. Accessed October 11, 2011.

Cobell v. Salazar Class Action website. http://www.cobellsettlement.com. Accessed July 19, 2010.

Covington, James W. *The Seminoles of Florida*. Gainesville: University Press of Florida, 1993.

Department of the Interior News Release, July 12, 1977.

Eisler, Kim Isaac. *Revenge of the Pequots: How a Small Native American Tribe Created the World's Most Profitable Casino.* New York: Simon and Schuster, 2001.

Fixico, Donad L. THE INVASTION OF INDIAN COUNTRY IN THE TWENTIETH CENTURY. Niwot, CO: University Press of Colorado, 1998.

Fixico, Donald L. "Modernization and the Native American Middle-Class." In *Sharing a Heritage*, special edition of *American Indian Culture and Research Journal, Contemporary American Indian Issues Series*, No. 5 (1985): 75–87.

Gover, Kevin. "Remarks of the Assistant Secretary-Indian Affairs, Department of the Interior at the Ceremony Acknowledging the 175th Anniversary of the Establishing of the Bureau of Indian Affairs" (National Apology for the Bureau of Indian Affairs), September 8, 2000, Box 13, Folder 2, Clinton Administration History Project, William Clinton Presidential Library, Little Rock, AK.

"The History Adoption Project." http://www.uoregon.edu/~adoption/topics/IAP.html. Accessed July 31, 2010.

"Indian Gaming Regulatory Act," P.L. 100-497, October 17, 1988, U.S. Statutes at Large, 102:2467–88.

"Indian Tribal Energy and Self Determination Act." August 8, 2005, as Title V of the Energy Policy Act, P.L. 109-58. *U.S. Statutes at Large*, 119.

Lane, Ambrose I., Sr. *Return of the Buffalo: The Story Behind America's Indian Gaming Explosion.* Westport, CT: Bergin and Garvey, 1995.

MacDonald, Peter with Ted Schwarz. *The Last Warrior: Peter MacDonald and the Navajo Nation.* New York: Orbis Books, 1993.

Nagel, Joane, Carol Ward, and Timothy Knapp. "The Politics of American Indian Economic Development: The Reservation/Urban Nexus." In *Public Policy Impacts on American Indian Economic Development*, ed. Matthew Snipp. Albuquerque, NM: Native American Studies Institute for Native American Development, 1988.

"National Museum of the American Indian Act." P.L. 101-185. November 28, 1989. *U.S. Statutes at Large*, 103, 1336.

"Native American Apology Resolution." P.L. 111-118. December 19, 2009. *U.S. Statutes at Large*, 123.

"Native American Graves Protection and Repatriation Act," P.L. 101-601, November 16, 1990, U.S. Statutes at Large, 104 pt. 4:3048-58.

Nixon, Richard. "Special Message to Congress." July 8, 1970. *Public Papers of the Presidents, 1970.* Washington, DC: National Records and Archives Administration.

The Office of Minority Health in the U.S. Department of Health and Human Services. http://www.hhs.gov. Accessed September 2, 2010.

Pearson, Maria D. "Give me Back my People's Bones: Repatriation and Reburial of American Indian Skeletal Remains in Iowa." In THE WORLDS BETWEEN TWO RIVERS: PERSPECTIVES ON AMERICAN INDIANS IN IOWA, edited by Gretchen Bataille, David Gradwohl and Charles L.P. Silet. (Iowa City: University of Iowa Press, 2000), 2nd edition, 131–141.

Public Law No. 638. June 4, 1936 (49 Stat. 1458; 25 U.S.C. 452–455).

Taylor, Theodore W. *The Bureau of Indian Affairs.* Boulder, CO: Westview Press, 1984.

The U.S. Department of the Interior Indian Affairs. http://www.bia.gov/FAQs/index.html. Accessed September 2, 2010.

Biographies of
Key Figures

Adams, Hank (1943–)

Hank Adams is an Assiniboine-Sioux and was born on the Fort Peck Indian Reservation in Montana at a place called Wolf Point, commonly referred to as Poverty Flats. He resisted being drafted into the army but reluctantly served. Following his service, he became involved in the struggle for Native fishing and treaty rights in the state of Washington during the 1960s. As a political activist, he helped to organize a march on the Washington State capitol in 1964. In 1968 he became the founding director of Survival of American Indians Association to fight for Indian fishing rights. He participated in the Trail of Broken Treaties March to Washington in 1972 where he helped develop the Twenty Points presented to the Richard Nixon administration. Adams also participated in the Wounded Knee takeover in 1973 and participated in the final negotiations that ended the 73-day occupation.

Banks, Dennis (1937–)

Born on the Leach Lake Reservation in northern Minnesota, Dennis Banks is an Anishinabee. He attended a boarding school and served in the U.S. Air Force. In 1968 he cofounded the American Indian Movement with Clyde Bellecourt and George Mitchell. As a leader of AIM, he helped to organize the Trail of Broken Treaties March in 1972 and participated in the takeover of the BIA in Washington. He also was instrumental in leading the takeover of Wounded Knee in 1973. He was arrested and tried for his activism in 1974, but all charges were dismissed in 1985. From 1976 to 1983, he earned an associate of arts degree at University of California, Davis, and he served as the first American Indian chancellor at Deganawide Quetzecoatl (DQ) University. Banks believes that running is an important part of Native life for good health and well-being, which led him to organize the Great Jim Thorp Longest Walk, a spiritual run from New York to Los Angeles.

Bellecourt, Clyde (1936–)

Clyde Bellecourt and his brother Vernon are Anishinabee from the White Earth Indian Reservation in northern Minnesota. They are among 11 siblings. Clyde attended Benedictine Missionary School and was later sent to a reform school in Red Wing, Minnesota. At age 16, his family moved to Minneapolis as a part of the BIA relocation program. In 1968 he cofounded the American Indian Movement with Dennis Banks and George Mitchell and served as the first AIM chairman. He participated in the Trail of Broken Treaties March and the BIA takeover in 1972 as well as the occupation of Wounded Knee in 1973. In the 1980s, Bellecourt helped to establish the International Indian Treaty Council, which focused on Nicaragua's civil war between Marxist Sandistas and right-wing Contras. In 1993 AIM split, and Bellecourt established the National American Indian Movement. In 1999 Bellecourt helped to lead the protest of two murdered American Indians in White Clay, Nebraska, and he continues to be an Indian rights activist in the 21st century.

Bennett, Robert L. (1912–2002)

Robert Bennett served as the second American Indian to hold the position of commissioner of Indian Affairs when President Lyndon Johnson appointed him in 1966. He served three years as commissioner but had a long career with the Bureau of Indian Affairs. From 1933 to 1938, he worked at the BIA agency on the Ute Reservation in Utah; for the following five years, he worked at the BIA in Washington, DC. During World War II, Bennett served in the U.S. Marine Corps and directed training programs for Indian veterans in Phoenix, Arizona. From 1949 to 1951, he returned to the bureau as a job placement officer in Aberdeen and was reassigned to the Washington, DC, office for the next three years before returning to Utah as Superintendent of Consolidated Ute Agency at Ignacio, Colorado. From 1956 to 1962, Bennett served as assistant director of the Aberdeen Area Office and as area director of Indian Affairs for the Alaska Region from 1962 to 1965.

Blount, William (1749–1800)

Born in Bertie County, North Carolina, to an elite family of merchants and planters, Blount rose to leadership in the American Revolution. Afterward he served in the North Carolina state assembly from 1780 to 1784 and 1788 to 1790, and as a delegate to the Continental Congress. He interceded to help negotiations with the Cherokee during these years and became Governor of the newly formed territory south of the Ohio River. He was appointed Superintendent of Indian Affairs for the Southern District, which he served from 1790 to 1796. During these years, he negotiated the Treaty of Holston with the Cherokee, also known as the Blount Treaty. In 1796 Blount was elected to the U.S. Senate of the new state of Tennessee. In 1797 Blount was discovered to be involved in a plot to incite the Cherokee and Creek to aid the British to take over Spanish territory in West Florida. He was expelled from the Senate, and impeachment proceedings started, but they were dismissed. Blount returned to Tennessee as a hero and became Presiding Officer of the state Senate.

Boldt, George (1903–1984)

In 1974 Judge George Boldt decided one of the most important Indian fishing rights cases that set a precedent for future cases in federal courts. His decision settled in favor of rights for the regional tribes in Washington based on the Treaty of Medicine Creek in 1854. This case is *United States v. Washington*, better known as the Boldt Decision. Boldt was born in Chicago, Illinois, and graduated from the University of Montana. He earned his LLB degree from the University of Montana Law School. In 1953 the U.S. Senate confirmed his appointment to the U.S. District Court for the Western District of Washington.

Brown, Edward F. (1945–)

Eddie Brown was appointed by President George Bush to serve as Assistant Secretary of the Department of the Interior and served from 1988 to 1993. In this capacity, Brown established a nationwide communication network that laid the foundation for federal partnership with tribal governments, implemented the Tribal Governance Demonstration legislation, and restructured the Office of Indian Education Programs. An enrolled Pascua Yaqui tribal member, Brown earned a doctorate in Social Work from the University of Utah in 1975. He has also served as associate dean and director of the Center for American Studies at the George Warren Brown School of Social Work at Washington University in St. Louis, Missouri. In addition, he served as executive director of the Department of Human Services for the Tohono O'odham Nation, the director of Arizona Department of

Economic Security, and as chief of the Division of Social Services for the BIA in Washington, DC. From 2004 to 2011, Brown served as the director of American Indian Studies at Arizona State University.

Burke, Charles (1861–1944)

Burke was born on a farm near Batavia in Genesee County, New York. In 1882 he moved to Dakota Territory and settled in Beadle County where he studied law. He was admitted to the bar in 1886. Burke was elected to the House of Representatives in 1895 and 1897. In Indian affairs, he amended the Dawes Allotment Act with the Burke Act of 1906, which shortened the 25-year period for Indian allottees, resulting in much more land being lost. Burke served as commissioner of Indian Affairs from 1921 to 1929. He believed in the forced assimilation of Indians and the suppression of their cultures. As commissioner, he opened reservation land to white settlement and petroleum as well as mineral resource business. He faced criticism, and the Meriam Report of 1928 confirmed that Indian conditions had not improved while he was in office.

Calhoun, John C. (1782–1850)

Calhoun was a prominent politician from South Carolina, and his Scottish and Irish father was an Indian fighter, named Patrick Calhoun, who was a landowner, legislator, anti-Federalist, and slave owner. John C. Calhoun served as the seventh vice president of the United States from 1825–1832, under John Quincy Adams and Andrew Jackson. He served as secretary of war from 1817 to 1825, leading to his vice presidency. Secretary of War Calhoun represented the federal government in relations with Indians. In 1824 he created the Indian Office within the War Department. He appointed Thomas McKenney as the first director of Indian Affairs. Calhoun believed that eastern Indian groups should be removed to the West, and he agreed with Jackson's Indian removal policy. He served as secretary of state from 1844 to 1845 under President John Tyler.

Cass, Lewis (1782–1866)

Cass was born in Exeter, New Hampshire, and educated at Exeter Academy. In 1799 he moved to Ohio and began a legal and political career. In 1813 and 1814 he served in the army at the rank of brigadier general. During this time, President Madison appointed Cass as governor of Michigan

Territory, and he served until 1831. Indian affairs became a part of his responsibility, and he negotiated the Treaty of St. Mary's of 1818, the Saginaw Treaty of 1819, and the Treaty of Sault St. Marie in 1820. President Andrew Jackson appointed Cass as secretary of war in 1831, and Cass served as American ambassador to France in 1836. In 1845 Cass was elected to the U.S. Senate, and he was nominated for the presidency by the Democrat Party in 1848, but he lost to Zachary Taylor. He held his Senate seat until 1857 when he became secretary of state, and he retired in 1860.

Clark, William (1770–1838)

Clark was one of nine children on a plantation in Caroline County in Virginia. He had little education, and his family moved to Kentucky where he joined the militia and became a lieutenant of infantry. He partnered with Meriwether Lewis to explore the Louisiana Purchase in 1803. From 1807 to 1838, Clark represented the United States in 37 treaties negotiated with Indians. During this time he served as Missouri's first territorial governor from 1813 to 1820. Clark was appointed as superintendent of Indian Affairs, which was headquartered at St. Louis, Missouri. He presided at the Peace Treaty of Prairie du Chein in 1825 and negotiated with Black Hawk and Keokuk after the Black Hawk War of 1832.

Cobell, Elouise (1946–2011)

Cobell is a member of the Blackfeet Nation and was born in Browning, Montana. She graduated from Great Falls Business College and attended Montana State University where she was later awarded an honorary doctorate. She founded the Blackfeet National Bank, the first national bank located on a reservation and owned by an American Indian tribe. She also helped to form the Blackfeet Reservation Development Fund, Inc., and is involved in the Individual Indian Monies Trust Correction and Recovery Project to reform the government's management of Indian trust assets. She is the executive director of the Native American Community Development Corporation, a nonprofit affiliate of the Native American Bank. In 1996, Cobell served as the leading plaintiff in the class action lawsuit against the U.S. government, originally known as *Cobell v. Norton*, then *Cobell v. Babbit*, then *Cobell v. Kempthorne*, and finally *Cobell v. Salazar*, resulting in 13 years in court and the largest Indian court settlement ever: in December 2009, $3.4 billion was awarded for mismanagement of Indian trust funds.

Cohen, Felix (1907–1953)

Cohen was born in Manhattan, New York. He earned a doctorate in philosophy from Harvard University and a law degree from Columbia University. He is credited for drafting the Indian Reorganization Act of 1934, and he drafted the Indian Claims Commission Act of 1946. From 1933 to 1947 he served as assistant solicitor for the Department of the Interior and worked with Commissioner John Collier. He is also known for writing and publishing the *Handbook on Federal Indian Law*. In his later years, he taught at Yale Law School and City College of New York. He also worked in private practice, largely on behalf of American Indians.

Collier, John (1884–1968)

Collier grew up in Atlanta, Georgia, and was educated at Columbia University. He also attended the Collége de France in Paris. In his early years, he worked as a social worker in New York and moved to Taos, New Mexico, where he learned about Indians. He helped to establish the American Indian Defense Association and served as its executive secretary. He helped to defeat the Bursum bill that threatened to give irrigated lands to white squatters on Pueblo communities in New Mexico. President Franklin Roosevelt appointed him as commissioner of Indian Affairs, and he served from 1933 to 1945 during which time he ushered in the Indian New Deal. He was instrumental in engineering the Indian Reorganization Act, known also as the Wheeler-Howard Act. This act stopped allotments to Indians and allowed them to reorganize themselves as governments and maintain economic control over their affairs. In 1940 he attended a conference that led to the establishing of the Inter-American Indian Institute, and he served as president of the organization until 1946.

Dawes, Henry L. (1816–1903)

Born in Cummington, Massachusetts, Dawes received his education at Yale University. He studied law and was admitted to the Massachusetts bar in 1842. In 1848 he was elected to the Massachusetts State House of Representatives with reelections in 1849 and 1852, and he served in the State Senate in 1850. He served as district attorney for the western district of Massachusetts from 1853 to 1857 and became a Republican member of the House of Representatives, serving from 1857 to 1875. He was elected to the U.S. Senate from 1875 to 1893. He sponsored what is known as the Dawes

Act in 1887. In 1895 he served as the chairman of the Dawes Commission to the Five Civilized Tribes to persuade tribal members to accept provisions of the law.

Deer, Ada E. (1935–)

Deer was born in Keshena on the Menominee Reservation in northeastern Wisconsin. The first 18 years of her life was spent in a one-room cabin without running water and electricity. She received a college education at the University of Wisconsin–Madison, and earned a master's degree in social work from Columbia University in 1961. She worked as a social worker, Peace Corps volunteer, and BIA service coordinator. She attended one semester of law school at the University of Wisconsin–Madison, but withdrew to help form the Determination of the Rights and Unity of Menominee Shareholders in 1970. She led the movement for the Menominee Restoration Act of 1973. In 1992 President Bill Clinton appointed Deer assistant secretary of the Interior over Indians Affairs, and she has been the only Native woman to ever hold this position. Afterward, she returned to the University of Wisconsin–Madison, where she became a lecturer and director of American Indian Studies.

Gover, Kevin (1955–)

Kevin Gover served as assistant secretary of the Interior from 1997 to 2000. Prior to his presidential appointment, he practiced law in Washington, DC, and in Albuquerque, New Mexico. He holds a law degree from the University of New Mexico and an undergraduate degree from Princeton University. Gover is an enrolled tribal member of the Pawnee in Oklahoma. In 2003, he joined the law school faculty at Arizona State University (ASU) and was a cofounding director of the American Indian Policy Center at ASU. In 2009, he began serving as the second director of the National Museum of the American Indian. As assistant secretary of the Interior, he made the first national apology by the BIA to American Indians for the long history of mistreatment of Indians, at the BIA's 175th anniversary ceremony.

Hawkins, Benjamin (1754–1816)

Benjamin Hawkins was born in North Carolina. He attended the College of New Jersey, which later became Princeton. He left during his last year and joined the Continental Army. Receiving a commission as a Colonel, he served several years on George Washington's staff with his primary duty as an interpreter of French. In 1789, Hawkins was elected as a delegate to the North Carolina convention that ratified the U.S. Constitution, and he served in the first U.S. Senate until 1795. In the same year, Hawkins participated in negotiations with the Muscogee Creek Indians that led to the Treaty of New York of 1785. Hawkins advocated civilization for the southern Indians and for them to advance their farming skills. He kept journals about the Creek language and culture that were later donated to the American Philosophical Society. As the agent to the Creeks, he helped to maintain nearly 20 years of peace until the Creek Civil War of 1813–1814. Hawkins helped Major William McIntosh by persuading loyal Creeks to fight for the United States. The final conflict, ending at the Battle of Horseshoe Bend, resulted in the decline of the Creek confederacy with the Treaty of Fort Jackson in August 1814.

Hitchcock, Ethan Allen (1798–1870)

Hitchcock was born in Vergennes, Vermont. He attended the U.S. Military Academy and fought in the Second Seminole War that lasted from 1835 to 1842. Hitchcock served in the military from 1817 to 1855 and from 1862 to 1867. The federal government asked Hitchcock to investigate the expenses of the removal of tribes from the east to Indian Territory. He discovered that the government contracted with private companies owned by friends of those in government. The Hitchcock Report revealed that contractors had short-weighted the removal parties, supplied them with spoiled meat, and bad grain. He kept a journal during his investigation and found evidence of bribery, perjury, forgery, and other tactics used to manipulate government monies and supplies that were promised to the Indian removal parties through treaty provisions. Hitchcock served briefly as the chairman of the War Board in 1862, and he also produced several published works, including *Remarks upon Alchemy and Alchemists* (1857), *Christ the Spirit* (1861), *Remarks on the Sonnets of Shakespeare* (1867), *Fifty Years in Camp and Field* (1909), and *A Traveler in Indian Territory: The Journal of Ethan Allen Hitchcock, Late Major-General in the United States Army* (1930).

Jerome, David H. (1829–1896)

Born in Detroit, Michigan, Jerome, an Episcopalian, started out as a merchant. He was also a Republican and spent much of the 1860s in the Michigan Senate. From 1876 to 1881, he served on the U.S. Board of Indian

Commissioners and as governor of Michigan in 1880. After being defeated for reelection as governor, Jerome received an appointment to chair the Cherokee Commission, also known as the Jerome Commission. His commission met with nearly 20 tribes, focusing initially on the Cherokee. The commission negotiated the opening of the Cherokee Outlet for settlement. Tactics used by the commission later led to tribal claims for lands lost to the Indian Claims Commission after 1946; this resulted in $41 million paid to those tribes in Oklahoma.

Johnson, William (1715–1774)

Born in Ireland, Johnson came to the province of New York as a young man to manage an estate purchased by his uncle. He became very influential in relations with the Iroquois during the French and Indian War. He learned to speak Mohawk, married a Mohawk woman, and recruited many Iroquois to British interests, earning him a baronet title. For his continued representation of British interests, he became Sir William Johnson. In 1756 he was commissioned as superintendent of Indian affairs for the northern colonies, and he served in this capacity until his death.

Knox, Henry (1750–1806)

Knox was born in Boston, Massachusetts, and he was a self-educated man. At age 18, he joined the local militia and became a general in the Continental Army and Chief of Artillery. He became secretary of war under the Articles of Confederation in 1785, and he served as secretary of war again in 1789. Knox negotiated with Joseph Brant of the Six Nations to end border disputes that continued after the Treaty of Paris, which ended the American Revolutionary War. He also participated in negotiations with the Creek and Cherokee and settled conflicts on the frontier with the Miami Indians in the Old Northwest Territory. Knox believed in first attempting to civilize Indians but in using force if necessary.

Lea, Luke (1810–1898)

Born in Grainger County in Tennessee, Lea helped to create the federal reservation system for the BIA to supervise. He was first appointed as an Indian agent at Fort Leavenworth in Kansas. Lea served as commissioner of Indian Affairs from 1850 to 1853. He played an important role in the negotiation of several treaties, including the Treaty of Fort Laramie in 1851.

He believed in the assimilation of Indians and that they had to be civilized to be ready to enter mainstream society.

Leupp, Francis (1849–1918)

Leupp was born in New York and received his education at Williams College. He became a journalist and later served as Washington's agent in the Indian Rights Association from 1895 to 1898. In 1905 President Theodore Roosevelt appointed him commissioner of Indian Affairs, and he served until 1909. Generally, Leupp worked to make treaties obsolete. However, he believed in treating Native people as individuals, not as members of a tribe. In 1910 he published THE INDIAN AND HIS PROBLEM about poverty on reservations and in 1914 he published, *Red Man's Land: A Study of the American Indian*, which explained treaty negotiations complicated by dishonest interpreters, translation difficulties, and the Native people's ignorance of the U.S. treaty process.

Marshall, John (1755–1835)

Marshall was born near Germantown on the Virginia frontier. He studied law at the College of William and Mary and was admitted to the bar in 1780. From 1782 to 1789 and 1795 to 1796, Marshall served in the Virginia House of Delegates. In 1788 he was elected to the Virginia Convention to debate the decision on ratification of the Constitution, and he led the fight for it. In 1801 President John Adams appointed Marshall as Chief Justice of the United States. He made landmark rulings involving Indian affairs in *Johnson v. M'Intosh* (1823), *Cherokee Nation v. Georgia* (1831), and *Worcester v. Georgia* (1832).

McKenney, Thomas L. (1824–1830)

Born into a prosperous family in Maryland, McKenney was influenced by his Quaker mother, although he was not officially a Quaker. During the War of 1812, McKenney served in local militias and reached the rank of Major. McKenney became the first unofficial head of Indian Affairs. Prior to taking charge of the Indian Office, McKenney served as superintendent of Indian Trade from 1816 to 1822. In 1822, Congress dissolved the U.S. Indian Trade Program. McKenney's influence grew in Washington as he seemed to be the individual who knew the most about Native people. In 1824, Secretary of War John C. Calhoun appointed McKenney to take charge of the newly created BIA. McKenney negotiated a series of removal treaties with several Native groups, and he believed in an educational program for Native youth. McKenney has been referred to as the father of federal services to Native people for bringing order to Indian relations.

Meriam, Lewis (1883–1972)

Meriam was born in Salem, Massachusetts. He earned degrees in English and government from Harvard University. In addition, Meriam earned law degrees from the National Law School and George Washington University as well as a PhD from the Brookings Institute. In 1926, Interior Secretary Hubert Work selected Meriam to lead a team of experts to study the federal-Indian policy of land allotment and conditions in Indian Country. The final result was the Meriam Report, officially known as *The Problem of Indian Administration*, released in 1928. The report of 847 pages consisted of eight sections of general policy; health; education; economic conditions; family and community life; and activities of women; migrated Indians; legal aspects of the Indian Problem; and missionary activities among Indians. Basically the report concluded that the allotment program had failed and recommended a new policy to take its place.

Myer, Dillon S. (1891–1982)

From Hebron, Ohio, Myer earned a bachelor's degree at Ohio State University and a master's degree from Columbia University. Throughout the New Deal, he worked at various government jobs. In 1941 he received an appointment as Director of the War Relocation Authority that relocated about 110,000 Japanese and Japanese American from their West Coast homes to internment camps. Afterward, he was appointed Commissioner of Indian Affairs by President Harry Truman. Under Myer, the Federal Indian Relocation Program began in 1951 and received its first applicants the following year.

Oakes, Richard (1942–1972)

Oakes was a Mohawk from Akwesasne, New York. At age 16, he became a high steel worker like a lot of his relatives and friends from the reservation. He traveled doing iron work in various cities and arrived in San Francisco in the early 1960s. Soon after, Oakes married his wife from the Pomo Nation and started a family. In the spring of 1969, he was asked to lead the White Roots of Peace, a Native organization that encouraged Indian youth to assert their sovereign rights with pride. In 1969, Oakes led a small group of Native activists in taking over Alcatraz Island, an abandoned federal prison. Oakes and others planned to start an Indian cultural center on the island, with a radio station to broadcast Indian issues and concerns, among other activities; the center was to become a focal point for Indian activism. In 1972 he got into an argument while defending Indian boys, and a YMCA camp manager shot him to death. The charges against the murderer, Michael Morgan, were dropped. The death of Oakes became a rallying point that helped to spark the Trail of Broken Treaties March in 1972.

Parker, Ely S. (ca. 1828–1859)

Parker was a Seneca Indian from the Seneca Reservation in upstate New York. He was elected leader of the Iroquois Nation in 1853. Parker's family had a history of loyalty to the United States. His father, William Parker, fought for the United States in the War of 1812 and was wounded. Parker attended a missionary school and later earned a law degree. Due to racial prejudice, Parker was banned from taking the bar exam. He then earned an engineering degree and worked on the Erie Canal and the Albemarle and Chesapeake Canal. Secretary of War William H. Seward disallowed him from joining the Union Army. But with the help of Grant, Parker did join the army, and he enlisted as a captain in 1863. For his loyalty to General Grant and his expertise, Parker served as the advisor to the general on Indian Affairs from 1865 to 1871. Grant named Parker as commissioner of Indian Affairs in 1869, and he served for two years. Parker was the first American Indian to serve as Commissioner of Indian Affairs.

Pike, Albert (1809–1891)

Pike was an attorney, soldier, writer, and Freemason from Boston. He went to school in Newburyport and Framingham. He was admitted to Harvard University but chose not to enter. Later he became a school teacher. He moved to Arkansas in 1833, studied law, and was admitted to the bar in 1837. Pike served in the Mexican-American War and was at the Battle of Buena Vista. In the Civil War, Pike was commissioned as a brigadier general in 1861 for the South. He was given command over Indian Territory, present-day Oklahoma. As a means to obtain more troops for the Confederacy and to disallow the Indian nations from joining the North, Pike was authorized to negotiate a series of treaties with Native leaders. In these agreements, known as the Pike treaties, the various nations in Indian Territory agreed to fight for the Confederacy.

Pratt, Richard (1840–1924)

From Rushford, New York, Pratt began a military career by enlisting in the Ninth Indiana Volunteer Infantry in the Civil War. Afterward, he returned to his home in Logansport, Indiana. He married and ran a hardware store for two years, then entered the military again in March 1867 as a second lieutenant in the Tenth U.S. Cavalry. He was in charge of an African American regiment that became known as the Buffalo Soldiers. He served in the Washita campaign of 1868–1869 and in the Red River War of 1874–1875. The military placed him in charge of Kiowa, Comanche, and Cheyenne prisoners at Fort Marion in St. Augustine, Florida, from 1875–1878. At Fort Marion, Pratt authorized giving military uniforms to the Native prisoners. He ordered the Indians' hair to be cut. Pratt also ordered the Indians to be given lessons in English, Christianity, and white civilization. Pratt believed that Indians could be changed with new surroundings. In 1879 Richard Henry Pratt received permission to use abandoned army barracks in Carlisle, Pennsylvania, to be converted into his Indian school. Carlisle Indian Industrial School became a model for other Indian off-reservation schools. From his experiences, Pratt wrote *Battlefield and Classroom: Four Decades with the American Indian, 1867–1904*, first published in 1964.

Taylor, Nathaniel Green (1819–1887)

Born in Happy Valley, Tennessee, Taylor attended private schools and Washington College Academy. He graduated from Princeton College, studied law, and was admitted to the bar in 1841. Taylor entered politics as a Whig and served in the U.S. House of Representatives in 1854 and 1855. President Andrew Johnson appointed Taylor to be Commissioner of Indian Affairs, and he served from 1867 to 1869. As Commissioner, he recommended an intensified program of tribal consolidation on reservations in his report, "Indian Hostilities on the Frontier." He believed that a strong acculturation program should begin once the tribes were relocated.

Later, Taylor headed the Indian Peace Commission, created by Congress to negotiate treaties with western tribes under President Ulysses Grant's peace policy.

Watkins, Arthur V. (1886–1973)

Born in Midway, Utah, Watkins attended Brigham Young University from 1903 to 1906 and New York University from 1909 to 1910. He graduated from Columbia University Law School in 1912. He was admitted to the bar in 1912 and practiced law in Vernal, Utah. He served as a district judge for the Fourth Judicial District of Utah from 1928 to 1933. As a Republican, he was elected to the U.S. Senate in 1946 and reelected in 1952. During the 83rd Congress, Watkins became the most outspoken congressmen to end the trust status of tribes under the Termination Policy that was established under the House Concurrent Resolution, passed in 1953. In his role as U.S. Senator, Congress terminated 61 tribes, communities, villages, and bands from 1954 to 1961.

Primary Documents

Delaware Treaty of 1778 (Treaty of Fort Pitt)

In 1778 President George Washington and Secretary of War Henry Knox agreed on the strategic benefit of obtaining recognition from the Delaware, one of the most powerful Indian nations in the northern region, and keeping them neutral. With the British presence so close at hand, the United States needed the Delaware as a military ally. Officials persuaded White Eyes, The Pipe, John Kill Buck, and other attending Delaware to make an alliance agreement, resulting in the first of 374 ratified treaties between the United States and Indian nations.

Article 1

That all offenses or acts of hostilities by one, or either of the contracting parties against the other, be mutually forgiven, and buried in the depth of oblivion, never more to be had in remembrance.

Article 2

That a perpetual state of peace and friendship shall henceforth take place, and subsist between the contracting parties aforesaid, through all succeeding generations: and if either of the parties are engaged in a just and necessary war with any other nation or nations, that then each shall assist the other in due proportion to their abilities, till their enemies are brought to reasonable terms of accommodation . . .

Article 5

Whereas the confederation entered into by the Delaware nation and the United States, renders the first dependent on the latter for all the articles of clothing, utensils and implements of war, and it is judged not only reasonable, but indispensably necessary, that the aforesaid Nation be supplied with such articles from time to time, as far as the United States may have it in its power, by a well-regulated trade, under the conduct of an intelligent, candid agent . . .

Article 6

Whereas the enemies of the United States have endeavored, by every artifice in their power, to possess the Indians in general with an opinion, that it is the design of the States aforesaid, to extirpate the Indians and take possession of their country: to obviate such false suggestion, the United States do engage to guarantee to the aforesaid nation of the Delawares, and their heirs, all their territorial rights in the fullest and most ample manner, as it hath been bounded by former treaties, as long as they the said Delaware nation shall abide by, and hold fast the chain of friendship now entered into.

Source: "Treaty with the Delawares. Sept. 17, 1778." Charles J. Kappler, comp. and ed., INDIAN AFFAIRS: LAWS AND TREATIES, Vol. 2 (Washington: Government Printing Office, 1904), 4–5.

First Indian Trade and Intercourse Act 1790

Congress passed the first of the Indian Trade and Intercourse Acts on July 22, 1790, the last one being made in 1834. These laws laid the specific guidelines for U.S. interaction with the Native nations. The initial act of 1790 authorized superintendents to distribute licenses to trade with Indians, and they had the power to revoke licenses from traders or stop illegal trading.

Sec. 1 Be it enacted by the Senate and House of Representatives of the United States of America in Congress assembled, That no person shall be permitted to carry on any trade or intercourse with the Indian tribes, without a license for that purpose under the hand and seal of the superintendent of the department, or of such other person as the President of the United States shall appoint for that purpose . . .

Source: "An Act to regulate trade and intercourse with the Indian tribes." July 22, 1790, *U.S. Statutes at Large*, 1: 137.

Indian Removal Act of 1830

More than three dozen Indian nations were forcibly removed from their homelands in the Eastern Woodlands to west of the Mississippi River. The Indian Removal Act, passed on May 28, 1830, was considered one of President Andrew Jackson's crowning achievements. Congress authorized $500,000 for the purpose of exchanging Indian lands in the East for new lands in the West and for the cost of the removals.

Sec. 1 An Act to provide for an exchange of lands with the Indians residing in any of the states or territories, and for their removal west of the river Mississippi.

Be it enacted by the Senate and House of Representatives of the United States of America, in Congress assembled, That it shall and may be lawful for the President of the United States to cause so much of any territory belonging to the United States, west of the river Mississippi, not included in any state or organized territory, and to which the Indian title has been extinguished, as he may judge necessary, to be divided into a suitable number of districts, for the reception of such tribes or nations of Indians as may choose to exchange the lands where they now reside, and remove there . . .

Sec. 3 And be it further enacted, That in the making of any such exchange or exchanges, it shall and may be lawful for the President solemnly to assure the tribe or nation with which the exchange is made, that the United States will forever secure and guaranty to them, and their heirs or successors, the country so exchanged with them; and if they prefer it, that the United States will cause a patent or grant to be made and executed to them for the same: Provided always, that such lands shall revert to the United States, if the Indians become extinct, or abandon the same.

Source: "Indian Removal Act." May 28, 1830, *U.S. Statutes at Large*, 4: 411.

Worcester v. Georgia 1832

The Cherokees set a legal precedent that would be a landmark in federal-Indian law for years to come. Chief Justice John Marshall ruled in favor of the Cherokee in Worcester v. Georgia in 1832. His ruling, which disturbed President Jackson, referred to the Cherokee as a sovereign nation that only the United States could deal with, not the state of Georgia.

"The Cherokee nation . . . is a distinct community occupying its own territory, with boundaries accurately described, in which the laws of Georgia can have no force, and which the citizens of Georgia have no right to enter, but with the assent of the Cherokees themselves, or in conformity with treaties, and with acts of congress. The whole intercourse between the United States and this nation, is, by our constitution and laws, vested in the government of the United States."

The act of the state of Georgia, under which the plaintiff in error was prosecuted, is consequently void, and the judgment a nullity.

Source: U.S. Supreme Court Reports, 6 *Peters*, 534–536, 558–563.

Act of 1871 Abolishing Indian Treaty Making

The Act of 1871 was an appropriation for the Indian Office to continue its operations in providing promised treaty annuities to Indian tribal groups, and a rider was attached that halted further treaty making with the Indian nations.

"An Act making Appropriations for the current and contingent Expenses of the Indian Department . . .

Provided, That hereafter no Indian nation or tribe within the territory of the United States shall be acknowledged or recognized as in independent nation, tribe, or power with whom the United States may contract by treaty: *Provided, further,* That nothing herein contained shall be construed to invalidate or impair the obligation of any treaty heretofore lawfully made and ratified with any such Indian nation or tribe . . .

Source: "Indian Appropriations Act," March 3, 1871. *U.S. Statutes at Large,* 16: 566.

Standing Bear v. Crook Decision 1979

In this landmark court case in federal-Indian law, Judge Elmer Dundy ruled that Ponca leader Standing Bear was a legal person within the laws of the United States and therefore had rights whereas previously, Indians were outside of U.S. laws and the U.S. Constitution. Dundy's first and fourth points in his conclusion are as follows:

"First. That an *Indian* is a person with the meaning of the laws of the United States, and has therefore the right to sue out a writ of habeas corpus in a federal court and before a federal judge, in all cases where he may be confined, or in custody under color of authority of the United States, or where he is restrained of liberty in violation of the constitution or laws of the United States . . .

Fourth. That the Indians possess the inherent right of expatriation as well as the more fortunate white race, and have the inalienable right to 'life, liberty and the pursuit of happiness,' so long as they obey the laws and do not trespass on forbidden ground . . ."

Source: United States *ex rel.* Standing Bear v. Crook, 25 Federal Cases, 695 (C.C.D. Neb. 1879) (No. 14,891).

Dawes General Allotment Act of 1887

This important law was heavily debated in Congress in the early 1880s and resulted in a drastic change in federal-Indian policy of individualiz-

ing Native people from their traditional communal lifestyle and provided separate allotments of land to them for farming and raising livestock as a means to civilize them for assimilation into American society. As a part of the process, Congress made the large surplus areas left over after allotment allocation available for settlers and railroad companies.

"An act to provide for the allotment of lands in severalty to Indians on the various reservations, and to extend the protection of the laws of the United States and the Territories over the Indians, and for other purposes.

Be it enacted . . . That in all cases where any tribe or band of Indians has been, or shall hereafter be, located on any reservation created for their use . . . the President of the United States be, and hereby is, authorized, whenever in his opinion any reservation or any part thereof of such Indians is advantageous for agricultural and grazing purposes, to cause said reservation, or any part thereof, to be surveyed, or resurveyed if necessary, and to allot the lands in said reservation in severalty to any Indian located thereon in quantities as follows:

To each head of a family, one-quarter of a section;

To each single person over eighteen years of age, one-eighth of a section;

To each orphan child under eighteen years of age, one-eighth of a section; and

To each single person under eighteen years of age now living, or who may be born prior to the date of the order of the President directing an allotment of the lands embraced in any reservation, one-sixteenth of a section . . .

SEC. 5 That upon the approval of the allotments provided for in this act by the Secretary of the Interior, he shall cause patents to issue therefore in the name of the allottees, which patents shall be of the legal effect, and declare that the United States does and will hold the land thus allotted, for the period of twenty-five years, in trust for the sole use and benefit of the Indian to whom such allotment shall have been made, or, in the case of his decease, of his heirs according to the laws of the State or Territory where such land is located, and that at the expiration of said period the United States will convey the same by patent to said Indian, or his heirs as aforesaid, in fee, discharged of said trust and free of all charge or incumbrance whatsoever; *Provided,* That the President of the United States may in any case in his discretion extend the period . . ."

Source: "General Land Allotment Act," February 8, 1887, *U.S. Statutes at Large,* 24: 388–391.

Curtis Act 1898

Introduced by Senator Charles Curtis of Kansas, a part Kaw Indian and later U.S. vice president, this devastating act nullified the tribal governments of the Five Civilized Tribes and other Native nations in Indian Territory that included their courts, lighthorse or police forces, as well as their schools.

"An Act for the protection of the people of the Indian Territory, and for other purposes . . .

SEC. 11. That when the roll of citizenship of any one of said nations or tribes is fully completed as provided by law, and the survey of the lands of said nation or tribe is also completed, the commission heretofore appointed under Acts of Congress, and known as the "Dawes Commission," shall proceed to allot the exclusive use and occupancy of the surface of all the lands of said nation or tribe susceptible of allotment among the citizens thereof, as shown by said roll, giving to each, so far as possible, his fair and equal share thereof, considering the nature and fertility of the soil, location, and value of the same . . .

SEC. 17. That it shall be unlawful for any citizen of any one of said tribes to inclose or in any manner, by himself or through another, directly or indirectly, to hold possession of any greater amount of lands or other property belonging to any such nation or tribe than that which would be his approximate share of the lands belonging to such nation or tribe and that of his wife and minor children as per allotment herein provided . . .

SEC. 26. That on and after the passage of this Act the laws of the various tribes or nations of Indians shall not be enforced at law or in equity by the courts of the United States in the Indian Territory .

SEC. 28. That on the first day of July, eighteen hundred and ninety-eight, all tribal courts of Indian Territory shall be abolished, and no officer of said courts shall thereafter have any authority whatever to do or perform any act theretofore authorized by any law in connection with said courts, or to receive any pay for same; and all civil and criminal causes then pending in any such court shall be transferred to the United States court in said Territory by filing with the clerk of the court the original papers in the suit; *Provided,* That this section shall not be in force as to the Chickasaw, Choctaw, and Creek tribes or nations until the first day of October, eighteen hundred and ninety-eight . . ."

Source: "Curtis Act," June 28, 1898. *U.S. Statutes at Large*, 30: 497–498, 502.

Winters Doctrine 1908

This is the most important Indian water rights court case to date. The U.S. Supreme Court ruled that the Assiniboine and Gros Ventre Indians of the Fort Belknap Reservation had "reserve" water rights to the Milk River that was a part of the reservation and that non-Indians upstream could not stop the water from flowing onto the reservation. This crucial resource was a part of the treaty, and Indians had a right to the water to develop their reservation.

"This suit was brought by the United States to restrain appellants and others from constructing or maintaining dams or reservoirs on the Milk River in the state of Montana, or in any manner preventing the water of the river or its tributaries from flowing to the Fort Belknap Indian Reservation . . .

Under the just and reasonable construction of this agreement [establishing the Fort Belknap Reservation], considered in the light of all the circumstances and of its express purpose, the Indians did not thereby cede or relinquish to the United States the right to appropriate the waters of the Milk River necessary to their use for agricultural and other purposes upon the reservation, but retained this right, as an appurtenance to the land which they retained, to the full extent in which it had been vested in them under former treaties, and the right thus retained and vested in them under the agreement of 1888, at a time when Montana was still a Territory of the United States, could not be divested under subsequent legislation either of the Territory or of the State . . ."

Source: *Winters v. United States*, 207 U.S. 564 (1908).

Meriam Report 1928

After surveying reservation conditions throughout Indian Country, the Lewis Meriam task force of several members submitted its very lengthy report to the commissioner of Indian Affairs in 1928. Upon disclosing its findings of the deplorable health conditions, extreme poverty, and poor living conditions in general, the report recommended major reform efforts be implemented, and declared that the previous Indian allotment program had failed.

Chapter IX Education

The most fundamental need in Indian education is a change in point of view. Whatever may have been the official government attitude, education for the Indian in the past has proceeded largely on the theory that it is necessary to remove the Indian child as far as possible from his home environment; whereas the modern point of view in education and social work lay stress on upbringing in the natural setting of home and family life. The Indian educational enterprise is peculiarly in need of the kind of approach that recognizes this principle; that is, less concerned with a conventional school system and more with the understanding of human beings . . .

The Question of Cost . . . It will cost more money than the present program, for the reason that the present cost is too low for safety. The real choice before the government is between doing a mediocre job thereby piling up for the future serious problems in poverty, disease, and crime, and spending more money for an acceptable social and educational program that will make the Indian cease to be a special case in a comparatively short time. At a time when states and cities everywhere and the national government likewise have found it necessary to adjust expenditures to a new price scale, the Indian school service has been kept as near as possible to the old level, with very unfortunate effects. Cheapness in education is expensive . . .

Undesirable Effects of Routinization. The whole machinery of routinized boarding school and agency life works against the kind of initiative and independence, the development of which should be the chief concern of Indian education in and out of school. What all wish for is Indians who can take their place as independent citizens. The routinization characteristic of the boarding schools, with everything scheduled, no time left to be used at one's own initiative, every moment determined by a signal or an order, leads just the other way . . .

Can the Indian be "Educated?" It is necessary at this point to consider one question that is always raised in connection with an educational program for Indians: Is it really worthwhile to do anything for Indians, or are they an "inferior" race? Can the Indian be "educated?" . . . the answer can be given *unequivocally: The Indian is essentially capable of education* . . .

Source: Lewis Meriam et al., *The Problem of Indian Administration.* Baltimore: Johns Hopkins Press, 1928.

Indian Reorganization Act of 1934

President Roosevelt signed this pivotal measure on June 18, 1934, and it became the heart of John Collier's Indian New Deal. Introduced as the Wheeler-Howard bill in the House, the combined efforts of William Zimmerman, Nathan Marigold, and Felix Cohen produced the original draft. Surely no one at the time realized that the IRA would set the foundation for present-day tribal governments. BIA wisdom divided the bill into four sections, and all of it proved exceptionally long, at 48 pages. Representative Edgar Howard sponsored the bill in the House, and it passed 258 to 88. Senator Burton Wheeler followed, introducing the bill in the Senate.

"An Act to conserve and develop Indian lands and resources; to extend to Indians the right to form business and other organizations; to establish a credit system for Indians; to grant certain rights of home rule to Indians; to provide for vocational education for Indians; and for other purposes.

BE IT ENACTED by the Senate and House of Representatives of the United States of America in Congress assembled, That hereafter no land of any Indian reservation, created or set apart by treaty or agreement with the Indians, Acts of Congress, Executive order, purchase, or otherwise, shall be allotted in severalty to any Indian . . .

Sec. 16 Any Indian tribe, or tribes, residing on the same reservation, shall have the right to organize for its common welfare, and may adopt an appropriate constitution and bylaws, which shall become effective when ratified by a majority vote of the adult members of the tribe, or of the adult Indians residing on such reservation, as the case may be, at a special election authorized by the Secretary of the Interior under such rules and regulations as he may prescribe. Such constitution and bylaws when ratified as aforesaid and approved by the Secretary of the Interior shall be revocable by an election open to the same voters and conducted in the same manner as hereinabove provided. Amendments to the constitution and bylaws may be ratified and approved by the Secretary in the same manner as the original constitution and bylaws.

Sec. 18 This Act shall not apply to any reservation wherein a majority of the adult Indians, voting at a special election duly called by the Secretary of the Interior, shall vote against it [*sic*] application . . .

Source: "Indian Reorganization Act," June 18, 1934. U.S. Statutes at Large, 48 pt. 1:984–88.

Indian Claims Commission Act of 1946

In a final effort to settle Indian land claims, Congress passed this law that established a commission of three members to help tribes prepare claims against the U.S. government for the first five years and for the commission to decide the cases for the next five years. Underestimating the work involved, the act was amended twice until the commission was dissolved in 1978.

"*An Act To create an Indian Claims Commission, to provide for the powers, duties, and functions thereof, and for other purposes.*

Be it enacted . . ., That there is hereby created and established an Indian Claims Commission, hereafter referred to as the Commission.

SEC. 2. The Commission shall hear and determine the following claims against the United States on behalf of any India tribe, band, or other identifiable group of American Indians residing within the territorial limits of the United States or Alaska: (1) claims in law or equity arising under the Constitution, laws, treaties of the United States, and Executive orders of the President; (2) all other claims in law or equity, including those sounding in tort, with respect to which the claimant would have been entitled to sue in the a court of the United States if the United States was subject to suit; (3) claims which would result if the treaties, contracts, and agreements between the claimant and the United States were revised on the ground of fraud, duress, unconscionable consideration, mutual or unilateral mistake, whether of law or fact, or any other ground cognizable by a court of equity; (4) claims arising from the taking by the United States, whether as the result of a treaty cession or otherwise, of lands owned or occupied by the claimant without the payment for such lands of compensation agreed to by the claimant; and (5) claims based upon fair and honorable dealings that are not recognized by any existing rule of law or equity. No claim accruing after the date of this Act shall be considered by the Commission . . ."

Source: "Indian Claims Commission Act," August 13, 1946. *U.S. Statutes at Large*, 60: 1049–1056.

House Concurrent Resolution 108

House Concurrent Resolution (HCR) 108 laid the foundation for the most dangerous Indian policy that the U.S. government ever devised. Once and for all, Congress intended to abrogate all obligations to American Indians as promised in 374 treaties signed with the United States. Senator Henry Jackson of Washington introduced HCR 108 in the Senate, and Representative William Harrison of Wyoming sponsored the legislation in the House of Representatives of the 83rd Congress, which was approved on August 1, 1953. The essence of this landmark resolution reads as follows:

"Whereas it is the policy of Congress, as rapidly as possible, to make the Indians within the territorial limits of the United States subject to the same laws and entitled to the same privileges and responsibilities as are applicable to other citizens of the United States, to end their status as wards of the United States and to grant them all of the rights and prerogatives, pertaining to American citizenship; and Whereas the Indians within the territorial limits of the United States should assume their full responsibilities as American citizens."

Source: "House Concurrent Resolution 108," August 1, 1953. *U.S. Statutes at Large*, 67: B132.

Kennedy Education Report 1969

Due to Indian activism and progress in the study of education, this task force, chaired by Senator Edward Kennedy, recommended that a national policy be developed to advance the low educational level of American Indians to conform with national norms at all levels, especially K–12. This report reinforced the idea that if Native people were going to improve their lives, then education would be a key area.

"For more than 2 years the members of this subcommittee have been gaging [sic] how well American Indians are educated . . . We are shocked at what we discovered . . .

We have concluded that our national policies for educating American Indians are a failure of major proportions. They have not offered Indian children—either in years past or today—an educational opportunity anywhere near equal to that offered the great bulk of American children. Past generations of lawmakers and administrators have failed the American Indian. Our own generation thus faces a challenge—we can continue the unacceptable policies and programs of the past or we can recognize our failures, renew our commitments, and reinvest our efforts with new energy.

It is this latter course that the subcommittee chooses. We have made 60 separate recommendations . . . We have recommended that the Nation adopt as national policy a commitment to achieving educational excellence for American Indians. We have recommended that the Nation adopt as national goals a series of specific objectives relating to educational opportunities for American Indians . . .

We have recommended that there be convened a White House Conference on American Indian Affairs. We have recommended—although not unanimously—that there be established a Senate Select Committee on the Human Needs of American Indians. We have recommended the enactment of a comprehensive Indian education statute, to replace the fragmented and inadequate education legislation now extant. We have recommended that the funds available for Indian education programs be markedly increased.

One theme running through all our recommendations is increased Indian participation and control of their own programs . . .

In this report, we have compared the size and scope of the effort we believe must be mounted to the Marshall plan which revitalized postwar Europe. We believe that we have, as a Nation, as great a moral and legal obligation to our Indian citizens today as we did after World War II to our European allies and adversaries . . .

In conclusion, it is sufficient to restate our basic finding: that our Nation's policies and programs for educating American Indians are a national tragedy. They present us with a national challenge of no small proportions. We believe that this report recommends the proper steps to meet this challenge. But we know that it will not be met without strong leadership and dedicated work. We believe that with this leadership from the Congress and the executive branch of the Government, the Nation can and will meet this challenge."

Source: *Indian Education: A National Tragedy—A National Challenge.* Senate Report no. 501, 91st Cong. 1st Session. Serial 12836–1.

Boldt Decision 1974

Considered the most important Indian fishing rights court case, the Boldt Decision favored tribal sovereignty in allowing Indian groups in Washington to fish in ceded water areas that had been negotiated in treaties with the United States. The Boldt Decision set a precedent for later Indian fishing rights cases that held that Native people would be allowed to continue to use this natural resource as part of developing their livelihood.

". . . 13. From the earliest known times, up to and beyond the time of the Stevens' treaties, the Indians comprising each of the treating tribes and bands were primarily a fishing, hunting and gathering people dependent almost entirely upon the natural animal and vegetative resources of the region for their subsistence and culture. They were heavily dependent upon anadromous fish for their subsistence and for trade with other tribes and later with the settlers. Anadromous fish was the great staple of their diet and livelihood. They cured and dried large quantities for year round use, both for themselves and for others through sale, trade, barter and employment. With the advent of canning technology in the latter half of the 19th Century the commercial exploitation of the anadromous fish resources by non-Indians increased tremendously. Indians, fishing under their treaty-secured rights, also participated in this expanded commercial fishery and sold many fish to non-Indian packers and dealers.

14. The taking of anadromous fish from usual and accustomed places, the right to which was secured to the Treaty Tribes in the Stevens' treaties,

constituted both the means of economic livelihood and the foundation of native culture. Reservation of the right to gather food in this fashion protected the Indians' right to maintain essential elements of their way of life, as a complement to the life defined by the permanent homes, allotted farm lands, compulsory education, technical assistance and pecuniary rewards offered in the treaties. Settlement of the West and the rise of industrial America have significantly circumscribed the opportunities of members of the Treaty Tribes to fish for subsistence and commerce and to maintain tribal traditions. But the mere passage of time has not eroded, and cannot erode, the rights guaranteed by solemn treaties that both sides pledged on their honor to uphold. . . ."

Source: *U.S. v. Washington,* February 12, 1974. U.S. Court of Appeals, Ninth Circuit, 1975. 520 F.2d 676, *cert. denied,* 423 U.S. 1086, 96 S. Ct. 877, 47 L.Ed.2d 97 (1976).

Indian Self-Determination and Education Assistance Act 1975

Indian self-determination became a federal-Indian policy, and implementation of this law indicated the significance that the Richard Nixon administration placed on education for Native people. According to this policy and law, American Indians would become more like partners in working with the federal government to advance tribal governments and reservation conditions.

"An Act to provide maximum Indian participation in the Government and education of Indian people; to provide for the full participation of Indian tribes in programs and services conducted by the Federal Government for Indians and to encourage the development of human resources of the Indian people; to establish a program of assistance to upgrade Indian education; to support the right of Indian citizens to control their own educational activities; and for other purposes . . .

Congressional Findings

1   SEC. 2 (a) The Congress, after careful review of the Federal Government's historical and special legal relationship with, and resulting responsibilities to, American Indian people, finds that—

(1) the prolonged Federal domination of Indian service programs has served to retard rather than enhance the progress of Indian people and their communities by depriving Indians of the full opportunity to develop leadership skills crucial to the realization of self-government, and has denied to the Indian

people an effective voice in the planning and implementation of programs for the benefit of Indians which are responsive to the true needs of Indian communities; and

(2) the Indian people will never surrender their desire to control their relationships both among themselves and with non-Indian governments, organizations, and persons.

(b) The Congress further finds that—

(1) true self-determination in any society of people is dependent upon an educational process which will insure the development of qualified people to fulfill meaningful leadership roles;

(2) the Federal responsibility for and assistance to education of Indian children has not effected [sic] the desired level of educational achievement or created the diverse opportunities and personal satisfaction which education can and should provide; and

(3) parental and community control of the educational process is of crucial importance to the Indian people.

Declaration of Policy

SEC. 3. (a) The Congress hereby recognizes the obligation of the United States to respond to the strong expression of the Indian people for self-determination by assuring maximum Indian participation in the direction of educational as well as other Federal services to Indian communities so as to render such services more responsive to the needs and desires of those communities.

(b) The Congress declares its commitment to the maintenance of the Federal Government's unique and continuing relationship with and responsibility to the Indian people through the establishment of a meaningful Indian self-determination policy which will permit an orderly transition from Federal domination of programs for and services to Indians to effective and meaningful participation by the Indian people in the planning, conduct, and administration of those programs and services.

(c) The Congress declares that a major national goal of the United States is to provide the quantity and quality of educational services and opportunities which will permit Indian children to compete and excel in the life areas of their choice, and to achieve the measure of self-determination essential to their social and economic well-being . . ."

Source: "Indian Self-Determination and Education Assistance Act," P.L. 93-68, January 4, 1975, *U.S. Statutes at Large*, 88: 2203–2217.

Cabazon Court Decision 1988

The state of California contested Indian bingo operations when the Cabazon Band opened a card club, offering draw poker and other card games to the public, predominately non-Indians. The state of California sought to apply two state ordinances, although the statute did not prohibit the playing of bingo. Almost a four-year legal process ensued until the most important Indian gaming court case to date was resolved. On February 25, 1987, the Supreme Court of the United States was divided, although it handed down a major decision in favor of Indian gaming tribes. In brief, Riverside County had no legal authority to enter the reservations and close the card playing, thus the small Cabazon and Morongo groups could reopen their gaming operations. Justice Byron White stated the ruling of the court.

". . . The Court has consistently recognized that Indian tribes retain 'attributes of sovereignty over both their members and their territory' . . . and that 'tribal sovereignty is dependent on, and subordinate to, only the Federal Government, not the States.' . . . It is clear, however, that state laws may be applied to tribal Indians on their reservations if Congress has expressly so provided. Here, the State insists that Congress has twice given its express consent: first in Pub. L. 280 in 1953 . . . and second in the Organized Crime Control Act in 1970 . . . We disagree in both respects . . .

We conclude that the State's interest in preventing the infiltration of the tribal bingo enterprises by organized crime does not justify state regulations of the tribal bingo enterprises in light of the compelling federal and tribal interests supporting them. State regulation would impermissibly infringe on tribal government, and this conclusion applies equally to the county's attempted regulation of the Cabazon card club. We therefore affirm the judgment of the Court of Appeals . . ."

Source: *Cabazon Band of Mission Indians et al. v. California*, 480 U.S. 202 (February 25, 1987), 205, 215, 247.

Indian Gaming Regulatory Act 1988

The Indian Gaming Regulatory Act was passed on October 17, 1988, to regulate Indian gaming according to three kinds of gambling: Class I gaming included traditional forms of Indian gambling, usually a part of tribal celebrations and social games for minimal prizes. Class II involved bingo and card games for prizes. Class III included casino gambling, especially baccarat, blackjack, and slot machines. The National Indian Gaming Commission was set up to supervise Class II and III gaming.

"Indian Gaming Regulatory Act," P. L. 100–497: "to establish federal standards and regulations for the conduct of gaming activities within Indian country;" [and] "as a means of promoting tribal economic development, self-sufficiency, and strong tribal governments," "to shield it [Indian gaming] from organized crime and other corrupting influences, . . . to assure that gaming is conducted fairly and honestly by both the operator and players," and to establish a National Indian Gaming Commission."

Source: "Indian Gaming Regulatory Act," P.L. 100-497, October 17, 1988. *U.S. Statutes at Large,* 102: 2467–2488.

Kevin Gover Bureau of Indian Affairs Apology 2000

On September 8, 2000, then Assistant Secretary of the Interior Kevin Gover made a national apology to American Indians at a ceremony commemorating the 175th anniversary of the founding of the Bureau of Indian Affairs. This long overdue apology was ironically made by an Indian person to Indian people and from the BIA—and not from the rest of the federal government.

"I do not speak for the United States. That is the province of the nation's elected leaders, and I would not presume to speak on their behalf. I am empowered, however, to speak on behalf of this agency, the Bureau of Indian Affairs, and I am quite certain that the words that follow reflect the hearts of its 10,000 employees. Let us begin by expressing our profound sorrow for what this agency has done in the past. Just like you, when we think of these misdeeds and their tragic consequences, our hearts break and our grief is as pure and complete as yours. We desperately wish that we could change this history, but of course we cannot. On behalf of the Bureau of Indian Affairs, I extend this formal apology to Indian people for the historical conduct of this agency. And while the BIA employees of today did not commit these wrongs, we acknowledge that the institution we serve did. We accept this inheritance, this legacy of racism and inhumanity. And by accepting this legacy, we accept also the moral responsibility of putting things right."

Source: "Remarks of Kevin Gover, Assistant Secretary–Indian Affairs, Department of the Interior at the Ceremony Acknowledging the 175th Anniversary of the Establishing of the Bureau of Indian Affairs" (National Apology for the Bureau of Indian Affairs), September 8, 2000, Clinton Administration History Project, William Clinton Presidential Library, Little Rock, AK.

Congressional Resolution of Apology to Native Peoples 2004

U.S. senators Sam Brownback (R-KS), Ben Nighthorse Campbell (R-CO), and Daniel K. Inouye (D-HI) introduced Senate Joint Resolution 37 on May 6, 2004. Senator Brownback issued Congress's first national apology to American Indians.

Many treaties were made between this Republic and the American Indian tribes. Treaties, as my colleagues in this Chamber know, are far more than words on a page. Treaties are our word, our bond. Treaties with other governments are not to be treated lightly. Unfortunately, too often the United States of America did not uphold its responsibilities as stated in its covenants with the Native American Tribes. Too often, our Government brokes its oaths to the Native peoples.

This is a resolution of apology and a resolution of reconciliation. It is a first step toward healing the wounds that have divided us for so long—a potential foundation for a new era of positive relations between Tribal governments and the Federal Government. It is time—it is past time—for us to heal our land of divisions, and bring us together as one people.

Source: "Joint Resolution of Apology to Native Peoples Introduced in the United States Senate," S.J.R 37 introduced by Senator Sam Brownback, Senator Ben Nighthorse Campbell, and Senator Daniel Inouye. U.S. Congressional Record—Senate, May 6, 2004, Vol. 150, S5002.

Cobell v. Salazar 2009

Elouise Cobell, a Blackfeet banker for her tribe in Montana, began to realize that the government had problems in accounting for the funds it held in trust for American Indians. She filed suit on June 10, 1996, with Mildred Cleghorn, Thomas Maulson, and James Louis Larose. The case is also known as Cobell v. Babbitt, Cobell v. Norton, and Cobell v. Kempthorne and also Cobell v. Salazar. In 2009 a federal court reached a final settlement in the Cobell case that the U.S. government mismanaged individual Indians' trust accounts and could not tell the individuals what had happened to their monies. President Obama signed the settlement *legislation calling for the federal government to create a $1.4 billion accounting/trust administration fund and a $2 billion trust land consolidation fund. In addition, the settlement created an Indian Education Scholarship fund of up to $60 million to improve access to higher education for American Indians.*

"We [Judges] recounted the long history of the Government's trust responsibilities to Native Americans in *Cobell VI*, and we therefore provide only an abbreviated version of that history here. Pursuant to the General Allotment Act of 1887, ch. 119, 24 Stat. 388 (formerly codified at 24 U.S.C. § 331 et seq.), lands that had previously been set aside for Indian tribes were allotted to individual Indians in fixed amounts, "surplus" lands were opened to non-Indian settlement. The Act crated a system in which allotted lands would be held in trust by the United States for 25 years or more, during which period an individual account ("Individual Indian Money" account or "IIM" account) would be created for each Indian with an interest in the allotted lands. The United States would manage the lands for the benefit of the allottees until the expiration of the trust period, at which time each allottee would be issued a fee patent. . . . In 1994 the Congress enacted the Indian Trust Fund Management Reform Act, Pub L. No. 103–412, 108 Stat. 4239 (codified as amended at 25 U.S.C. § 4001 et seq.) (1994 Act"), recognizing these responsibilities an identifying some of the Government's duties to ensure it meets them. The plaintiffs' lawsuit alleges a breach of these responsibilities."

Source: www.CobellSettlement.com. Accessed July 19, 2010; Cobell Case, 334 F.3d 1128.

Glossary

Alaska Native   Native people who are indigenous to Alaska and share many of the legal rights of American Indians through federal law and court cases.

Allotment   The Indian General Allotment Act of 1887 authorized that Indian reservations be divided into separate tracts of land for individual tribal members. This is also known as allotment in severalty. These typical tracts, 160 acres for Indian heads of households and 80 acres for the unmarried, were to be used for farming and cattle grazing. Some cases of tribal allotments were larger in size.

Area Office   As of 2010, there were 12 regional offices—Alaska, Eastern, Eastern Oklahoma, Great Plains, Midwest, Navajo, Northwest, Pacific, Rocky Mountains, Southern Plains, Southwest, and Western. The dozen regional offices contain 83 agencies that report to the BIA deputy director of Field Operations. Each regional director is responsible for all BIA activities except education, law enforcement, and administrative procedure.

Assistant Secretary of the Interior   This position was created in 1978 to be specifically in charge of federal-Indian affairs and is one of five assistant secretaries answering to the secretary of the Interior.

BIA Takeover   From November 3–9, 1972, the American Indian Movement occupied the BIA building in Washington, DC. Damages to the BIA building and its contents amounted to $2.28 million.

Bureau of Indian Affairs   Created in 1824 as the Indian Office, Secretary of War John C. Calhoun established this office within the War Department. Upon creation of the Department of the Interior in 1849, the BIA was transferred. With a central office located in Washington, DC, the Indian Bureau operates with a series of 83 regional or area offices strategically located throughout what has been called "Indian Country." At the end of the first decade in the 21st century, an estimated 12,000 employees work for the BIA.

Bureau of Indian Education   This bureau started in 2006, and it administers an education program with 184 schools and dormitories, 48,000 elementary and secondary students, and 28 tribal colleges, universities, and postsecondary schools.

Commissioner of Indian Affairs   This position was established in 1832. Until 1978 a commissioner of Indian Affairs presided over the BIA, and since then this office has been advanced to a higher level, known as the assistant secretary of the Interior. The commissioner and later the assistant secretary were named by the secretary of the Interior and appointed by the president of the United States.

Competent   A person deemed by a court of law to be literate and able to run his or her own business affairs. This term was used to classify Indians receiving land allotments.

Department of the Interior   This department was created in 1849, and the secretary of the Interior at present has five assistant secretaries. The Bureau of Indian Affairs is within the Interior.

Department of War   Created by Congress in 1798, the secretary of War was the highest U.S. authority next to the president in charge of Indian affairs until the Indian Office was established in 1824. The War Department was dissolved in 1947 when it became the Department of the Army and Department of the Air Force; it joined the Department of the Navy as a part of the joint National Military Establishment and was renamed the U.S. Department of Defense in 1949.

Domestic Dependent Nation   The status given to federally recognized tribes, with the primary charge that indigenous nations have the authority to govern themselves. Chief Justice John C. Marshall first used this term in the 1831 Supreme Court case *Cherokee Nation v. Georgia* to characterize Indian tribes. He wrote that this legal relationship is "that of a ward to his guardian."

Federal Acknowledgement Process   A formal, highly bureaucratic, controversial process that the federal government follows in acknowledging the existence of an American Indian tribe. After a tribe is acknowledged, a "government-to-government" relationship is established between that Indian group and Congress. Federal acknowledgement allows tribes to draw upon BIA services.

Federally Recognized Tribes   Tribes that share a "government-to-government" relationship with Congress. Congressional obligations to these tribes include protection of land, health care, education, and economic assistance. There are presently 564 federally recognized tribes. (See State Recognized Tribes.)

Federal Paternalism   The firm supervision of affairs of a group by another group or organization in federal-Indian relations such as the Bureau of Indian Affairs or War Department that took a fatherly approached toward tribes.

Fee Simple   Also called fee patents, in the distribution of land allotments to individual Indians, the Dawes Act originally stipulated fee simple ownership without trust restrictions. This policy of absolute ownership intended for Indians to become individual landholders for farming or raising livestock or both.

Government-to-Government   A unique political relationship between the U.S. government and federally recognized Indian tribes. The Clinton administration stressed this new approach in Indian affairs.

Headright   The Osage tribal members held their mineral rights in common so that all of them had a share of the oil royalties paid by oil companies to the individual allottees. Each share was a headright.

Incompetent   A person deemed by a court of law to be illiterate and not able to run his or her own business affairs. This term was used to classify Indians receiving land allotments.

Indian Agent   Also know as a subagent, the agent usually lived among Indians and was appointed by the federal government. Agents were created in the late 1700s, and they became known as Indian superintendents in the late 1800s and were in charge of Indian agencies on reservations.

Indian Country   The BIA is responsible for 326 federal reserved lands for Indian tribes and Alaska Natives. Federal-Indian reserved lands exist in all but 18 states. Treaties, congressional laws, and presidential executive orders have created federal-Indian reserved lands.

Indian Health Service (IHS)   IHS refers to federally run hospitals and health clinics serving American Indians, which have been contracted with tribes since the late 1970s. An act in 1954 transferred Indian health services from the BIA to the Public Health Service in the Department of Health, Education, and Welfare.

Indian Preference   Commissioner of Indian Affairs John Collier started this policy guideline to hire Indians to fill positions in the BIA, but it only became heavily implemented in the early 1970s during Commissioner Louis Bruce's tenure. Today over 70 percent of BIA employees are American Indian or Alaska Native, and an Indian has served as commissioner or assistant secretary since 1966.

Indian Treaty Rights   From 1778 to 1871, the United States' relations with individual American Indian nations were defined and conducted largely through the treaty-making process. These "contracts among nations" recognized and established rights, benefits, and conditions for tribes who agreed to cede millions of acres of their homelands to the United States and accept its protection. These treaties are the foundation upon which federal-Indian law and the federal Indian trust relationship is based.

Jurisdiction   P.L. 280, passed in 1954 as part of the termination movement, Congress transferred criminal and civil matters from tribal to state control. It also decentralized some BIA authority by giving certain states (Wisconsin, Minnesota, Nebraska, California, Oregon, and later Alaska) the responsibility for overseeing these matters.

Land Lease   As trustee to American Indians whose tribes signed treaties with the United States, the Department of the Interior and the BIA have the power to determine leasing of land to other parties in regard to livestock grazing, timberlands, and mining areas.

Native   The condition or identity of being indigenous to North America.

Office of Indian Affairs   Also known as the Indian Office, this precursor to the BIA was created in 1824 to supervise Indian policy. From 1824–1849, the War Department, Congress, and the president regulated Indian relations. After 1849, the Indian Office became known as the Bureau of Indian Affairs. After the Indian Reorganization Act of 1934, the BIA moved into a more advisory rather than authoritative role.

Per Capita   Payment of a certain amount of money to members of an Indian tribe from the tribe itself or from the federal government.

Plenary Power   This legal doctrine holds that Congress has the power to dissolve treaties under its authority by passing legislation.

Relocation   The BIA created this program under Commissioner Dillon Meyer in 1951, and the following year all Indians were offered assistance in finding jobs and accommodations if they would relocate. This program changed to Employment Assistance and operated until 1973.

Reservation   An area of land reserved for a tribe or tribes under treaty executive order, federal statute, or administrative action as a permanent tribal homeland; and these land bases resulted when the nations signed (often under duress) treaties with the U.S. government, surrendering much of their homelands. The federal government holds title to the land in trust on behalf of the tribe.

Restoration   In 1973 Menominee activist Ada Deer and other grassroots activists overturned the Menominee termination with new legislation, starting a new federal policy of "restoring" terminated tribes as federally recognized tribes.

Royalty   Monies received as a percentage of lands leased, mined, or used to generate income but usually referring to funds paid to individuals or tribes per agreement for using natural resources.

Self-determination   The recognition that American Indian tribes have autonomy over their own social, economic, educational, cultural, and linguistic needs and customs. It was first heard in the 1966 National Congress of American Indians to counter the termination threat.

Sovereignty   In 1832 Chief Justice John Marshall explained tribal sovereignty as a "pre-existing condition among self-governing entities and acts as a legal shield protecting all rights and privileges reserved and implied by nationhood."

State Compacts   These are agreements between states and gaming tribes, which started with the implementation of the Indian Gaming Regulatory Act of 1988. They are overseen by the National Indian Gaming Commission.

State Recognized Tribes   As of 2010 there were some 70 tribes recognized only by state governments (and not the federal government), and they have formed working relations with the states.

Termination   Started by House Concurrent Resolution 108 as a federal policy approved in 1953 by Congress to end the trust status between the U.S. government and a tribe usually; but also a community, band, or individual who has land or properties in trust with the United States. There were 109 cases of termination by legislation in 1974.

Treaty   An official agreement between Indian tribes and the U.S. government with a total of 374 ratified treaties and additional agreements; and there are also state-tribe treaties that have been called state compacts since 1988.

Tribal Courts   In the late 1970s, tribes began to develop their own modern court systems on reservations that paralleled the federal court model, but tribes traditionally had justice systems that operated like tribal courts when tribal members committed crimes.

Tribal Self-Government   The authority for tribes to administer the programs and services formally administered by the BIA for their tribal members. It is the recognition that tribes possess nearly all powers of self-government, such as the right to form their own governments; to make and enforce laws, both civil and criminal; to tax; to establish and determine membership (i.e., tribal citizenship); to license and regulate activities within their jurisdiction; to zone; and to exclude persons from tribal lands.

Trust   Because Indian tribes' legal status is domestic dependent nations, the federal government has a legal obligation to these tribes' treaty rights, lands, assets, and resources. The government holds money accounts for Indian tribes and individual Indian people, and it agrees to protect and advance tribal interests. The BIA's principal focus is to develop programs and policies to allow the government to fulfill its responsibilities.

Trust Land   Because of the trust relationship between tribes and the federal government, the United States holds legal title to tribal assets, including real property (land). The users of the property hold a beneficial title, which allows them to use and benefit from that land.

Trust Responsibility   When trusts were established, both sides of the treaties agreed to maintain a trust responsibility. *Cobell v. Salazar (2010)*, the largest lawsuit brought by Native peoples against the United States to date, indicates the severe mismanagement and broad negligence in keeping track of monies for Native Americans.

Wardship   The legal relationship such as that of the U.S. government serving via the BIA as the trustee over Indians regarding their lands and properties.

Annotated Bibliography

Books

Bee, Robert L. *The Politics of American Indian Policy* (Cambridge, MA: Schenkman Publishing, 1982).

Bee seeks to bridge the gap between local community and national studies in federal-Indian policy. He focuses on the constraints that guide decision making in Washington, DC; why tribal leaders maintain relationships with federal officials in spite of poor self-determination policies; and how political processes go beyond reservation boundaries. As an ethnographic study in the milieu of federal-Indian policy, this book offers detailed descriptions of the workings of the Washington environment in which Indian policies are made.

Burton, Lloyd. *American Indian Water Rights and the Limits of the Law* (Lawrence: University Press of Kansas, 1991).

Burton presents an overview of historical Indian-U.S. relationships in relation to water rights law. He analyzes the historical background of Indian water rights, with particular attention to the *Winters* Doctrine and its consequences. He also presents an analysis of 20th-century legal disputes over that resource and its effects on both Indians and non-Indians.

Cahill, Cathleen D. FEDERAL FATHERS & MOTHERS: A SOCIAL HISTORY OF THE UNITED STATES INDIAN SERVICE, 1869–1933 (Chapel Hill: University of North Carolina Press, 2010)

Cathleen Cahill analyzes the social history of the Indian Bureau from 1869 to 1933. She focuses on how women, men, bureaucrats and Indians formulated federal policy in efforts to assimilate Native people.

Clarkin, Thomas. *Federal Indian Policy in the Kennedy and Johnson Administrations 1961–1969* (Albuquerque: University of New Mexico Press, 2001).

Clarkin's analysis of the shift in American Indian and white relations between 1961 and 1969 traces American Indian efforts to gain control over the creation of Indian policy and the operation of government programs. This period was a time of transition, as termination slowly gave way to Indian self-determination, and Clarkin is careful to give particular attention to the opposition from senators who tried to continue termination policies of the 1940s and 1950s. While some supported termination, many others reacted against it with a surge of American Indian political activism.

Clow, Richmond, and Imre Sutton. eds. *Trusteeship in Change: Toward Tribal Autonomy in Resource Management* (Boulder: University Press of Colorado, 2001).

Clow and Sutton offer an array of chapters on environmental, American West, and Indian history related to resource management. This compilation of essays includes 11 case studies in the evolution of resource management from the 19th century through the end of the 20th. The three sections of the book focus on the trust relationship between Indians and the federal government at the beginning of the reservation system, increasing tribal participation in managing their own resources, and self-determination toward control over those resources.

Daily, David W. *Battle for the BIA: G.E.E. Lindquist and the Missionary Crusade against John Collier* (Tucson: University of Arizona Press, 2004).

Covering the years from the 1920s to the 1950s, this study examines the difficult relationship between John Collier and the BIA and G.E.E. Lindquist leading the Protestant missionary crusade against Collier's dominance in federal-Indian relations. During the early decades, the BIA and missionary organizations became dependent upon each other in Indian affairs, but Lindquist's belief in the urgency of converting Indians to Christianity ran counter to Collier respecting Native religions while trying to build tribal communities.

DuMars, Charles T., Marilyn O'Leary, and Albert E. Utton. *Pueblo Indian Water Rights: Struggle for a Precious Resource* (Tucson: University of Arizona Press, 1984).

The authors focus on the Rio Grande Pueblos as a case study of all Pueblo Indian water rights. They provide analysis of historical actors contending for this resource in New Mexico's Upper Rio Grande Basin and of laws and legal precedents that resulted. Written from a legal standpoint, the book analyzes various challenges that Indians faced in claiming their rights from an indigenous viewpoint.

Echo-Hawk, Walter R. IN THE COURTS OF THE CONQUEROR: THE 10 WORST INDIAN LAW CASES EVER DECIDED (Golden, CO: Fulcrum Publishing, 2010).

Legal scholar Walter Echo-Hawk reviews the ten worst cases on injustice in federal-Indian law. He contextualizes the politics of the time periods for each case, stating the motives for these noted court rulings.

Ellis, Richard. *General Pope and U.S. Indian Policy* (Albuquerque: University of New Mexico Press, 1970).

This biography of General John Pope and his interactions with the BIA reveals his influence on federal-Indian policy. Ellis offers a slightly revised dissertation on Pope's reform efforts based on his understanding of the issues and problems with Indian policy. Ellis also comments on various Indian wars that Pope did not influence, although it is largely a study of federal interactions with western tribes, through Pope's position of administrator.

Fixico, Donald L. *Termination and Relocation: Federal Indian Policy, 1945–1960* (Albuquerque: University of New Mexico Press, 1986).

From World War II to JFK, this book explores the origins of termination and relocation as two damaging federal policies that strove to end the trust relationship between the government and tribes and individual Indians. This book also examines the beginning of the urbanization of Native people by promising them jobs and homes in cities.

Hagan, William T. *Indian Police and Judges: Experiments in Acculturation and Control* (New Haven, CT: Yale University Press, 1966).

At the close of major warfare on the plains, the secretary of the Interior formed the reservation police system to ensure compliance with BIA policies. Government programs to destroy tribal culture—such as farming, schools—and missionaries, also eliminated local control over individuals' behavior. Hagan examines how police and judges acted as agents of acculturation in the climate of limited local control.

Hill, Edward E. *The Office of Indian Affairs, 1824–1880: Historical Sketches* (New York: Clearwater Publishing, 1974).

This reference volume provides helpful information on all of the Indian and Alaska Native agencies as well as the superintendencies. This information lists the Indian agents and acting agents who worked among the tribes. The information on each agency also provides both the location and very brief history of each one that reported to the Indian Office from 1824 to 1880.

Hoxie, Frederick. *A Final Promise: The Campaign to Assimilate the Indians, 1880–1920* (Lincoln: University of Nebraska Press, 1984, 2001).

Hoxie places the economic, political, and social issues and motives of the assimilation campaign into historical perspective through his analysis of white and Indian people and organizations. In addressing why the assimilationist campaign failed, Hoxie analyzes changing and increasingly negative assumptions concerning Native American improvement. He demonstrates how the rejection of social homogeneity led to the rejection of assimilation.

Jackson, Helen Hunt. *A Century of Dishonor: A Sketch of the U.S. Government's Dealings with Some of the Indian Tribes* (Boston, MA: Roberts Brothers, 1881).

Hunt chronicles the injustices against Native Americans sanctioned and driven by the U.S. government. This book consists of the histories of seven different tribes by describing white settlers' landgrabs and other activities designed to secure Indian lands. At her own expense, Hunt sent a copy of the book to every senator in 1881, hoping to persuade her or him to reform Indian conditions.

Kneale, Albert H. *Indian Agent* (Caldwell, ID: Caxton Printers, 1950).

Former Indian agent Albert Kneale worked among western tribes for 36 years prior to writing *Indian Agent*. His compilation of his interactions with various tribes is demonstrated in his cursory treatment of various subjects of concern to the BIA, such as tribal languages. Somewhat autobiographical, *Indian Agent* provides substantial detail in the culture of various tribes that Kneale interacted with, as well as agent duties and procedures.

Leupp, F. E. *The Indian and His Problem* (New York: Charles Scribner's Sons, 1910).

As former U.S. commissioner of Indian Affairs, Leupp documents his perspective of the problems Indians routinely faced at the turn of the 20th century. His goal is to provide a "birds-eye view" (vii) of Indian affairs, with suggestions for future commissioners and government leaders on how to improve their situations. Leupp, for example, established the first real Indian health services in 1908, and described the ongoing challenges the clinics were not able to meet.

Mardock, Robert Winston. *The Reformers and the American Indian* (Columbia: University of Missouri Press, 1971).

This early study focuses on the scope of the Indian reform era from its origins and humanitarian role to failures of the Dawes Allotment Act of 1887. The author addresses the origin of President Grant's peace policy, the civilization of Indians movement, and the Ponca removal culminating in Standing Bear's famous Supreme Court case. The author supports the Indian reformers who hailed the passage of the Dawes Act as their greatest achievement, although it led to many problems of land exploitation of Indians and their tribes.

McGillycuddy, Julia B. *McGillycuddy, Agent: A Biography of Dr. Valentine T. McGillycuddy* (Stanford, CA: Stanford University Press, 1941).

The book is an account of experiences in the life of Dr. McGillycuddy, as dictated to the author. As a surgeon and Indian agent, McGillycuddy describes people he interacted with, such as Sitting Bull and Red Cloud; and problems he encountered, such as agency investigations, intertribal relationships, and the death of Sitting Bull.

McKenney, Thomas L. *Memories, Official and Personal: Thomas L. McKenney*, with an introduction by Herman J. Viola (1846 Reprint, Lincoln: University of Nebraska Press, 1973).

As the title indicates, this memoir is purely descriptive of McKenney's travels and observations. The former commissioner of Indian Affairs tries to situate Native Americans as the principle characters in his book, detailing their social and cultural practices.

Meriam, Lewis et al. *The Problem of Indian Administration* (Baltimore, MD: Johns Hopkins Press, 1928).

Secretary of the Interior Hubert Work requested this report on the economic and social conditions of Indians in 1926. The report divides the issues of the BIA and those it serves into eight sections: (1) A General Policy for Indian Affairs, (2) Health, (3) Education, (4) General Economic Conditions, (5) Family and Community Life and the Activities of Women, (6) The Migrated Indians, (7) The Legal Aspects of the Indian Problem, and (8) The Missionary Activities among the Indians.

Miller, Mark Edwin. *Forgotten Tribes: Unrecognized Indians and the Federal Acknowledgement Process* (Lincoln: University of Nebraska Press, 2004).

Miller provides the first monographic treatment of the federal recognition process for Indian tribes. He analyzes the historical development of the process and attempts by unrecognized tribes to gain recognition as political and legal entities. Miller offers four case studies of successful and unsuccessful tribes, with analysis of why they failed or succeeded.

Otis, Elwell S. *The Indian Question* (New York: Sheldon and Company, 1878).

Elwell Otis (1838–1909) served a long military career that spanned the Civil, Indian, Philippine-American, and Spanish-American Wars. He addresses a variety of Indian-white issues and eras, including the alarming rate of depopulation, colonial Indian policy, the treaty system, and the "civilization" of Indians.

Philp, Kenneth L. *John Collier's Crusade for Indian Reform, 1920–54* (Tucson: University of Arizona Press, 1977).

Philp outlines the path of Collier's career, from 1907 to the early 1960s. He focuses particularly on Collier's opposition to acculturation and the resulting development of the Indian New Deal. Philp analyzes Collier's efforts to create new federal-Indian programs and reinstitute tribal governments, cultures, and religions.

Prucha, Francis Paul. *American Indian Policy in Crisis: Christian Reformers and the Indian, 1865–1900* (Norman: University of Oklahoma Press, 1976).

Prucha argues that Christian humanitarians and philanthropists heavily influenced Indian policy during Grant's peace policy and formation of nearly 200 reservations in Indian Country. During years of turmoil for the BIA to be turned over to the War Department, Prucha explains a civil service reform of the BIA occurred with Christian reformers pushing for Indian education.

Prucha, Francis Paul. *American Indian Policy in the Formative Years: The Indian Trade and Intercourse Acts, 1790–1834* (Lincoln: University of Nebraska Press, 1962).

Prucha provides great detail in his analysis of early federal policy regarding American Indians, including trade and intercourse, alcohol, trespassing, crime, and property laws. Writing from the lens of the written records in the National Archives, Prucha links laws that destroyed tribal cultures and economies to the Christianity and humanitarianism of the federal law-makers.

Prucha, Francis Paul. *American Indian Treaties: The History of a Political Anomaly* (Berkeley: University of California Press, 1997).

Prucha constructs a comprehensive history of American Indian treaties and their roles in the lives of indigenous peoples. He specifically addresses how the development and meaning of treaties, meant to be used as a tool between two sovereign nations, created inequality and imbalances for the Indian nations that signed them.

Prucha, Francis Paul. *The Great Father: The United States Government and the American Indians*, 2 vols. (Lincoln: University of Nebraska Press, 1984).

This is the most comprehensive, 200-year history of federal-Indian policy, concerned primarily with the federal side of Indian-American relationships. Prucha emphasizes the role of paternalism, Christian humanitarianism, and militant Americanism in shaping federal policy, such as the early government's efforts to "protect" the Indians by passing the Trade and Intercourse Laws.

Satz, Ronald. *Indian Removal: The Emigration of the Five Civilized Tribes of Indians* (Norman: University of Oklahoma Press, 1968).

As the white population expanded in the southeastern United States, they pushed against the ever-shrinking reservations and homelands of the Choctaw, Cherokee, Chickasaw, Creek, and Seminole Indians. Satz details how whites increasingly demanded that the federal government work to extinguish Indian title and remove its original occupants to lands west of the Mississippi River. He addresses how the subsequent removal uprooted Indians' cultural, social, and economic lifeways; and the trials of the march to Oklahoma.

Schmeckebier, Laurence. F. *The Office of Indian Affairs* (Baltimore, MD: Johns Hopkins University Press, 1927).

This detailed but dated volume was one of the earliest and most complete histories of the Office of Indian Affairs. Schmeckebier, a political scientist, describes the nature of the government agency and gives a broader context of the federal government's Indian policy. The volume is a part of a series that strives to detail the history, structure, and activities of each governmental service agency.

Seymour, Flora Warren. *Indian Agents of the Old Frontier* (New York: D. Appleton-Century, 1941).

Seymour offers sketches of various and unrelated Indian agents from the Civil War to the turn of the century, a period when the United States attempted to reform its Indian policy by allowing various religious denominations to provide agents. Quakers, Methodists, and others sent missionaries to the Apaches, Comanches, and many other western tribes in an attempt to acculturate American Indians through a combination of religious instruction and federal law.

Taylor, Theodore W. *The Bureau of Indian Affairs* (Boulder, CO: Westview Press, 1984).

Taylor systematically surveys the structure and selected policy issues the BIA encountered during its development and evolution. The focus of the book is primarily on the bureau of the late 1970s and mid-1980s, tribal issues that affected policy development, and future options. More descriptive than analytic, *The Bureau of Indian Affairs* offers a considerable amount of information of the state of affairs between the federal government and Indian tribes in the 1980s.

Taylor, Theodore W. *The States and Their Indian Citizens* (Washington, DC: U.S. Department of the Interior, Bureau of Indian Affairs, 1972).

In an Interior-commissioned study, Taylor examines the relationship between Native Americans and their local and state governments. Taylor raises issues and concerns within these relationships and offers alternatives and recommendations. One-half of the book contains 15 appendices, including demographic tables; tribal lists; and presidential remarks concerning American Indians.

Tatum, Lawrie. *Our Red Brothers and the Peace Policy of President Ulysses S. Grant* (1899 Reprint, Lincoln: University of Nebraska Press, 1970).

Indian agent Lawrie Tatum oversaw Indian affairs for the Fort Sill, Oklahoma, Kiowa and Comanche in the late 1860s and 1870s. Although he tried to promote agriculture, the Kiowa and Comanche held onto their raiding and hunting culture. Tatum eventually used the military to arrest several tribal members for their attack on a wagon train. Tatum wrote about his experiences in *Our Red Brothers* in 1899.

Ulrich, Roberta. *American Indian Nations from Termination to Restoration, 1953–2006* (Lincoln: University of Nebraska Press, 2010).

In this recent publication, Ulrich provides an overview of several cases of termination and restoration in the second half of the 20th century and into the 21st. This book is the first to consider all terminations and restorations together, thus illuminating national trends as well as drawing out regional and tribal differences.

Viola, Herman J. *Thomas L. McKenney: Architect of America's Early Indian Policy: 1816–1830* (Chicago, IL: The Swallow Press., Sage Books, 1974).

Viola analyzes the short, history-defining career of Thomas McKenney through the lens of public service in shaping federal Indian policy. In this biography, Viola details three sections of McKenney's work: his management of the government factory system, the Office of Indian Affairs, and his efforts to regain political office after his dismissal. He examines McKenney's role in several federal-Indian policies and details the day-to-day operations of managing a national Indian office.

Wallace, Anthony F. C. *Jefferson and the Indians: The Tragic Fate of the First Americans* (Cambridge, MA: Harvard University Press, 1999).

In this two-part study, Wallace examines both 18th-century attempts to understand Indians and a political history of Jefferson's Indian policies. Wallace particularly emphasizes Jefferson's beliefs that American Indians were on their way to extinction and his policies that hastened them toward that end. He focuses on Jefferson's actions within the context of the national policies of eradicating Indian land claims and cultures.

Wilkins, David, and K. Tsianina Lomawaima, *Uneven Ground: American Indian Sovereignty and Federal Law* (Norman: University of Oklahoma Press, 2002).

Competing legal precedents in Indian law created inconsistencies in interpretation for tribal justice and tilted the balance of power toward whites. Wilkins and Lomawaima analyze the six key doctrines of Indian law from an indigenous perspective—the Doctrines of Discovery, Trust, Plenary Power, Reserved Rights, Implied Repeals, and Sovereign Immunity.

Wilkinson, Charles. *Blood Struggle: The Rise of Modern Indian Nations* (New York and London: W. W. Norton and Company, 2005).

Wilkinson, a former attorney for the Native American Rights Fund and now a law professor at the University of Colorado, focuses on the "Indian Sovereignty Movement" as a social reaction to termination and total assimilation in the 1950s. He divides the book into four parts: termination as a federal policy; the rise of the anti-termination movements among Indians, including its philosophy, leadership, and organization; modern policy; and the social movement of "revitalization," or the reemergence of tribal leadership and culture.

Websites

http://www.bia.gov

This government website provides information on the BIA's organizational structure and services, as well as updates on current news and events. Further, the website includes a list of documents the organization has available and an interactive map through which those interested can gain more information on the indigenous populations of various regions. Contact information is also provided.

http://www.loc.gov/rr/mopic/findaid/indian2.html

This website lists all the documentaries on American Indians housed in the Library of Congress. Entries provide the title, producer, film length, and a brief annotation.

Films

Burns, Ric, dir. *The WayWest: How the West was Lost & Won, 1845–1893*. DVD. Hollywood, CA: WGBH Educational Foundation and Steeplechase Films, 1995.

This six-hour educational series chronicles relationships between the federal government and American Indians from the time of the Gold Rush to the Wounded Knee Massacre.

Gage, Beth, dir. *American Outrage*. DVD. New York: First Run Features, 2009.

This award-winning film centers on the current struggles of two elderly Western Shoshone to keep their land. The film demonstrates the centrality of land negotiations between the federal government and indigenous tribes, as well as the fact that such negotiations are not only found in the past but remain contentious issues in the 21st century.

Ritchie, Chip, dir. *Our Spirits Don't Speak English: Indian Boarding School*. DVD. Dallas, TX: Rich-Heape Films, 2008.

Gayle Ross, a descendant of Cherokee leader John Ross, stars in this film that directly confronts the negative aspects of the removal of Native children to BIA boarding schools and the government's more general policy to assimilate children by severing ties with their families and cultures.

Appendix

Commissioners of Indian Affairs and Assistant Secretaries of the Interior

1824–1830 Thomas L. McKenney
1830–1831 Samuel S. Hamilton
1832–1836 Elbert Herring
1836–1838 Carey A. Harris
1838–1845 T. Hartley Crawford
1845–1849 William Medill
1849–1850 Orlando Brown
1850–1853 Luke Lea
1853–1857 George W. Manypenny
1857–1858 James W. Denver
1858–1858 Charles E. Mix
1858–1861 Albert B. Greenwood
1861–1865 William P. Dole
1865–1866 Dennis N. Cooley
1866–1867 Lewis V. Bogy
1867–1869 Nathaniel G. Taylor
1869–1871 Ely S. Parker
1871–1871 H. R. Clum (acting)
1871–1872 Francis A. Walker
1872–1873 H. R. Clum (acting)
1873–1875 Edward P. Smith
1875–1877 John Q. Smith
1877–1879 Ezra A. Hayt
1880–1880 E. M. Marble (acting)
1880–1881 Roland E. Trowbridge
1881–1885 Hiram Price
1885–1888 John D. C. Atkins
1888–1889 John H. Oberly
1889–1893 Thomas Jefferson Morgan

1893–1897 Daniel M. Browning
1897–1904 William A. Jones
1905–1909 Francis E. Leupp
1909–1912 Robert G. Valentine
1913–1921 Cato Sells
1921–1929 Charles H. Burke
1929–1933 Charles J. Rhoads
1933–1945 John Collier
1945–1948 William A. Brophy
1948–1949 William R. Zimmerman (acting)
1949–1950 John R. Nichols
1950–1953 Dillon S. Myer
1953–1961 Glenn L. Emmons
1961–1966 Philleo Nash
1966–1969 Robert L. Bennett
1969–1973 Louis R. Bruce
1973–1976 Morris Thompson
1976–1977 Benjamin Reifel

Assistant Secretaries of the Interior for Indian Affairs

1977–1981 Forrest Gerard
1981–1984 Kenneth L. Smith
1985–1989 Ross Swimmer
1989–1993 Eddie F. Brown
1993–1997 Ada E. Deer
1997–2001 Kevin Gover
2001–2001 James H. McDivitt (acting)
2001–2003 Neal A. McCaleb
2003–2004 Aurene M. Martin (acting)
2004–2005 Dave Anderson
2005–2007 Jim Cason (acting)
2007–2008 Carl J. Artman
2008–2009 George Skibine (acting)
2009–present Larry Echo Hawk

Index

Wilson, Richard, 139
Winters v. United States, 96
Witt, Edgar, 124
Wolcott, Oliver, 8
Women Accepted for Volunteer
   Emergency Service (WAVES),
   119
Women's Auxiliary Army Corps,
   119
Women's National Indian Associa-
   tion (WNIA), 56, 88, 89
Wood, Robert E., 125
Woosey Deer, 98
Worcester v. Georgia, 16, 48, 55
Work, Hubert, 100, 101

World War I, land allotment and,
   97–98
World War II, tribal reorganization
   and, 119–20
Wounded Knee Creek, 63–64
Wounded Knee occupation,
   139–40
Wovoka (Paiute Indian), 62–63
Wright, Alfred, 69

Yazzie, Allen D., 131

Zimmerman, William, 111, 118,
   124–25
Zokosky, Peter, 153

About the Author

DONALD L. FIXICO (Shawnee, Sac and Fox, Muscogee Creek, and Seminole) is Distinguished Foundation Professor of History and Affiliate Faculty in American Indian Studies at Arizona State University. He is the author and editor of ten books, including *Termination and Relocation: Federal Indian Policy, 1945–1960* (1986); *The Invasion of Indian Country in the Twentieth Century: American Capitalism and Tribal Natural Resources* (1998); *The Urban Indian Experience in America* (2000); and *The American Indian Mind in a Linear World: Traditional Knowledge and American Indian Studies* (2003).